ECONOMIC INVESTIGATIONS IN TWENTIETH-CENTURY DETECTIVE FICTION

For Oscar

Economic Investigations in Twentieth-Century Detective Fiction

Expenditure, Labor, Value

YAN ZI-LING

National University of Tainan, Taiwan

Routledge
Taylor & Francis Group

LONDON AND NEW YORK

First published 2015 by Ashgate Publishing

2 Park Square, Milton Park, Abingdon, Oxfordshire OX14 4RN
52 Vanderbilt Avenue, New York, NY 10017

Routledge is an imprint of the Taylor & Francis Group, an informa business

First issued in paperback 2019

British Library Cataloguing in Publication Data
A catalogue record for this book is available from the British Library

The Library of Congress has cataloged the printed edition as follows:
Zi-Ling, Yan.
  Economic investigations in twentieth-century detective fiction: expenditure, labor, value
    / by Yan Zi-Ling.
    pages cm
  Includes bibliographical references and index.
  ISBN 978-1-4724-5253-5 (hardcover: alk. paper)
  1. Detective and mystery stories, American—History and criticism. 2. Detective and mystery stories, English—History and criticism. 3. Labor in literature. 4. Value in literature. 5. Economics in literature. I. Title.
  PS374.D4Z55 2015
  813'.087209—dc23

                                                                    2014036139

ISBN 978-1-4724-5253-5 (hbk)
ISBN 978-0-367-88100-9 (pbk)

Contents

Acknowledgments   *vii*

1   Ideology Critique and Economics in Detective Fiction   1

2   Conservationism, Enclosure, and Totalitarianism   25

3   Expenditure and Discursive Recuperation   57

4   Clue, Value, and Counterfeit   93

5   Detective Labor   125

6   Hard-Boiled Gift-Labor and the Aneconomic Gift   151

Conclusion: The Theatrical Economy   175

Works Cited   *183*
Index   *199*

Acknowledgments

This study benefited materially from two National Science Council grants: NSC #099-2410-H-024-010 and NSC #100-2410-H-024-023.

An earlier, abbreviated version of Chapter 4 was presented as "Value and Clue: From Restricted to Token Economies in Major Detective Story Sub-Genres" at the 2011 PCA/APC Conference in San Antonio. Parts of Chapter 6, likewise a preliminary study, were presented as "Towards the Pathological Gift: Calculation and Expenditure in Detective Fiction" in the Special Session "The Gift of Literature" at the 2012 MLA Conference in Seattle.

Chapter 1
Ideology Critique and Economics in Detective Fiction

The Scope of This Study

Although the detective story properly has its origins in Poe, the detective-centered narrative does not attain maturity until the late nineteenth century. The heyday of this form, roughly 1890 to 1950, encompasses three detective subgenres of enduring popularity: the Classical analytic tale, the Golden Age detective novel, and the hard-boiled detective story. A precise definition of these subgenres gives rise to dispute—period, theme, style, and national origins are common methods; more theoretically engaged readings look to social, political, psychological, and philosophical underpinnings to make distinctions. My approach favors the second group: I argue that the subgenres, particularly the Golden Age and hard-boiled, may be differentiated by the way they structure knowledge vis-à-vis the economic categories of expenditure, value, and productive labor. In general, two distinct pathways are evident, so that in this study the Classical analytic tale, exemplified by Doyle, Chesterton, and the early Freeman in the United Kingdom and Futrelle and Reeve in the United States, will be understood as the soil which nurtured its novelistic outgrowth in the Golden Age. Thus, in shorthand, the sharpest economic distinction lies between the Golden Age and the hard-boiled detective text since the Golden Age intensified the structural and character-related aspects of the Classical tale. As it pertains to detective fiction, the "economy of literature," to allude to Marc Shell's influential book of that name, is more than a sociological study of textual production; it is certainly not a mere cataloguing of economic metaphors. Rather, this method demands an understanding of economy as conterminous with narrative structure—in Shell's words, "money talks in and through discourse in general," and "the monetary information of thought, unlike its content, cannot be eradicated from discourse without changing thought itself" (*Money* 180). This point may be amplified to disclose economic distinctions between discursive modes of representation, or, to cite another significant theoretical contributor, Jean-Joseph Goux, "*a mode of writing is representative of a mode of signifying exchange*" (*Symbolic* 72).

In addition to Shell and Goux, I am indebted to a third figure whose philosophical concerns inform my economic readings of literature, namely Georges Bataille. Bataille's work on nonproductive expenditure from the 1920s and 1930s supplies the terms *homogeneity* and *heterogeneity*. These concepts, outlined in Chapter 1 and applied in Chapters 2 and 3, illuminate epistemological tendencies in detective stories, especially when coupled with later Bataillian ideas like summit and decline. The sociopolitical context in which authority figures determine events and construct boundaries or frames have an economic resonance that offers insights into how detectives or the institutional forces they represent establish parameters in which truth can function. Detectives, visibly buttressing social order, frequently underwrite outcomes supporting narrow ideological interests. The detective's truth-generating capacity, most often characterized as a process of discovery rather than creation, demands scrutiny given the institutional and class biases he or she is often called upon to serve. Complicity with or resistance to cooptation by authority-bearing agencies is tied to the discursive reduction and eventual transmission of the text—a process that differs noticeably between subgenres. The double bind involved in this process, particularly in hard-boiled texts where alienation is overt, is analyzed in Chapter 3 through another of Bataille's ideas, the *crochet* from his aphoristic study *Guilty*.

More recent critical activity is brought into play with Goux's *Symbolic Economies* and *The Coiners of Language*. I employ these contributions to the sociology of literature to establish conceptual boundaries related to knowledge and the determinations of value, the central problem of Chapter 4. Essays from the former text shed light on the detective's function as general equivalent, as a measuring function which nonetheless circulates. Goux's insights in this and other texts help to construct a Marxist trajectory that complements Ernest Mandel's Trotskyist ideology critique of detective fiction. Instead of only reflecting evolving class interests, detective stories also indicate anxiety over a vanishing fund of meaning whose visibility guarantees the viability of exchange, the stability of value in circulation, and the "genuine." This anxiety, which deepens in the Interwar period, is observable even within the works of individual authors like Doyle. To narrow this part of the investigation, I highlight the theme of counterfeiting against the social effect of leaving the gold standard—areas in which Goux's works prove especially insightful.

The final category, labor, generates the sharpest distinctions between subgenres. In Chapter 5 I argue that the representation of detective work places it closer in spirit to the gift than wage labor or professional or artisan labor. In Chapter 6 I coin the term *gift-labor* to define a range of labor positions among hard-boiled detectives in Coxe, Nebel, and Whitfield. Analyses of these less frequently discussed authors are preliminary to an examination of Chandler and Spillane, whose detectives embody the aporias of poststructuralist gift theory.

The Historical Specificity of the Detective Text

Literary critics, confronting the dynamic nature of genre, must avoid the chimera of false analogies created by importing anachronisms into historically determined rhetorical forms. If approached self-reflectively, genre provides adequate grounds for comparative analysis. The genre-determining criteria must be scrutinized since, in their role as mediators between text and context, genres may either yield insights into cultural change or be employed to confirm the ideological assumptions of the researcher. Michael Denning aptly observes that the desire to objectify the confluence of history and cultural forms above the fray of the textual confusion on the ground "can reify generic categories" (*Mechanic Accents* 75). The resulting classifications become ossified, and they obscure certain questions like whose interests are served, whose value system is vanquished (and thus rendered invisible), what fantasy of social order is endorsed, and how audiences are manipulated into supporting or acquiescing in the interests of powerful Others. All of these questions are vital to detective fiction.

Although certain stable, widely accepted detective subgenres are intuitively grasped by readers, attempts at discrete categorization involve a jumble of timelines, national traditions, thematic elements, and narratological assumptions. Detective story writers have not helped matters: S.S. Van Dine's and Ronald Knox's semi-comic rule lists are as ineffective in establishing genre boundaries as Chandler's engaging, though likewise distorted, polemic in "The Simple Art of Murder." Most of the critical tradition, exemplified by scholars such as Symons, Knight, or Dove, is more balanced.[1] Formalist definitions of detective fiction, for instance in George Dove's *The Reader and the Detective*, are useful inasmuch as they articulate categorical boundaries. Dove's four formal demands include a detective-centered narrative focus, the precedence of investigation over other plot elements, a complex "secret that appears impossible of solution," and closure (*Reader* 10). This last point, he adds, reflects the audience's knowledge and not necessarily that of the detective or other characters. The value of Dove's regulative conventions lies in their descriptive rather than prescriptive basis.[2] However, as general categories, they must be supplemented to analyze the representation of social interests, since these interests are neither ahistorical nor acultural.

Generic classification is further complicated by a range of critical methods by which objects are defined within interest parameters. Historical surveys, sociological studies, reception theory and reader response, ideology critique, and sociopolitical and culture studies potentially condition the objects they are employed to examine. Certain structural constants are nevertheless widely acknowledged by researchers, for instance, the "bottleneck" idea, which asserts the influence of major figures like Poe or Doyle on subsequent developments. Several general historical conditions are also understood to be structurally necessary for detective fiction to emerge: a reliance on or openness to science and scientific method, a commitment to rational explanations within a dominant secular culture, individualism instead of collective action, especially in terms of the specialist (but also the criminal), and bourgeois sensibilities (Scaggs 19; see also Knight, *Form*

---

[1]   Julian Symons suggests that generic classifications, particularly squabbling over rules, essentially fall down in real world applications (3); George Dove rejects the need for strict detective typologies (*Police* 47); and Stephen Knight argues that blanket terms like *Golden Age* are "unduly homogeneous" ("Golden" 77). See also Scaggs (2).

[2]   Greene, for example, is prescriptive in his insistence on the social recognition that the crime is wrong, the unsympathetic criminal, and the exclusion of the supernatural (96–99).

40; Shaw and Vanacker 13). Whereas these factors no doubt are discernible in late nineteenth-century texts, they are partly determined by historical developments that predate these texts' appearance.

Despite Sayers' playful argument for its Aristotelian origins ("Aristotle" 25–26), the detective story is not an old genre. There is wide consensus that the genre takes distinctive form in Poe in the 1840s, a suggestive debut given the contemporaneous social, political, and economic upheavals in the United States and Europe. Sean McCann understands Poe's work to emerge under the twin influences of "the advent of populist democracy and the transformative energies of a 'market revolution'—in a society ... that had definitively traded its republican and agrarian legacy for a liberal, capitalist order" (6–7). Terence Whalen, in an invaluable essay on economic dimensions in Poe, details how Poe's brainchild originated in the throes of capitalist contradiction and depression rather than Poe's own psychological problems (386). He goes on to remark that Poe's economic vulnerability as a writer in this market heightened this tension (387).

In his three Dupin stories Poe channeled the American individualist impulse reflective of his epoch into a triad of highly imitated plot structures. "The Murders in the Rue Morgue" establishes the sensationalist-deductive pattern, in which the detective-protagonist employs arcane knowledge (though not fair play)[3] to decipher clues and assemble them into a narrative by which he explains a baffling and sensationalist crime. "The Mystery of Marie Rogêt," a second type, dispenses with all but intellectual activity in a Baconian assemblage of discrete factual data, whose detached, almost disinterested arrangement becomes the focus. Finally, "The Purloined Letter" proceeds along the lines of inversion and the caper; the interest lies in the denouement and in the outwitting of a criminal opponent rather than a suspenseful train of events that culminates in a surprise unmasking. From our perspective, these modes illustrate the limits of Poe's socioeconomic context in that his innovation does not encompass the "beads-on-a-string" structure found in some of Hammett's and Chandler's plots, nor critiques of institutions, nor a structure founded upon professional collectivism—these developments are by their very historical and socioeconomic specificity unavailable to Poe. Nonetheless, Poe's creative genius synthesizes narrative strains that had been developing during detective fiction's prehistory, an area of study which has generated a large body of scholarship.

I will not rehearse at any length the findings of authors like Stephen Knight, Ian Bell, or Heather Worthington, all of whom give detailed information about the state of British justice, the early development of a police force, the popularity of the Newgate Calendar, Godwin's *Caleb Williams*, and other historical developments prior to Poe and the formalizing of the detective genre on both sides of the Atlantic. These historicocritical studies demonstrate that before the police emerged as a formal institution, crime was already prevalent in fiction and nonfiction alike. Bell's

---

[3]   Many critics dismiss the demand for fair play in the Classical and Golden Age periods. See Dove (*Reader* 4, 20); Herzel (77); Joshi (104); Panek (*Probable* 91–92; *Watteau's* 23); and Aydelotte (78).

work on the crime theme in English literature of the previous century correlates real or imagined perceptions of sociopolitical reality in the management, policing, and punishment of criminal behavior and its literary representation. Bell remarks how this intense interest in crime, evident in eighteenth-century literature, was treated differently from its subsequent appearance in detective fiction (7). The nineteenth century witnessed the disassociation of the detective hero from other social forces, a departure from melodramatic holdovers in the hybrid mystery-adventure combination. The impetus behind the detective's appearance, however, has been attributed to different sources. Dennis Porter, writing about the United Kingdom, claims that "by the 1840s a greater diffusion of the nation's wealth into the middle and lower-middle classes resulted in a form of *embourgeoisement* that led to a more positive perception of the forces of order" (*Pursuit* 149–50). Though viewed as repressive by Thomas (3), Porter maintains that this change is one condition of the detective or police hero. Others go further to emphasize another need: the fantasy of a champion who confronted the corruption of extant legal institutions and a grossly class-based system of punishment (Bell 14; Worthington 4).

LeRoy Panek details developments in American detective fiction, which he views as distinct from Britain's for social and historical reasons. As for the former point, he claims an interest in "unmasking corruption and hypocrisy in high persons" and the eschewing of "artificial problems" characteristic of its British counterpart (*Probable* 19). Regarding the latter, Panek argues that the growth of the genre paralleled a perceived growth in crime, warranted or not, that can be linked to historical events like the Civil War, or, as he and coeditor Mary Bendel-Simso write in their introduction to the anthology *Early American Detective Stories*, to the burgeoning problem of counterfeiting (176). The core of his argument in *Probable Cause*, however, follows market developments concerning the format in which stories were distributed to the public, mostly through serial fiction in weekly publications. By the 1870s newspapers containing fiction along with news had greatly expanded in circulation and were in competition with dime novels. Production procedures also changed as publishers discovered ways of turning greater profits. Salaries for writers declined and factory-like production went into effect (Panek, *Probable* 12). The fascination with social scandal, the appearance of detective fiction in bourgeois magazines, and the rise of popular interest in science cooperated to generate sales. Panek's investigation of American publishing from the Civil War onwards suggests that trends in reading tastes were perhaps as dependent upon changes in the postal regulations as the perceptions of social reality promulgated by somewhat less than trustworthy media organs (*Probable* 154; see also Panek and Bendel-Simso 15–16).[4] By tying together these

---

[4]   This point is raised for the UK by Colin Watson, who opines that advances in printing, distribution, and format were essential to the development of a certain kind of fiction and its audience (15–16)—although these remarks are made in reference to the standard big nineteenth-century novel, they foreshadow the popular market of detective fiction.

disparate threads, Panek astutely distinguishes between a generalized British and a generalized US experience, though overlap and influence are discernible, for instance through the pirating of foreign titles, and later, the conduit of Arthur Conan Doyle, whose "legitimate" imports were featured in the slicks. Nonetheless, distinct cause-and-effect relations are difficult to establish in this epoch: perception was molded by media, but those selfsame media depended upon sales, indicating the guiding force of reader demand. Although technology, advertising (in the link between sales and ads as a percentage of revenue), and the opening of a national market facilitated change, the impact of middle-class tastes appears to have been central to cycles of production and consumption. Though the market potentially constituted an arena of "freedom," whatever was produced was irretrievably linked for the starving artist with whatever was consumed: the texts he or she produced must be consumable (marketable), first, and actually profitable, second. Artistic "freedom," founded upon competition, reflected a chaotic form of capitalism between individual producers.[5]

To summarize the preceding points, genre-focused critical methods must be sensitive to large-scale sociopolitical developments and the technical aspects of production and consumption in the context of markets, as well as to the influence of individual writers. That said, individual, historically situated texts nonetheless embody ideological commitments, and, given the enormous audience of detective fiction, allow the transmission of ideas whose influence belies overdetermination by an economic base. The ideological content is not transparent, though; rather, it is refracted through the complex artificiality of the genre in both its British and American tendencies. This artificiality requires the examination of realism claims in the genre, since the appeal of the core historical forms beginning in the late nineteenth century (that is, the subgenres under study here) implies a response to specific historical conditions. The social, political, and economic climates, reworked within the generic limits of detective fiction subgenres, suggest different textual economic modes. The rules of exchange, value, and circulation, ideas derived from economics, indeed have their structural expression in these texts. Before turning to this problem in its theoretical dimension, we must examine why detective fiction makes only weak claims to realism and how this weakness favors ideology critique.

Detective Fiction and Verisimilitude

The contention over realism in detective fiction is well represented by Chandler's dismissal of Golden Age plots and characters as generally implausible. Most critics maintain that his American colleagues weren't much closer to realism themselves, if realism is taken to mean the conformity of character, language, and plot to everyday experience. Indeed, critics have rejected the notion of

---

[5]   Raymond Williams documents this change ("The Writer" 23–24). See also Williams's *Culture and Society* (50).

realism in detective fiction, both Golden Age and hard-boiled, almost without exception.[6] Hard-boiled authors' use of violence is "too frequent and too romantic to be absolutely real" (Panek, *Probable Cause* 112); such romanticism tends to reduce narrative elements to a "literary device" or "metaphor" (Grella 118; see also Mahan 31). The "purely literary conceit" and "outlandish" plot of most hard-boiled writers reaches its apex in the "nightmare" of Mickey Spillane (Collins and Traylor 74). The recognition of formal implausibility suggests an internal divide in readers, who are both detached from and engaged by the antirealist elements in detective fiction. As with other artificial genres from science fiction to fairy tales, readers concede an in-text reality founded upon generically or historically prescribed conventions. Conventional verisimilitude is discarded for a so-called higher realism that reduces the text to a function; thus the stock features of the detective tale might be "predicated upon and reflect basic assumptions about the way of the world and the nature of reality" (Malmgren, *Anatomy* 6). In terms of sociology, they are permitted because they serve as vehicles to address historically defined problems, or, if these problems are no longer current, they grant insight into how writers, readers, and cultural formations perceived both problems and solutions within the parameters of their historical consciousness.

To give an example, this limit is quite noticeable in Arthur B. Reeve's scientific gadgetry—readers a century later are unimpressed by mobile recording equipment or lie detectors. Underneath the technological applications, we critically eye the so-called scientific content of the ratiocinative detection process of which gadgetry is an epiphenomenon. Even for Doyle's more lasting contributions, Kayman discloses how Holmes's method is hardly scientific; though it may register as believable within the tales as presented by Watson, it cannot be taken seriously (48–50). This pseudorealistic scientific content is actually a representation of science as it is thought to operate by nonscientists, or, as Belsey perceptively writes, "it [positivistic science] reveals itself to a deconstructive reading as ideology at the moment that classic realism, offered as verisimilitude, reveals itself as fiction" (387). In detective fiction this ideology is a form of secularization, whereby truth claims must have some ostensibly empirical basis; in this context evidence is a foundation for belief and, juridically, a demonstration of culpability beyond mere sworn testimony.

The tendency of Golden Age texts in particular (for example, Carr, Sayers, Berkeley, and Crispin) to self-referentiality and even self-parody further distances the reader from the illusion of reality. Holmes's remark to Watson at the beginning of "The Adventure of the Copper Beeches," that fiction cannot approach the *bizarreries* afforded by truth, is a contrivance—an ironic one, given that this

---

[6] For examples of such statements, see Alewyn (69); Roth (23); Joshi (100); Porter (*Pursuit* 42); Aydelotte (68); and Rabinowitz (129). Geherin is an exception; he asserts that "beginning with Hammett, writers in the [hard-boiled] genre have aimed at depicting realistically the society in which they lived" (200).

viewpoint is expressed in an example of sensationalist fiction.[7] The byzantine plots of much Golden Age fiction and conventions like the least likely suspect, the elaborate and improbable murder method, the intricate time schedule, and the detective's arcane knowledge or dubious psychological theories contrive to weaken believability. Nonetheless, the hard-boiled tradition fares little better, notwithstanding Hammett's much-remarked practical experience. The detective loner who opposes institutionalized corruption is a theatrical hypostatization which simplifies the confrontation of individual and institution. Ruehlmann's citation of the New York code concerning private detectives makes short shrift of a private detective's involvement in a murder investigation (3–4). And thus, with good reason, Dove maintains that "the conventions and formulas of the classic and hard-boiled schools are almost entirely mythical" (*Police* 4)—the likelihood of the audience's first-hand knowledge of private detectives is probably nil, at least in terms of criminal cases. And although real life experience of police officers is commonplace, we are just as much in the dark over the activities of official crime investigators as we are with the private variety. Even when the lone investigator is displaced by the collectivism of the procedural, we find the contrivances of neat closure and the telescoping of much of the routine that would otherwise make the narrative unbearably tedious. In addition to the impossible solve-rates customary in the genre as a whole, the highly truncated timelines are unrealistic, the fantasy of a quick resolution epitomized by Hammett's apt title "One Hour." The rationale for these obfuscations is not simply that our interest must be captured, something hard to imagine with a faithful record of boring and inconsequential interviews leading to failure. Rather, detective independence functions to obscure the institutional and ideological frames around labor—the detective is a refutation, at a certain historical juncture, of economic collectivism. This Bataillian *non serviam*, however, is not uniform since *within the confines of the text* the refusal to be integrated into collectivism in the Golden Age is not typically an attack upon the class whom such collectivism benefits the most. When it resembles this among hard-boiled writers, we understand why overstated chivalric themes sit uncomfortably upon the detective's shoulders—they are quixotic inasmuch they come up against economic rather than simply ethical barriers. Thus, we are confronted with two concerns that should not be conflated: improbability in the tortuous meanderings of plot construction on the one hand, and implausibility in the ideological construction on the other. The former is an intensification of all fictional representation that hopes to capture the popular interest and imagination; the latter, in the case of detective fiction, is the sleight of hand that surreptitiously defines interests.

Agatha Christie's highly unrealistic short story "The Jewel Robbery at the Grand Metropolitan" (1924) serves to demonstrate this distinction and to provide a

---

[7]   John Dickson Carr puts similar speeches into the mouths of his characters; see dialogue between Bencolin and Marle in *The Lost Gallows* (77) or the opening of Fell's locked room lecture in *The Three Coffins* (160).

measure by which to compare later generic developments. The plot involves Poirot's recovery of a set of pearls stolen from the wealthy Mrs. Opalsen. The theft, set up to implicate Mrs. Opalsen's maid, turns out to have been carefully orchestrated by a pair of jewel thieves posing as staff at the hotel where the characters are guests. The story brims with implausible action: the unnecessarily complex plan of the criminals, who hide a fake necklace instead of simply replacing the real one with its duplicate; the easy deception of the victims, Mr. and Mrs. Opalsen, by a string of false pearls whose duplication would require the handling of the real set; the time coincidences in which one criminal awaits the actions of another on the off-chance that a servant will leave the room twice; and so on. But underneath these impossibilities, our attention is *not* drawn to the criminal activity of the purported victims and their coterie, or to the suspicious behavior of the detective himself. At the story's outset Hastings invites Poirot to a luxurious Brighton resort hotel, which is made possible by the "killing" he made on the stock market ("A friend in the City put me on to a very good thing" [Christie, "Jewel" 112]). An oblique reference to insider trading does not faze the reader; neither do the exploitive methods used by Mr. Opalsen or the rest of the "gay throng," of whom many are "plastered with gems" at the Grand Metropolitan Hotel (Christie, "Jewel" 113), whose money has been "earned" from market speculation in colonial industries. Their exploitation at a distance raises no eyebrows, nor do we think much about the class complicity of the police who detain and strip search members of the working classes in the pursuit of justice (namely, the restoration of the upper middle class's right to expensive accoutrements which double as investments). Poirot's devious acquisition of incriminating fingerprints, despite his unofficial position, is taken in stride by the police, who permit his access to their institutional inner workings. The plot's departures from realism do not necessarily draw attention to the social imbalances implied by the action. This antirealism, certainly in line with readers' blindness to such concerns, is an exemplary case of hegemonic cultural control—one of the most enjoyable, it seems.

Once we foreground the construction of narrative sympathies we are compelled to give interpretative weight to ideology critique. This focus is not only warranted by the tendency to downplay classist notions of justice in the aesthetic pleasure of the text. A mere 30 years later the detective's complicity in reinforcing the class divide is overt and expanded to the level of the nation state. The jewel theme in Ian Fleming's *Diamonds Are Forever* (1956), for example, is a long cry from the benign restoration of the Opalsen pearls by the omnicompetent Poirot's subterfuge. Somewhat unlike the persona cultivated by his film roles, the James Bond portrayed on the opening page of Fleming's novel is a bureaucratic functionary and yes-man who cannot tell a real diamond from a fake; he is briefed on the international diamond situation and instructed to shut down a cartel that threatens British imperialist interests. None of this needs to be interpretatively extracted, nor does it offer any apology; rather, it is the substantive and sympathetically portrayed content of the story itself.

Towards Ideology Critique in Detective Fiction

The intersection of reader, author, text, and society in critical treatments of detective fiction structures sophisticated reflective readings. Some critics propose hierarchical theories: Edward Margolies, for instance, maintains that the popular author "conceals from his reader something that the reader already knows or secretly believes," in contrast to "elitist fiction" with "its ability to surprise or communicate a fresh, original, or unusual understanding of experience to an audience" (2). A more detailed reflective assessment is developed in Cawelti's pioneering study *Adventure, Mystery, and Romance*, where deterministic and reflective models are systematically contrasted. In Cawelti's view, stories mirror values and social concerns, but these are part of larger rhythms that find common ground in universals. Such topoi allow "popular stories [to be] embodiments of archetypal story forms in terms of specific cultural materials" (6). The "formula genre" refers to texts sharing a sufficient number of traits to justify linking them as a group to a specific historical context; the "archetype-genre" consists of regularities that stretch beyond these groups' historical limits. Cawelti's rejection of deterministic theories does not exclude socioeconomic or psychoanalytic readings as much as limit them to the panoply of analytic methods. One might criticize Cawelti in his reduction of deterministic theories to what he calls "a single fundamental social or psychological dynamic" (*Adventure* 30), a monolithic quality they typically do not possess. Neither Marx nor Freud could have survived to inspire contemporary literary interpretations if they were so constituted—though they are, as Cawelti might rejoin, made simplistic in the hands of unimaginative interpreters. Cawelti's subtle nod to historical limits helps him to remain viable and to weather his detractors' claims.

Hannah Charney criticizes Cawelti, and by implication other critics who oscillate between socially specific readings and broad psychological readings—namely, exclusive versus inclusive readings. Relatively narrow class readings, for instance, are rejected as "vague" since they do not "elucidate the catharsis that the detective novel provides" (xvi), presumably for any reader. By rejecting amalgamations in which the subject loses distinct boundaries and agency, we presumably move to individual psychology. Charney pursues the thesis that class should be rejected in favor of individual reader psychology. Within such parameters, we question how social readings are recuperated from individual experience. This apparent problem partly resolves itself by examining the assumptions underpinning this divide—namely, by noting that the society-individual problem is a historically specific construction to begin with.[8] Given this historical blind spot, a sustained

---

[8]   Raymond Williams remarks in *Culture and Society* that "nearly all theoretical discussions of art since the Industrial Revolution have been crippled by the assumed opposition between art and the actual organization of society .... Individual psychology has been similarly limited by an assumption of opposition between individual and society which is in fact only a symptom of society's transitional disorganization" (244).

discussion of class, economics, or sociology is absent from most reception theory: Dove, for instance, suggests the individualization of the reading experience in a world designed as private stage for the fantasies of the subject. This privatized, aesthetic experience unsurprisingly lends itself to the charge of escapism. And indeed, Dove argues that detective fiction's "transitory" quality lacks "long-range goals or purposes," and though "fundamentally an intellectual undertaking," is in the end "intended primarily to relax" (*Reader* 2). When approached within the historical context of its heyday, critics like Maugham juxtapose the detective story with contemporaneous avant-garde experimentation, claiming that the former offers the satisfaction of a story told "briefly," "with dispatch," and geared to "arouse curiosity, excite suspense," and "maintain the reader's interest" (110). In light of the obvious social terrors coincident with detective fiction's ascendency and twentieth-century triumph, the genre is easily perceived as stress-reducing and therapeutic (Dove, *Reader* 41), "consoling" (Knight, *Form* 4), anxiety-dispelling (Defino 75), or simply escapist (Aydelotte 69–70).[9]

The charge of frivolity tends towards ambivalence, since few critics claim that detective fiction is an inappropriate vehicle for the study of serious cultural and theoretical concerns. One of the most engaging studies, Ernest Mandel's *Delightful Murder*, places the popular form within a Trotskyist theoretical framework. Though R. Gordon Kelly complains that Mandel engages in distortions by reducing authors to mere functions, underemphasizing the power of readers, and attributing an ominous independence to an abstract ideology (158), Mandel has the distinct advantage of offering a theory of change operating within a concrete and limited historical matrix; we must recognize that read critically, he provides a meeting point between reflective theory and psychology, bridging the lacuna between them in ideology critique. Mandel dismisses vulgar Marxist readings that reduce literary texts to epiphenomena of an economic base, and instead inquires into the dialectic between readers in their perceptions of culture and authors in their representations of culture. The complexity of our problem in its economic dimension lies in establishing a theoretical ground for this relation.

Mandel sketches the generalized historical changes in detective fiction from its mid-to-late-nineteenth-century origins to the period immediately following World War II. Specifically, he is interested in how consumption (reading) prompts us to speculate on the reformulation of fantasies with specific relations to ideological problems—these naturally involve representation. Representation in fiction, to follow Eagleton, is not so much a reflection of a social reality as a deformation of that reality (47), though a deformation which can be recognized as such. Indeed, Eagleton asserts that "literature ... does not stand in some reflective, symmetrical, one-to-one relation with its object. The object is deformed, refracted, dissolved— reproduced less in the sense that a mirror reproduces its object than, perhaps, in

---

[9]   Claims of escapism are echoed by other critics, for instance Greene (102), Rabinowitz (122), and Alewyn (65). A sustained and careful analysis that avoids these generalizations is found in McCann (6–7).

the way that a dramatic performance *reproduces* the dramatic text" (48). Unlike the living experience of theater, however, the detective text is a secondary representation in that point of view is determined in ways that the immediacy of a theater space cannot reproduce. And it is here that the ideological framing of the text comes to the forefront—though historical investigation suggests that this frame is unstable or malleable.

In explaining the rise of crime fiction, Mandel begins with the relation between authority and criminal, suggesting that in its origins, crime fiction is antiauthoritarian and procriminal. Reader perception shifts over time, indicating changes in the social and class structure in western societies. As authority and the associations around it move from an irrational and traditional order retaining vestiges of feudal privilege to the bourgeois legal system, earlier relations of privilege are reversed. The ideology of crime fiction, as it reached more mature forms in the late nineteenth and early twentieth centuries, tended to defend the bourgeois order. Moreover, the structure of these stories precluded the effort, except in readers so predisposed, to contest the order portrayed therein. Although we find the buttressing of property rights and a definition of crime to function within bourgeois parameters, the victory of bourgeois legal norms in the nineteenth century did not quash anxiety, despite its self-representation as the logical evolutionary culmination of western historical development. The assumption of unshakable and eternal laws epitomized by the capitalist system was challenged by the need for a literature that vigorously mandated such a worldview. From the consumption side of the equation, popular literature including crime fiction "reconciled the upset, bored and anxious individual member of the middle class with the inevitability and permanence of bourgeois society" (Mandel 29). Indeed, within the Classical and Golden Age text, anxiety is often premised upon bourgeois norms gone awry—acquisition, individuality, competition are turned into sources of criminality which must be combated by other conventionally bourgeois traits, namely hyper-rationality steeled by positivistic "science."[10]

The foregrounding of bourgeois individualism neutralizes the larger scope of conflict (that is, inter- and intraclass conflicts); we confront individual criminal acts and, typically, individualized responses from the detective. The detective is supported by a sympathetic institutional framework portrayed in recognizable individuals instead of the faceless representatives of a bureaucratic machine. The characters in conflict spur a sequence of events ending in resolution and closure. Psychologically, the singling out of individuals as criminals and delivering them over to institutional mechanisms of enforcement and judgment are regarded as an enjoyable experience. This is especially true of the Classical and Golden Age periods in which apprehension—in the sense of both arrest and knowledge—

---

[10]   Stephen Knight analyzes this conflict in Sherlock Holmes stories, demonstrating that crime and its detection do not simply represent abnormality and corrective, respectively. They are, in fact, degrees of bourgeois normality—both excessive, either in acquisitiveness or rationality, but both recognizable class traits ("Case" 372).

is sufficient, and the distasteful aspects of incarceration or execution remain discreetly hidden away. And yet, contradictions cannot remain forever masked. Mandel foresees the breakdown of the genre (always a risky prediction, given the form's adaptability) for reasons of internal crisis in an outworn bourgeois worldview—once epitomized by the genre, these values are under attack by its inheritors.

Building upon Eagleton's claim that "significant developments in literary form … result from significant changes in ideology" (23), Mandel argues that shocks to emergent nineteenth-century bourgeois institutions were registered in generic changes. By late century, the hegemony of bourgeois rationality, embodied in the superhuman guise of the omniscient detective, was in decline. Such figures, who ostensibly worked through scientific methods or through a complex system of intuitive psychological typologies, were contested by American developments, in which "the abandonment of an investigative structure became increasingly common in narratives of both private and public crimes" (Horsley, *Noir* 44). In fact, this omniscient figure was displaced, in line with Mandel's critique, by "criminal protagonists" (*Noir* 44), which in 1930s films, before the intrusions of the Hays Office, allowed audiences "the double satisfaction of vicarious participation in gangster violence and of seeing violence turned against the gangster himself" (*Noir* 45–46)—again, a sort of hybrid division of identification tendencies registering social transformation.

The central premise is this: boundaries become visible when conventions can no longer sustain previously unquestioned structures, a transformation indicated repeatedly and more or less simultaneously in the oeuvres of several productive and long-lived authors (Christie, Mitchell, Carr, and Marsh are obvious examples). This claim is illustrated by Robin Woods for the Golden Age worldview in her analysis of Christie's boundary-defining novel *Curtain*. Woods explains how Classical texts, in this instance including the Golden Age, confront the problem of sympathy generated for criminals who have entered the spotlight of public interest "by presenting a fictional detective who absorbs the attention previously accorded the criminal"—this individual constitutes a "moral buffer" in these earlier texts (104), that is, those as a rule preceding World War II. Stories carefully exclude the criminal voice, reducing it to nodding confirmation or confession at the conclusion of the detective's summing up (Woods 104). Taking on this role of buffer, the detective necessarily becomes taboo, sacred in the ambiguous sense of exceeding socially determined norms. In this role he or she can come into contact with criminality, itself an excessive force, without risk of corruption. The detective serves as mediator, but this role entails prohibitions against contact and full integration into "normal" society. The detective's antisocial misanthropy partly arises from the threat of contamination,[11] but the detective's role also aids

---

[11]   In contrast, Bargainnier views the detective's isolation as a mark of objectivity unavailable to the suspects—freedom from bias, rather than contamination arising from proximity to the criminal (43).

in the compartmentalization of criminal and noncriminal, a pressing requirement in any detective text. The aim of many Golden Age narratives, particularly of the country house weekend variety, is to set these categories straight. Once they are established, the wrath of the group can be mobilized against the unmasked person. This aggressive impulse is a form of self-interested retaliation against the criminal: he or she has been instrumental in revealing the assorted misdeeds of the entire community, and thus of threatening the fundamental integrity of all preestablished categories. In such cases the power of language must be invested with care; given the fact that criminal intentions are revealed to be widespread, the detective's narrative-generating capacity may radically reconfigure reality. Whereas many characters may harbor murderous intentions, the detective can be relied upon as an incorruptible force and point of reference. The abandonment of this principle is the opening of criminal self-consciousness in the reader. To be sure, this argument does not seriously question the means by which criminality is established or in whose interest justice is operating. The origins of this process lie within the villain (or specific type of villainy). But villainy must be locatable since "the law cannot punish universal guilt" (Woods 109). The management of guilt is not only the establishment of boundaries but the nature of what is bounded in relation to an observer who is invested with the power of discourse. This complex idea requires a theoretical basis which draws from Marc Shell, Jean-Joseph Goux, and, more contemporaneous to the focus texts, Georges Bataille.

Economics and Literary Form

Economies may be understood in abstract terms, distinct from the prosaic concerns of stock markets, unemployment rates, and GDP. An economy denotes a dynamic process involving circulating elements within boundaries and responsive to conventions which are sometimes highly artificial. As a process, an economy consists of components in flux—points and frames of reference, flows and circulation, sites of production and expenditure, notions of value and correspondence. Although these analytic terms are applicable to fiscal systems, they are in fact concrete instances of a fundamentally modern experience, and therefore possess wider application than conventional notions of money. Following Marc Shell's insights on this point, and despite a persistent critical conjoining of language and money, we would be ill advised to assert primacy to a narrowly conceived money economy to serve as template for literary analysis. In his introduction to *The Economy of Literature*, Shell remarks the propensity among literary critics over the last 300 years to confuse economic language with economic structure and to reduce literary language, particularly that which consciously or unconsciously evokes economic imagery, to permit the conflation of the marketplace with literary texts.

Despite widespread interest in economic applications to literature, few scholars employ economic analysis in the context of detective fiction. Nonetheless, Shell's warnings concerning simplistic overstatement apply well to the most overt example, William Breit and Kenneth Elzinga's "Economics as Detective Fiction." Breit and Elzinga, two real-life economists (and collaborative authors of the Marshall Jevons mysteries), reverse the primacy of literary applications by stating that "almost all good economic analysis is structured like classical detective fiction," inasmuch as the detective-economist is scientific, predisposed "to find rational explanations for seemingly irrational behavior," and, most tellingly, engaged in a fundamentally epistemologically centered enterprise (368). Although reasons may be adduced for this reading, such evidence merely supports a highly reductionist approach to the subject that errs on the side of a narrow, disciplinary sense of economics.[12] To avoid this reduction the structural points expressed by relation, circulation, and boundary will guide much of my discussion, at least tacitly—these terms are more suited to my literary focus than the etymological derivations employed by Shell, namely, "the conventions (*nomoi*) of and distribution (*nemesis*) within the household (*oikos*)" (*Economy* 89), though his formulation is, in fact, the basis for my own. In this study, I am using the relation-circulation-boundary structure as a tool for comparative analysis rather than an end in itself. And so, as already stated, I am not interested in money *per se*, but rather the categories that inform economic thought such as (nonproductive) expenditure, guarantor, value, and (productive) labor in the context of the detective's impact on social structure and organization, the clue's convertibility, and the status of labor involved in establishing truth claims. To shift the point of view to authorial production, we are concerned with the tools that enable analysis of the production and consumption of texts at specific historical moments; perhaps unsurprisingly, these moments turn out to be eras of monetary crisis (Goux's preoccupation, but also an overt concern of Shell's [*Economy* 152]).

Shell is a point of departure, specifically in the set of conventions and distributions within the bounded relation already mentioned (*Economy* 89–90), the *nomos* and the *oikos*—though, of course, the *oikos* refers to a domestic situation which necessarily must be successively broadened in literary contexts. The family as the locus of crime, characteristic of *The Adventures of Sherlock Holmes* (1892), widens in scope as we approach the country house and its enclosed substitutes. Establishing the nature of this boundary is a pressing first concern which is facilitated by turning to Jean-Joseph Goux, especially in essays from *Symbolic Economies* (collected from his *Freud, Marx: Economie et Symbolique* and *Les Iconoclastes*). The erection of boundaries, which regulates the interface between detective and crime scene and which, furthermore, aids him or her in determining the nature of the event and the scope and propriety of any solution, may be linked explicitly to Goux's work on the general equivalent. This application is not only

---

[12] More astute economic readings, both interestingly derived from Hammett, are found in Cooper and Murphy's "Taking Chances: Speculation and Games of Detection in Dashiell Hammett's *Red Harvest*" and Freedman and Kendrick's "Forms of Labor in Dashiell Hammett's *Red Harvest*."

relevant to the Golden Age detective, but extends also to the hard-boiled operative, though in a different sense.

The logical derivation of the general equivalent as it figures in Marx's analysis of money is the means to move on to "other domains, where values are no longer economic, where the play of substitutions defines qualitative values" (Goux, *Symbolic* 3). We question how authority functions within a system to valorize substitutions and to establish boundaries, that is, to determine which spaces are valid for exchange, which naturally enough regulates what passes as just. For literary criticism this authority is initially linked to authorship embedded in a sociohistorical situation. For Goux, it seems that common perceptions of boundary or limit—which he terms *"certain distinctive poles"*—are erected through repetition and systematic behavior (*Symbolic* 10). Such boundaries preexist self-conscious acts of exchange and so problematize locating any origin. That said, such functional and ideological blocks are not delimiting in the case of literary representations.

In the Golden Age text and its immediate precursors (those of the quarter-century preceding World War I), the detective assumes the function of general equivalent, reproducing its problematic relation to social relations on more than one level. Goux's description of the general equivalent as "not simply an equivalence but a privileged, exclusive place, that of measuring object" (*Symbolic* 3) is an apt description of such detectives. This role, however, "stands in a double relationship with the world of elements which it governs and represents: both a privileged relationship ... and a correlated relationship of exclusion" (*Symbolic* 18). The privilege is not only the conventional presumption of the Golden Age detective's innocence in terms of the crime; this vantage enables the definition of boundaries so that the crime is contained and, subsequently, a plausible solution is forthcoming. And yet, such a vantage implies a measure that can only take place from outside, from a lack of full integration into the system which is now visually contained and at least tacitly endorsed. Goux continues: "The logical exclusion of the general equivalent, along with its sovereignty and its monopoly, imprints it with a transcendent character. It functions from the other world" (*Symbolic* 18), but once it does appear, "the analysis of value can begin" (*Symbolic* 22). The "theological character" of this other world generates a profoundly ambiguous understanding of the detective, who offers salvation (for some) but who also takes on the authoritarian role of the punishing Father.

The detective's transcendental status, the "sovereign element," itself possesses "no equivalent"—"it is out of the ordinary, placed for this reason outside the community it governs." Goux anticipates my later critique of latent authoritarianism in such figures by stating that "it legislates as an exception" (*Symbolic* 31), redolent of both Hobbes and Carl Schmitt. These remarks also pertain to the hard-boiled subgenre, though in the special sense that the hard-boiled detective's claim to outsider status takes a different semantic tack—he or she is an outsider in terms of powerlessness to act upon the boundary-defining function. To summarize: Classical or Golden Age detectives *appear* anterior to the problem to be solved (the exceptional event), and this appearance typically establishes the measure by which the bounded system comes into focus. The site's hermetic qualities, essentially a cliché composed of the isolated crime scene with its well-defined cast of suspects, certainly helps strengthen the boundaries of the criminal economy; however, this is just a subconscious response in the reader to what is already present—the potential (in the detective) to establish a totality by which deviancy and degrees of guilt are assigned without being tainted in the process. The detective's isolation, what Goux calls "excommunication," is a mark of taboo status, highlighted socially in Holmes's drug abuse, Miss Marple's sexual and economic marginality, or Mrs. Bradley's grotesque cackle and wardrobe. In contrast, the hard-boiled hero is commonly understood to be caught up inside the action so that the only recourse to totality is negation; skepticism towards the outside is a gesture towards relativism but also a concession to the detective's own indistinguishability from the criminal world he or she engages. Generally consigned to the outside, hard-boiled operatives are excluded from the community, though it may well be a community in which they feel ill at ease. Such exclusion contrasts with the positive exclusion of their Classical and Golden Age counterparts in their role of admired guarantors of community.

The significance of this point for this model is that an outside and inside must be discernible (putting aside for the moment the problem of defining the location whence this relation is grasped). This binary relation is not only a structural device; it also entails an economic logic. The connection between this logic and literature is not merely an analogy, as we shall see in the application of Georges Bataille's work from the 1930s. Bataille helps us discern an ideological continuum between relevant philosophical and juridical debates arising in the 1920s and developments in contemporaneous and subsequent popular culture. The poles may be grasped in concerns over the basis for law that become acute in the confusion following World War I, and whose poles are defined by normativism (Hans Kelsen) and decisionism (Carl Schmitt). Specific to detective fiction, the outside-inside divide extends to a set of "rules" by which foreigners, colonials, racial minorities, and the servant class are excluded from active participation in the Golden Age murder game. Of course, this does not exclude them from various petty offenses, but unless they are unmasked as imposters who merely play at being invisible, they are not part of the so-called microcosms familiar in writers like Christie.

The country house is simply the most obvious physical boundary of this microcosm—the airplane, boat, train, snowbound lodge, and remote archaeological dig are its avatars. The communities established in these locations are more porous and in fact larger than they seem, since the marginalized underclass is barely acknowledged. The chief Golden Age dramatis personae are ascribed value by virtue of their appearance within the closed economy of the restricted site, though the authority grounding their licitness remains hidden. The calculation of value inevitably turns out to be misaligned since someone is a counterfeit, merely appearing to pass muster as currency. The detective's task is to expose this counterfeit who threatens our trust of any identity within the prescribed boundaries. And so, we require an individual with certain traits who can penetrate the closed system, but as an element whose value is not conditioned or questioned by circulating within it. Within this generic formula the detective thereby takes on the metaphorical role of a *circulating* general equivalent.

In practical terms, the closing off of the site protects the economy of meaning from the threat of outside pressures or epistemological disequilibrium, of which the hermeticism of the locked room represents the extreme case. The detective helps to delimit the field of inquiry, drawing up boundaries in the confrontation with a plenum of meaning and an explosion of signification which overloads the possibility of immediately assigning proper values. Readers and characters alike defer to the detective's judgment, his or her limiting function. In confronting the excess of signification, the detective disengages the clue from its misascribed meanings to establish objective relations. Goux illuminates this process in general terms when he writes, "supplementary (superfluous) elements are what govern the circulation of substitutes. The surplus is excluded to act as measure of the replacements. In general, whatever the register, the universal exchange-value is linked to excess" (*Symbolic* 31). Only by escaping the chains of substitution can a guarantee be established by which to achieve certainty. The curious nature of this performance is its very theatricality, its reduction to aesthetic pleasure. Not only was this model suggested contemporaneously to the fictional texts under study by Georges Bataille, he also offers a theory of symbolic expenditure to explain this aesthetic turn.

Bataille's Economic Perspectivism

Bataille's first systematic venture into economic theory appears "precisely at a turning point in the history of capitalism, in the 1920s and 1930s" (Goux, "General" 210). To be sure, this "turning point" had been on the horizon for some time: Lewis Corey's cogent and statistic-filled diagnoses of economic change written in the mid-1930s could build upon Lenin's *Imperialism, the Highest Stage of Capitalism* from 20 years earlier. Like Trotsky and his collaborators (for instance, Daniel Guérin), Corey understood fascism in conventional Marxist terms: as an intensification of existing capitalist practices. Bataille differs from these authors in his grudging admiration for a fascist "solution" that was not forthcoming in previous regimes of capitalist exploitation, though this is pursued at a psychological level and is linked to his understanding of nonproductive expenditure. Nonproductive expenditure contrasts with the spectacular waste that is carried out under and as part of capitalism with the object of maintaining or increasing profits—hinted at by Marx in *Capital* I (741) and remarked by diverse writers such as advertising critic James Rorty (11), economist Henryk Szlajfer (299, 307), and Goux in his "General Economics and Postmodern Capitalism."

Bataille's early philosophical essays identify a contradiction which will become more acute over time, namely, the discursive reduction and tabulation of objects and categories of experience which are themselves ill suited to categorization. Though often employing a nontraditional philosophical language, the structural problem concerns the framing of abjection and waste to represent them as objects of knowledge and scientific inquiry. This tension, recognized and developed by critics like Jacques Derrida, Michel Foucault, and Jean-Luc Nancy, is at the root of Bataille's interrogation of dialectical thought. For our purpose, this situation is best described by Joseph Libertson, who emphasizes Bataille's refusal to offer a synthesis; instead, Libertson reads Bataille's philosophical vocabulary as a series of posited and retracted terms which displace each other, a trend which begins in "The Psychological Structure of Fascism" (1933) but is already discernible in "The Use Value of D.A.F. de Sade" (c. 1930). In these early works "the characteristic structure of Bataille's dialectic" is comprised "of two terms which violently oppose each other, and simultaneously condition each other so intimately as to compromise the univocity of their opposition" (Libertson 679). Before pursuing this line of thought further, some terms and arguments require clarification.

"The Use Value of D.A.F. de Sade," an early effort at revaluating scarcity, productive capacity, and the role of positivistic science in shaping economic relations and "useful" knowledge, erects "two polarized human impulses" (Bataille 94), namely excretion and appropriation: both are relevant to detective fiction's epistemological concerns. These categories are not sequentialized, spatialized, or overtly hierarchicized—they are interpenetrating modes which must be understood as alterities that resist a neutralizing synthesis. The terms *homogeneity* and *heterogeneity*, developed in greater depth in later essays, are introduced in this fundamentally ambivalent way: "The process of appropriation is ... characterized by a homogeneity (static equilibrium) of the author of the appropriation, and of objects as final result, whereas excretion presents itself as the result of a heterogeneity, and can move in the direction of an ever greater heterogeneity, liberating impulses whose ambivalence is more and more pronounced" (Bataille, "Use Value" 95). Whereas these descriptions seem geared towards observable practices—the mobilization of productive forces in the creation of commodities or the sacrificial destruction of useful goods—Bataille is in fact pointing to an underlying substrate of concepts, concepts that have been normalized and endorsed by the efforts of science and philosophy. The typical practice of philosophy, Bataille holds, is to erect reference points whose value arises from privileged categories ultimately grounded in power, the object of which is to insure the homogeneity of social (and thus productive) relations. The theology of a homogeneous religious practice functions to guarantee a system of relations which neutralizes the transgressive eruption of heterogeneity, typically, in a world represented by *individual* acts that threaten the homogeneous social fabric. The tendency of the Golden Age, within the parameters I propose, sustains such a society.

In "The Notion of Expenditure" (1933) the privileging of consumption that reproduces the means to production is contrasted with a second consumption, whose object is the wanton destruction of resources (termed *nonproductive expenditure* to differentiate it from the first meaning). Such consumption proceeds without the promise of return so that investment and recuperation are swept aside. The favoring of productive relations entails expenditures that are limited and conservationist in nature (Bataille, "Notion" 116). Detective labor is difficult to situate in the larger scope of capitalist relations: the detective is neither a producer of tangible products nor a provider of services quite like other services. We witness such confusion in unpaid or coopted labor, as well as the absent, corporate, abstract, or recalcitrant client. Nonetheless, detective labor is historically coincident with the outcomes of successful bourgeois revolutions and the global triumph of capitalism. Instead of accumulation, the function of detective labor is often the securing and guaranteeing of a ground upon which homogeneous relations can operate; a technical scientific basis for this justification, while perhaps understandable, is not actually necessary. The conservationism of the Golden Age, however legitimated, is also its conservatism in service to those classes which benefit most from stable conditions of production. The ideological contradiction arising from an avid readership with only tenuous investments in such outcomes is not hard to see, but the hard-boiled, more often connected to the pulps and proletarian popular readership, seems less prone to such manipulations. The hard-boiled tale, with its blatant intrusions of nonproductive expenditure and its foregrounding of a world less obviously genteel-bourgeois, may well be understood differently. These tendencies of action and setting raise the question whether the hard-boiled detective really serves different interests or whether hard-boiled action leads to the retrenching of homogeneous relations. This question will be taken up in Chapter 3.

To the degree that the detective tale of any genre offers an approach to dissolution (death, loss, taboo violence or sexuality), the approach is nonetheless made within safe tolerances which typically criminalize archaic agonistic impulses. For Bataille, the stakes wagered by not admitting the "value" of nonproductive expenditure, or its curtailment into diluted forms of individual dissipation, are great. The class-based restriction on consumption, which ironically penalized the predominantly wage-earning producers for their enormous productive capacity, is only tangentially related to the lurid picture painted by Bataille—with his far-flung and overstated reduction of historical and anthropological examples as "evidence" for his expenditure thesis.[13] The real historical focus is the failure of democracy, the victory of monopoly State capitalism, and the potential rise of fascism in France, the United Kingdom, and the United States, the three most enthusiastic early producers and consumers of detective fiction. The renunciation of expenditure, particularly in Bataille's Weber-derived Protestant ethic, is in fact only a "theoretical negation" (Bataille, "Notion" 125), sometimes a negation whose object is rehabilitated as a form of investment.

The terms *homogeneous* and *heterogeneous*, central to "The Notion of Expenditure," are overtly politicized in "The Psychological Structure of Fascism." The homogeneous corresponds to a state of normalcy; it is antithetical to the exceptional state. The homogeneous is the world of rules which fix relations between persons and things in familiar situations and which subordinates consumption to productive activity (Bataille, "Psychological Structure" 137–38).

---

[13]   Bataille's anthropological claims concerning nonproductive expenditure are faulty. Eric Wolfe untangles some of the confusion regarding potlatch, pointing up Bataille's misunderstandings, in the chapter "The Kwakiutl" in *Envisioning Power*; see especially the section "Potlatching" (111–23).

In developed capitalist societies, the impetus to maintain social homogeneity is not uniform; it is disrupted by disequilibrium resulting from exploitation, and so the greater incentives to its maintenance are located in the class which controls the means of production. The interests of this class, and of the State, are nonetheless upheld by the workers' psychological investment in homogeneity, despite the fact that it may not reflect their immediate interests. Challenges to this "precarious form" are met in different ways, depending upon the character of the State—democratically through parliamentary neutralization, or, under totalitarianism, through autocratic violence (Bataille, "Psychological Structure" 139).

Homogeneity is linked to the scientific scrutiny of phenomena, which integrates and explains within a defined field of vision so as to promote self-consciousness. In this, homogeneity is analogous to the space surveyed by the Classic and Golden Age detective, who acknowledges the trangressive act and goes about explaining it, usually in the interest of re-establishing legitimate social relations or to remove those who block their operation. The hard-boiled detective, typically lacking the elevated vision of the bounded social totality, ostensibly cannot reduce the chaotic social milieu to the object of science (discourse), taken as a type of comprehensive knowledge and a reliance upon known, measurable quantities underpinning "true" assertions. The detective is a heterogeneous element, irreducible to a grid of productive relations and certainly opposed to official institutional organs linked to the State. Nonetheless, the hard-boiled voice, often transmitted in the first person, survives a series of life-threatening ordeals and social explosions.

Having associated the Golden Age detective with the confirmation, guarantee, and maintenance of homogeneous social relations (by virtue of being beyond them) and the hard-boiled investigator with heterogeneous elements, we must also make some mention of Bataille's treatment of fascist leaders. The fascist leader directs the energies of society, including its violence, independently of the rule of law; thus the leader is exceptional and necessarily beyond the boundaries of homogeneous life. The leader's transcendence makes boundaries visible, but the conditions by which homogeneity can continue seem to be spontaneously generated, that is, the myth of universal democratic rights and freedoms, of fraternity between classes or at least the paternalistic benevolence of the official rulers. In short, I refer to the "different human situations" by which it "is possible to dominate and even to oppress one's fellows," situations that appear under the "diverse circumstances" which Bataille lists ("Psychological Structure" 145) and which, in this case, appear because of "the inability of homogeneous society to find in itself a reason for being and acting," which "makes it dependent upon imperative forces" ("Psychological Structure" 146–47). But it is not simply stagnancy or alienation that impels homogeneous society towards creating the conditions for the heterogeneous to emerge—it is this society's "internal contradictions": "the development of heterogeneous forces necessarily come to signify a solution to a problem posed by the contradictions of *homogeneity*" ("Psychological Structure" 156), and, Bataille makes clear, the solution inevitably will benefit the capitalist insofar as this enterprise is aligned with the State.

Absolutism and Relativism as Generic Determiners in Detective Fiction

Economic frames, and the relation of the detective to those frames, entail questions of how truth is bounded—when the frames are determined outside of a necessary human agency (extreme scientific positivism) or, alternatively, relativized due to an inability to define phenomena. Truth can operate within a bounded economy whereby signs normally accepted without question are brought into doubt—this takes the form of a mystery and the clues associated with it. As we shall see, the disruption, frequently violent, does not indicate a departure from the status quo; rather, what we note is the fragility and indeed the myth of that status quo, which must continually be guaranteed to remain operational. That guarantee breaks down from any number of causes. When it does, the fragility of what is known is revealed—the transformation of places and objects, especially those which had neutral or positive meanings and associations, into sites of mystery or deviance. The conviction that stable meanings can be restored is problematic, as implied in Knight (*Crime* 86, 107) and Horsley (*Twentieth-Century* 10). The process of repair itself undermines the faith in the validity of signs and identities, since the event brings to light the weakness of the State, its institutions, and its institutional representatives, or some other guarantor, whether psychological, ethical, or ontological. The role of the detective in the Golden Age clue-puzzle form is to temporarily reestablish stability and a tenuous faith in the system (Knight, *Crime* 5), at least until the next crisis appears, since it is clear that crises will reappear— as certain, in fact, as the periodic economic crises concomitant with capitalism.

In constructing valid determinations of truth, detectives articulate relations between language and event. Sometimes their efforts take the form of an unmasking and revelation (the discovery of truth understood to exist independently of the players), sometimes as a function of institutional authority or its representatives (truth as mediated by power). In both operations the events themselves must be determined, sorted, modified or discarded, sequentialized, and encoded with meaning and self-sufficiency. Meaning is contingent with the establishment of boundaries that are ideologically charged, since what is brought into vision exists within limits. As readers of detective fiction, we negotiate between our position of limited vision and a posited totality. Visual metaphors are unstable because the system is dynamic and truth is part of an economy in which tokens are revalued and boundaries redrawn. But the reconstitution of truth also threatens to undermine conviction, a potential that is comically highlighted in parodies like *The Poisoned Chocolates Case*. The question of power, never far removed from questions of value, depends in part on (transcendental) guarantees and boundary-establishing regimes which can be impersonal and abstract. Yet the detective is sometimes in competition with institutional players who threaten misalignment with powerful interest groups.

How truths are guaranteed within different modes of detective fiction, namely, how they are made visible, is significant to determining generic and economic *tendencies*. The different tendencies in detective fiction are not metaphors for specific forms of economic activity (a weakness in Mandel's study); they are economic in structure. What the texts represent and what they are do not have some one-to-one relation; instead, beyond specific plot elements, the definition of events within texts tends towards specific economic modes. Within this model two generic forms tend towards Absolutism and two towards Relativism. Of these four, I will only discuss two in this study—the Golden Age tends towards an externalized Absolutism, externalized in that its guarantors are lodged in figures whose actions stabilize institutions with specific ideological aims and are beholden to specific interest groups. A large number of Classical texts, and the ones which have in fact best survived, adhere to this tendency. Compared to their Golden Age counterparts, hard-boiled detectives are premised on an internalized Relativism whose guarantors are ill-aligned with institutions and strong interest groups, though, ironically, they often serve them. Moreover, these guarantors, unlike Golden Age detectives, are weak, ineffectual, and typically unrewarded for their efforts. Their quests for personal or social stability remain tenuous, save in hyperbolic cases like Mike Hammer. The contradiction in this type, to simplify somewhat, is that the illusion of interiority is premised on a tacit recognition of totality that is *not* supposed to exist. These complicated statements sketching economic tendencies need expansion. They will be clarified in Chapters 2 and 3 through Bataille and Goux, who give us some tools to understand more fully these economic frameworks.

Two other types deserve mention. A second Absolutist type is one which invokes scientific positivism and is epitomized by Arthur B. Reeve's Craig Kennedy stories, but is also present with some frequency in R. Austin Freeman. This system is Absolutist in that it holds events and psychology to be reducible to knowable facts (or, alternately, to exclude some data from any positive, and thus scientifically significant, value). These truth quanta are subject to correct interpretation, which, presumably, any other competent scientist could discover under similar circumstances. R. Austin Freeman's creation, Dr. John Thorndyke, is a case in point. Freeman's lawyer-physician, from his 1907 debut in *The Red Thumb Mark*, encourages his colleagues to come to their own conclusions, confident that since they possess the same data as he, they will arrive at the same result. His mantra—"collect facts, make hypotheses, test them and seek verification" (Freeman, *Red* 22)—never undergoes self-scrutiny in the sense of questioning the nature of a fact or the socially-mediated aspect of a test, and it remains pronounced in Freeman's work to his last series of Thorndyke novels 35 years later.

The United States produced its own version of this robust confidence in scientific method. In the introduction to one of Reeve's first efforts, his volume *The Silent Bullet* (1910), Kennedy remarks to his Watson, Walter Jameson, "I am going to apply science to the detection of crime, the same sort of methods by which you trace out the presence of a chemical, or run an unknown germ to earth" ("Craig Kennedy's" 3). Kennedy invokes a methodology which "escapes" ideological distortions—cold deduction instead of creative abduction, despite the stories' sensationalism. In the title story, "The Silent Bullet," Kennedy asserts that "the forcing of man's secrets is like the forcing of nature's secrets. Both are pieces of detective work. The methods employed in the detection of crime are, or rather should be, like the methods employed in the process of discovering scientific truth" (25). In the end, the scientist demonstrates a truth which leads irrevocably to consequences (legal and, by extension, moral) that we are not permitted to question.

The final mode corresponds to postmodern and metaphysical detective fiction, a comparatively restricted genre in terms of both texts and readership. The instability of meaning in such texts points up their Relativism, which appears in a far more radicalized form than that found in the hard-boiled. Here the notion of totality is genuinely dispensed with, leading to infinite deferral. Within popular notions of detective fiction technique, these deferrals often make the texts look like failures in that clues have little stability, solutions are not forthcoming, the means of transmission are paradoxical, focalization is problematic, and all manner of conventions are overturned. This mode, if developed, would belong to a separate study, particularly given the more canonical associations around Borges, Robbe-Grillet, Eco, Auster, and their postmodern colleagues.

In the two chapters which follow, I build upon the theoretical concerns elaborated in this introduction. Chapters 2 and 3 complement each other: the former explains how Classical and Golden Age detectives engage in acts of framing by which the criminal event is identified and placed within parameters that allow its "proper" solution. The means of framing, despite appearances of factual, scientifically informed investigative methods, frequently entails an ideological construction which supports a system of homogeneous, productive relations. The latter, in which I examine hard-boiled examples, demonstrates degrees of difference from this framing action, commencing with technologically mediated forms of framing. These forms replace the human dimension of detective authority to bring into vision the collapse of the detective's ability to neutralize events, a development exemplified in the haptic relations that dominate many texts by Hammett and Chandler.

Chapter 4 turns to the means by which evidence is ascribed value, a process that depends upon the detective's role as guarantor, a sort of gold standard operating within a social frame. Over time, the anxious inability to affix meaning to any discrete element in the system grows as the detective's power vis-à-vis institutions declines. Chapters 5 and 6 take on the problem of detective labor, first examining how such labor differs from most experiences of capitalist work regimens and then turning to the different aims of this work within the subgenres (what I term *gift-labor*). The Classical and Golden Age genres are aligned in the eventual subordination of labor to "social" interests, further revealed to have a class rationale. The hard-boiled requires more detailed examination in that it displays a much broader range of gift-labor than the general tendency of its Classical and Golden Age counterparts. The Classical/Golden Age detective functions to guarantee boundaries that delimit the gift, to reinscribe it within economic modes of thought, despite initial impressions to the contrary. In contrast, hard-boiled authors describe a trajectory that modifies (Coxe), then challenges (Nebel, Whitfield), then becomes self-conscious of (Chandler), then becomes unselfconscious of (Spillane) detective gift-labor; this multistage process moves towards an aneconomic form. The dialectic illustrating this process is demonstrated in Chapter 6 through a series of textual analyses.

Chapter 2
Conservationism, Enclosure, and Totalitarianism

The Closed System: Conservationism and Entropy

Mid-nineteenth-century scientific and sociological theories like Darwinian evolution and Marxist class conflict were not only instrumental in weakening belief in a transcendental God; such theories lent prestige to scientific explanations of the world which could in fact serve as new grounds for meaning. Van Dover suggests that nascent detective fiction, with its ostensibly scientific basis, might be read as taking on this function in a popular context (10). As quasiscientific figures, detectives nonetheless demand scrutiny, given their power to discursively formulate truth. In this they possess an agency that differs significantly from the impersonal historical mechanisms of natural selection or class struggle—detective agency is both highly individualized and somewhat isolated. Roger Caillois, having the Golden Age operative in mind, understands the detective as "not quite assimilable into the body social" (38), referring both to the detective's bohemianism or eccentricity and to the detective's authoritative anteriority. By transcending the system they engage, Golden Age detectives register the limits by which transgression is measured and thereby anchor and stabilize meaning. In addition to defining boundaries, the Golden Age detective is instrumental in defusing the exceptional situation when it threatens the integrity of preexisting boundaries. Detective eccentricity—taken literally as off-centeredness—is the critical distance that brings the totality into vision. Speaking from the margins of that totality, defined positively or negatively, confirms that the detective is not fully a member of the society he or she defends, upholds, guarantees, makes possible, or, in the hard-boiled, negates.

These ideas resonate in Hilfer, who maintains that the detective "guarantees the rationality of the world and the integrity of the self" (2). This guarantee is one of grounded meaning emerging through the discursive operations of the denouement. If the detective of the Golden Age serves to close the social wound inflicted by criminal behavior, that closure is also the reestablishment of limits challenged by criminal transgression. In its more threatening guise, the logic employed to repair damage can likewise be used casuistically to justify any number of social imbalances, even to soothe the anxieties of those who victimize themselves by supporting the interests of exploitative Others. Whether or not that logic endorses conservatism,[1] it definitely tends towards *conservationism*, a conservationist

---

[1]   The conservatism of the Golden Age is discussed in Horsley (*Twentieth-Century* 18); Symons (108); Kelly (162); and Bargainnier (17).

principle threatened by the entropic effects of criminal transgression. Golden Age authors consistently underwrite a conservationist principle to counteract entropic diffusion: their management function involves identifying, reducing, and neutralizing the exceptional event to bring about discursive closure.

Peter Hühn demonstrates that the artificiality of much closure in detective fiction is a consequence of a system intrinsically incapable of preventing deviancy. We infer, therefore, that any restoration would be a return to a flawed state, since what logically is restored is the potential of repeated deviance.[2] For Hühn, crime destabilizes "because the system of norms and rules regulating life in the community has proved powerless"—the detective is a narrative necessity because those entrusted with the maintenance of order have failed, and the guardians of social order cannot encode events with meaning: "their inability to discover and tell the story of the crime, thus threatens the validity of established order" (452). The detective's magical act of language is tied to the historical contexts in which the Classical and Golden Age texts thrived on both sides of the Atlantic. In the case of the latter, the rattled middle classes were escaping from the aftermath of World War I, in which the evolutionary discourse attuned to the unquestioned leadership of the British Empire over its vast colonial possessions had been seriously undermined. The ideology that "inferior" populations could look forward, at least in fantasy, to advancing along the path already blazed by their colonial masters was challenged, occasioning a shock to prestige and a demand for introspection. Moreover, deep insecurity arose with the victories of monopoly capitalism, which converted broad sections of the work force into propertyless wage earners at the mercy of gigantic concentrations of trustified capital.

Given these doubts, we should look skeptically at Classical and Golden Age denouements. They are not the restoration of Eden through the identification and expulsion of the offender; neither do they function, in Symons's phrase, as a religious experience by which guilt is expiated "through ritual and symbolic sacrifice" (9; see also Cawelti, *Adventure* 106–7). In the postlapsarian world, no return to a state prior to knowledge is possible, only a consciousness of loss brought about by knowledge of the transgressive act. The legacy of this act is sequential violence, just as the outcome of the first novel is almost invariably the series. The return to a status quo is a return to the conditions by which violence can and does erupt once more, but the cyclical function of this violence is not so much a concern with guilt or even the need to seek justice or redress for the victims; instead, the victim and the punishment of a culprit are a means to solidify group identity (Heissenbüttel 84, 88) on the one hand, and, on the other, to meet definite psychological needs that a system dedicated to homogeneous productive relations cannot satisfy. In its economic dimension, this return is the temporary

---

2   Following the lead of W.H. Auden, many critics maintain that detectives in Classical and Golden Age stories mend a torn social fabric. See, for example, Kennedy (185); Laura Marcus (248); Klein (5); Johanna Smith (86); Mahan (2); Bargainnier (10); Aydelotte (70); and Evans (2). For an opposing view, see McCann (91).

and precarious balance that Marx perceives between cyclical crises in Volume 3 of *Capital* (357).

To address these demands, the social fabric is rent by the exceptional situation which the managers of homogeneous society appear unable to repair. The detective helps bring the exceptional event within tolerable limits, which, to use Bataille's parlance, corresponds to a decline. The exception or summit experience—the immediacy of sacrifice or ecstatic sexual engagement, for instance—is understood by Bataille to be an event destined to undergo decline, namely, the containment of taboo violence or eroticism through its conversion into discourse or containment within prescribed social norms. We might argue that this summit experience, particularly in the lack of immediacy characteristic of reading, was never a true gamble since meaning itself is not wagered (as it might be in postmodern fiction). The sacrificial victim merely becomes a preordained vehicle for discursive reduction and serves as a disappointing safety valve for the system's expenditure requirements. Arguably, the return to and definition of a stable self and community is possible after participating vicariously in transgression, which in Foucault's reading of Bataille is, in any case, necessary to demarcating a limit. This double movement is foremost an aesthetic experience in the closed theatrical space of the Golden Age, and our own aesthetic engagement entails a cathartic risk about as great as a night at the theater.

The exceptional event, usually a violent disruption, challenges an implied normative worldview. This worldview, particularly as it comes to us through Classical and Golden Age detective fiction, is premised on norms of gender, ethnicity, sexuality, and familial relations. These can be adduced and are intimately connected to a problem which the detective must set right. To say that this correspondence between the object of detective labor and the interests of the moneyed elite is simply self-serving egotism and self-celebration would be overstated. To be sure, the genre's American origins correspond to the flowering of bourgeois entrepreneurial hegemony, but its heyday in fact arrives during twentieth-century crisis, and its popularity, even in so-called vestigial forms like the locked room and romantic hard-boiled detective, has not been eclipsed. Nonetheless, the forms of bourgeois power we associate with Classical and Golden Age fiction, built around specific forms of imperialism and self-conscious class differences, no longer exist in their nineteenth-century forms.

We certainly can find evidence that detectives are aligned with this value system, but often enough, this alignment issues a challenge to the ethics emerging from late eighteenth- and nineteenth-century bourgeois revolutions, specifically the notion of equality under law and the divorce of rights from social status or other arbitrary qualities of the individual. We see this strikingly in Holmes, who repeatedly refuses to act upon his knowledge when middle-class criminals are concerned. In "The Adventure of the Devil's Foot" (1910) the crime is essentially committed twice but only acted upon once. Holmes seems prepared to bring the perpetrator of the first crime to justice, but this murderer is himself killed in an act of revenge. The second killer, a solvent member of the educated professional classes, is let off; moreover, we are asked as an audience to condone the crime and Holmes's attitude towards it, and to disdain the pathetic fumbling of an incompetent police force. Even in cases where the detective is sworn to uphold the law, as in Freeman's Dr. Thorndyke stories, we find a definite lack of enthusiasm to pursue a certain class of "sympathetic" murderers, victims of blackmail like Rufus Pembury in "A Case of Premeditation" (1912) or Marcus Pottermack in *Mr. Pottermack's Oversight* (1930). Of course, it doesn't hurt that the blackmailers are vulgar representatives of the lower orders and their victims refined gentlemen.

In the system I have sketched, conservationism applies to the ethical and political frame of reference in which the interests of the dominant group are reestablished after a transgressive disruption, typically emerging from within the group itself. This distinction differentiates the Classical and Golden Age subgenres from the hard-boiled and the police procedural. And so it is not the ethical and political conservatism of the Golden Age authors, American or British, which is thematized so much as their attempts to manage entropy in the systems they engage. This idea brings us to an examination of how enclosures are formulated and defended and how, over time, they tend towards dissolution within the Golden Age subgenre.

Metaphors of Enclosure

The closed site, which allows for the isolation of bodies and objects, is central to Golden Age settings, whether events transpire in the country house or the space station—a closed site, however, is more than a physical barrier. Importantly, temporal limits are closely aligned with enclosed space: both dimensions are complementary, given that bodies can be assigned specific coordinates at a given moment. The complicated timeline, pushed to absurd complexity in writers like Freeman Wills Crofts, may therefore function as effectively in defining bodies as an impassable spatial barrier. As if to emphasize the plottable aspect of bodies, the maps common to Golden Age fiction are elevated views that imply visual power over space with the assumption that these spaces are simply what they are: they merely literalize an abstract problem. Used in conjunction with the timetable, sometimes calculated to the second, they present themselves as objective (albeit sometimes disputable) displays of data. Questioning the calculable appearance of bodies in spatiotemporal terms is tantamount to rejecting the rational laws of nature, and the denouement only reaffirms this truism. Although the exceptional event, in the guise of a crime, is often linked to the apparent defiance of these laws, the detective astutely reestablishes the validity of the natural order, the regularized, predictable quality of the universe. Perhaps unsurprisingly, such qualities parallel a bourgeois value system—the convergence of time, space, and bodies instrumental to the calculation of productive output or wages.

The sociological and psychological dimensions of detective fiction lead us on to another set of approaches to enclosure, one which focuses attention on a discernible moral and legal order. If we concede the genre to be about more than the vicarious or intellectual thrills of engaging a complicated criminal case, we also come to see the trajectory of the Classical and Golden Age stories as a complex interaction between social fears of crime among the middle classes (stoked by the news media) and the need to be reassured about the legitimacy and strength of that order. Roth goes so far as to claim such engagement is "the story of a compulsive fascination between the detective and some extralegal order" (153). The "restoration" of that order is, according to Kestner, precarious, in that the "reassert[ion] [of] stability through narrative closure," in this case the confirmation of the dominant order, reveals that this ideological point is "inwardly conflicted" (*Edwardian* 15). The economy of the Golden Age is not founded merely upon the gold standard of detective discourse, a security that is usually taken for granted; rather, the potential arbitrariness of any standard subsists in the reader's mind, and sometimes requires rituals of proof. Holmes's role in "The Red-Headed League," for instance, is not only to assemble clues into a plausible narrative but also visibly to demonstrate his underwriting of an unseen ground, lending validity to the institutions that themselves underpin concrete social relations (see Chapter 4).

Class configurations, obvious upon reading any pre–World War II text by Christie, Carr, or Marsh, comprise our last criterion of closure. The limits imposed by class are obviously connected to spatial arrangements inasmuch as the country house, the ocean liner, or the exclusive hotel erects class barriers—they bring into vision the characters who will enact the drama while consigning the servant, the foreigner, and artisan labor to invisibility. In one of its best-known Classical formulations, Father Brown remarks how context influences the granting of identity and individuality to a human being: the question of whether someone is staying at a house depends upon his or her status within the house as much as who is asking the question (Chesterton, "Invisible" 92). The invisibility of stock characters like the lodgekeeper and the second chambermaid is explained by these framing devices of social custom and power, and thus allows us in this case to look through Chesterton's mailman, ironically reducing him and other lesser mortals to the status of the automata in "The Invisible Man" which populate the victim's flat—the robots likewise do not count. To this question of social perception, we add the property requirements to produce plausible motives that would not normally touch the lower orders, unless, of course, the servants themselves turn out to be operating under an alias or in disguise (as happens, for instance, in Christie's *The Murder of Roger Ackroyd* and *Three Act Tragedy*, respectively). The artificiality of this enclosure is clear enough, particularly after World War I had played havoc with Britain's class structure (Panek, *Watteau's* 11), but its ideological necessity is also clear in an author like Christie, whose "criminals are traitors to the class and world which is so calmly described" (Knight, "Golden" 82).

If the closed/open configuration is viewed from the perspective of the detective hero, the problem tends to be understood as an outside/inside relation, respectively, where the outside is defined through the omniscience, expert status, or omnicompetence of a detective (Classical/Golden Age), to whom we cede power and who typically serves as the trusted vehicle of truth. The insider, whose range of vision may exceed our own, nevertheless is limited by forces outside his or her control. Knight's claim that unity depends upon an external reference point can be accommodated to the hard-boiled inasmuch as the narrative convention of the first-person narrator both limits our vision and conveys the assurance of survival.[3] And so the hard-boiled detective does not necessarily differ radically from the Classical/Golden Age detective in being anterior to the text.[4] In both instances, the detective as reference point is the condition of possibility for signification, and one that allows us to remove ourselves from the closure but also to see its "proper" outlines.

Establishing the contours of a problem is essential to its mastery, a process which generally ends up taking two routes, the second of which is the more important for us. The first route consists of a logic which exists independent of the investigator and which is uncovered with the aid of incontestable facts. This form finds its purest expression in figures like Jacques Futrelle's Thinking Machine, Professor S.F.X. Van Dusen. For Professor Van Dusen, the establishment of correct parameters serves as a point of embarkation that, once fixed, leads to inevitable conclusions—for instance, in "The Problem of the Knotted Cord," Van Dusen complains to Hutchinson Hatch, his chronicler, that he cannot proceed without an incontestable reference: "There is no starting point. I have all unknown qualities" (242). We find it elaborated in "The Problem of the Broken Bracelet": "You have heard me say frequently, Mr. Hatch, that logic is inevitable .... That is true; but it must have an indisputable starting point,—the one unit which is unassailable. In this case unit produces unit in order, and the proper array of these units gives a coherent answer" (194). In reference to my schema at the close of Chapter 1, Van Dusen's Absolutism is reductionist; it is repeatedly emphasized by the dicta that pepper the pages: "'Knowledge is progress. We gain knowledge through observation and logic—inevitable logic'" (Futrelle, "Leak" 505). The popularity of this worldview has not waned, if we understand contemporary forensic-based detective fiction to be its successor, but the scientific basis of the starting point is in flux and thus threatens the survival of such stories (until they are sufficiently eclipsed to serve as vehicles for nostalgia). Whereas the first path makes claims to deductive reasoning, the second is linked, at least in the popular imagination, with induction, about which we will have more to say. Christopher Jervis, John Thorndyke's sometime narrator, expresses this side of the problem in his admiration of his friend: "[Thorndyke's] marvelous power of co-ordinating apparently insignificant facts, of arranging them into an ordered sequence and making them tell a coherent story, was a phenomenon that I never got used to; every exhibition

---

[3]   The Spade stories are disquieting because of Hammett's shift to the third person: not the reversion to a comforting omniscience, but, as Charles Rzepka confirms, the vulnerability of the detective (195–96).

[4]   That is, in the tradition stemming from Poe. If we were to take Wilkie Collins as our archetype, we find a much more fractured textual reality in the dismembered narratives of *The Woman in White* and *The Moonstone*.

of it astonished me afresh" (Freeman, "Case" 27). It is Thorndyke's storytelling ability that gets the emphasis here, which points to the idea that the frame is part of the story's very structure rather than just something to be discovered.

Representations of enclosure in their spatiotemporal, ethical/legal, and socioeconomic forms turn out to be unstable hankerings for order. As remarked in Chapter 1, Woods demonstrates the collapse of distance between the detective and the criminal voice in Christie's *Curtain* (1945), which forms a limit to the Golden Age paradigm. The approach to this limit is discernible in progressively more radical treatments of enclosure as we near World War II—and the limit's collapse is marked by comparison with postwar texts. Indeed, by examining three of Christie's most popular novels over a space of little more than a decade (and one by Christianna Brand for comparison), we perceive a growing self-consciousness of how any system's meaning is guaranteed. This process is tied to the dissolution of the clear-cut barrier between a homogeneous field of normal social relations and the transcendental guarantor which patrols the boundary between this and its heterogeneous Other.

"'From now on, it is our task to suspect each and every one amongst us.'" (Christie, *And Then There Were None* 149–50)

Three novels by Agatha Christie—*The Murder of Roger Ackroyd* (1926), *Murder on the Orient Express* (1934), and *And Then There Were None* (1939)—illustrate the shifting terrain of literal and figurative enclosure and discursive reduction. Perhaps most troubling, the means by which the frame is justified in the guise of a guarantor—typically the detective or some agent working on behalf of justice—increasingly comes under scrutiny, so that an institutionally mandated normative homogeneity can no longer function as given. Ironically, as the means of generating the frame is questioned, the murder events transpire within ever more elaborately isolated sites of enclosure. *The Murder of Roger Ackroyd* presents the most straightforward of these closed situations—a bolted study with a planted clue on the windowsill. The number of physical barriers increase in *Murder on the Orient Express*: enclosed spaces within enclosed spaces, themselves blocked off by natural barriers as well as a time schedule calculated not by the actors but by institutions beyond their direct control. *And Then There Were None*, the most contrived, but in its artificiality the most theoretically engaging, establishes even more extreme geographical and logical barriers to a solution. These types of enclosure are in fact more complex than the literalized space-time elements with which we began discussion of the closed site.

The economy of the three texts is varied, in part due to the different ways in which the narratives are transmitted—the first person of Dr. Sheppard (which nonetheless takes place in retrospect and conveys a feeling of omniscience), the third-person omniscient narrator of the second novel, and the fragmented individual perspectives coupled with a third-person narrator in the third. The first and third novels, contrary to convention, have criminal narrators, both of whom are closely linked to institutional power, representing medicine (Dr. Sheppard) and the courts (Judge Wargrave). The corruption of institutions extends to the officials in *Murder on the Orient Express*, who are complicit with the misdeeds of their fellow passengers—in all three cases, transmission is ironic and self-contradictory, if not impossible. Indeed, the relation of truth to frame becomes progressively more problematic as we consider each book in turn. One disruptive influence is the undermining of character roles normally regarded as outside the economy of the text—namely, the narrator and the detective. The conflation of the criminal with the Watson-figure or the victim brings the guarantor function under observation, revealing it to be a mechanism by which transgressive violence is safely bottled up in discourse—quite literally, in the third novel.

The locked-room aspect of *The Murder of Roger Ackroyd* is, for us, a cliché—the bolted door which must be broken down, the open window with its all-too-obvious clue—and this spatial cliché extends to establishing the time aspect: the heat of the fire that interferes with determining time of death, the regularity of servants and the late post, the church clock, small lies that have to be uncovered before the parameters can be well defined. All of these frames are common to locked-room situations, though the closed aspect of this crime is somewhat more complicated in that there are professional, class, and other forms of social closure. For example, we rely upon Dr. Sheppard's professionalism to establish facts, and we perceive Ackroyd to be a social climber (Sheppard's implied meaning when he writes: "Of course, Ackroyd is not really a country squire. He is an immensely successful manufacturer of (I think) wagon wheels" [Christie, *Roger Ackroyd* 10]). Additionally, we note prejudices towards foreigners, especially in the obviously closed system of the village. The village is of particular interest since, reflected in Sheppard's sister Caroline, a virtual hive mind exists in the deep networks of gossip that exert a powerful centripetal force, tying everyone to everyone else through forms of knowledge and hearsay that compete successfully with the official investigation.

The radical closure to be overcome, though, is Sheppard's narrative, which speaks to us from beyond life itself, though we are unaware of this until the end. The security of the first-person narrative reported from a vantage of safety and closure, notwithstanding the dangers and risks that comprise the narrative, logically posits the survival of the speaker. This security has more than one aspect—it ties us to a voice that presumably is capable of disclosing the truth, having lived through the ordeal, having witnessed it, or having been close to those who did, and therefore possesses authority; it implies closure, not only in that the criminal's actions have been contained or neutralized, but in that we stand temporally removed and outside the boundaries of that neutralized criminal "space" with the narrator, whom we presume to be blameless. From the start, this reporting of the past is done with the knowledge of outcomes: "I [Dr. Sheppard] am not going to pretend that at the moment I foresaw the events of the next few weeks. I emphatically did not do so" (Christie, *Roger Ackroyd* 1) or "I think I can safely say that it was at this moment that a foreboding of the future first swept over me. Nothing tangible as yet—but a vague premonition of the way things were setting" (Christie, *Roger Ackroyd* 14). In Stephen Knight's phrase, Christie "casts doubt on the very conventions of narrative fiction" (*Form* 112), which, as it turns out, constitute the real locked-room mystery, namely that the living narrative voice actually emerges from the tomb. Taking up Knight's able commentary on this novel in *Form and Ideology*, we are reminded that Christie's novels commonly entail a "murderer [who] somehow misrepresents himself against the map, the clock or, because of their tight interrelation, frequently against both" (120). Plotting, moreover, is underpinned by positivist notions of evidence relying upon the idea of space as a container which is neither distensible nor "produced" in the Lefebvrian sense. Sheppard's character, however, undermines the time-space foundations of bourgeois epistemological norms. The first dimension of this subversion is superficial but effective: Christie's manipulation of sympathy (harnessing a well-established though not universal convention). But in terms of the closed site, Sheppard challenges two other norms—the locus of narration is imprecise, outside of the conditions of any narrative, and the guarantor is not the detective addressing us but the criminal, thus merging the criminal and the Watson figure and placing both one step ahead of the detective. These narrative dimensions arguably remain within the bounds of stylistic innovations; a more pressing challenge to enclosure arises in the next work.

In *Murder on the Orient Express* we once more find several layers of enclosure, some of which are simply concrete, physical boundaries—the snowbound train, the locked door to Ratchett's compartment, the guarded egress to the next carriage—but others which are more abstract: the distance from urban areas, the marginalized political Otherness of the volatile Balkans, its unstable and unreliable institutions and "uncivilized" and inadequate legal prescriptions. In themselves, these concentric barriers do not seriously challenge epistemological norms. However, new and surprising obstacles do appear. I have argued against the idea that the purgation of the community proceeds through the focusing of attention on the criminal-scapegoat whose expulsion returns society to an ordered state of normalcy. More accurately, we frequently observe that all members of the community turn out to be *potential* criminals whose plans (or wishes) are only blocked by circumstances. Chandler is unimaginative in his diatribe against the Golden Age, and in particular against this novel ("Simple Art" 984), in that he does not see Christie's abstract moral argument, only the absurd but enjoyable plotting device through which it is delivered. In this case, Christie violates convention by giving us an absolute correspondence between the community and criminality, and to take this somewhat further, it is a community composed of a much deeper class range than she is accustomed to depict. By extending her larger, though still stereotyped, cast, which includes various nationalities and social positions, the depth of guilt spills out of its customary class-bound borders (including the tacit ban on the servant, the colonial, or the foreigner as criminal). Christie allows her characters—male or female, servant or master, youthful or aged, vigorous or infirm—to give vent to their murderous impulses; their actions are justified by making the victim the personification of evil. This democratization of violence is endorsed, presumably, by the failure of official justice to bring to heel a child murderer, but our very sympathy is in fact a ruse that occludes the sinister implication of universal guilt and the predilection to criminal violence. Moreover, criminality extends to the complicity of Poirot, M. Bouc, and Dr. Constantine, whose silence condones if not approves the impulses of the group.

The complicity of authority figures forges a link between this novel and *The Murder of Roger Ackroyd* in the sense of narrative limits. The impossibility in this text concerns transmission, which constitutes the real problem of closure in its resemblance to a locked-room situation. As Sheppard turns the narrative inside out so that we unknowingly end up inside the locked room with the killer, so does *Murder on the Orient Express* spirit us into the locked room to hear a solution that presumably will never achieve public disclosure. Whereas the locked room is typically the site of the crime, the larger context of the crime scene is converted into a locked room whose solution will never be revealed; rather, the criminally false solution is disseminated. Dove rightly remarks that whether or not the detective or fictional public knows this truth, the reader demands access to it, but here again, how is such access achieved if that truth has no outlet to the outside? The complicity of the detective, who typically serves as guarantor, erects a false standard, a convincing counterfeit which is probably more plausible than the fanciful crime that actually transpires. The transmission of the other truth, then, is only possible because we share the criminals' perspective on events as well as acquiesce in their actions.

And Then There Were None, though sharing qualities with the other two novels, radicalizes the self-consciousness of limits encountered in those texts. In common with *The Murder of Roger Ackroyd*, transmission of the text occurs through disembodied means—for most of the novel we oscillate between a detached, apparently omniscient third person and a series of fragmented, partially omniscient, sometimes stream-of-consciousness narrative perspectives from the characters/victims; in the epilogue, we are given a solution through a "truthful" first-person narrative voice from beyond the grave, a voice that belongs to a killer, but one which also suggests a divine injunction delivered in wrathful and retributive terms. The transmission of truth is even more fanciful than in *Murder on the Orient Express*, dependent literally upon a message in a bottle, but as we do in the other two novels, we note the instability of roles that permeates the character list. The community of criminals, while certainly more restricted than the train passengers, is radicalized in another way in that each participant in the holiday weekend is, if we are to believe Judge Wargrave, morally guilty of murder. The space reserved for the detective, taking the detective to be the mouthpiece of truth, corresponds with the character who is arguably the guiltiest, having killed 10 people, including his accomplice, Morris, instead of just one, and having committed the murders in ways that outstrip all the others in meticulous planning and the purposeful incitement of terror. And yet, the motive for his crime inverts expectations, ostensibly serving the interests of justice. As in *Murder on the Orient Express*, the interest in murder is abstract and grotesquely altruistic rather than a violation of its cult of property or legitimate gain, in that the star chamber sits when the regular mechanisms of justice break down. In addition to taking the detective's and the primary criminal's roles, the judge is likewise a victim—most obviously in his faked death with Dr. Armstrong's complicity, but also in his suicide, which copies the circumstances of his faked murder and renders the real and the fake indistinguishable to the police investigators.

The textual economy of *And Then There Were None* is threatened by the absence of a personified guarantor. Its collapse (in the sense that everyone dies) is aptly characterized by Merrill, who suggests that the novel is "unredeemed by the detective's saving competence" ("Christie's" 99)—with emphasis, no doubt unintentional in Merrill, on the suggestively economic dimension of *unredeemed*. The disorganization of the community, which survives Sheppard's death and which is likely strengthened through the sharing out of guilt in the second novel (though not through mutual fear of incrimination), is absolute in that no exteriority can be established to the Hobbesian war of all against all. The prejudices and guilty reticence among its members, which we have oblique access to through witnessing the thoughts of individual minds, cannot be overcome, even in the solidarity of fearful self-preservation. Progressively, we understand this anticommunity to be premised upon the universality of guilt, this time confined to a more conventional range of social positions associated with the new middle classes of the mid-twentieth century. The avenue of self-determination through the negation of an unmasked criminal Other is effectively closed off. The inevitability of the rhyme ("Ten Little Indians"), accentuating a juggernaut of unrestrained violence, effaces any semblance of community unified by proximity to a corpse. Such a community, though, is never really in question in this novel, as is evident from the start: "Rather doubtfully, Miss Brent permitted herself to be helped into the boat. The others followed suit. There was as yet no fraternizing among the party. It was as though each member of it was puzzled by the other members" (Christie, *And Then There Were None* 24). The crystallization of a structure around a dead body momentarily surfaces after the first murder: "It was past twelve o'clock. The suggestion [to go to bed] was a wise one—yet everyone hesitated. It was as though they clung to each other's company for reassurance" (Christie, *And Then There Were None* 71). But the judge's enjoinder turns out to be ironic, in his stern warning to his companions: "'I would ask you all to consider this carefully and to give me any suggestions that may occur to you. In the meantime I warn everybody to be upon his or her guard. So far the murderer has had an easy task, since his victims have been unsuspicious. From now on, it is our task to suspect each and every one amongst us'" (Christie, *And Then There Were None* 149–50). Later still, we find a reversal in that the basis of community is founded upon the negation of its other members: "There was little pretence now—no formal veneer of conversation. They were five enemies linked together by a mutual instinct of self-preservation" (Christie, *And Then There Were None* 191)—which externally differs little from the lack of fraternization and puzzlement described at the start.

To suggest that this situation is brought about by the unnatural manipulations of Wargrave's God complex is insufficient, and not only in the sense that all are guilty. A killer is able to induce, through divide and conquer techniques, murderous impulses in those who might not normally harbor them, especially since none of the party is likely to purposely kill again. Wargrave coerces Dr. Armstrong into open betrayal of the others to (unsuccessfully) insure his own safety. If we are given a microcosm of bourgeois relations, then those relations are reduced to accusation, systematic attrition, and coercion. Even before there is a hint of violence, Blore misrepresents himself with an alias (and later fakes his own death), Philip Lombard carries a gun to a peaceful weekend retreat, and Morris, Wargrave's accomplice, juggles accounts, names, and identities to fan the self-interest of the victims. This disturbing novel, Christie's darkest, would indeed be perfect if Wargrave's text never arrived, and yet this is too much to ask. We have come to expect that the institutional powers are incapable of guaranteeing the stability of the closed site so that we also can participate in the thrill of exteriority. But here the problem is taken to an extreme that indicates a boundary has been reached, one which is crossed a few years later in *Curtain*.

Extrapolating the trajectory established by Christie's novels, we arrive at Christianna Brand's 1955 *Tour-de-Force*. Appearing a decade after the break established by Woods in her analysis of *Curtain*, Brand's novel seems to be historically situated beyond the Golden Age clue-puzzle, though in a specific way—not so much in the formal trickery of its construction, a hallmark of Brand's style, but in vulgarization and the loss of standards for any valid judgment. Brand dispenses with the concentric layers of class conventions and bourgeois attitudes undergirded by wealth, which we find, for instance, in a less sinister form in Christie's 1941 *Evil under the Sun*. Instead, power is forcibly and visibly exerted: we find a parody of aristocratic whim in the form of a local absolute ruler up against a parody of middle-class mendaciousness. Those imprisoned on the Grand Duke's island-state are "victimized" by an inept and dangerous authority more concerned with the State-endorsed smuggling trade than the administration of justice. Solutions achieved by ratiocinative fireworks and the careful assemblage of clues are revealed to be ridiculous, inconsequential play. Although Brand does create a feeling of helplessness and anxiety in the face of an impersonal and threatening authority, the optimistic belief in the triumph of reason channeled through the detective proves hollow. The participants, although varied, represent a range of stereotypes: a lisping gay fashion designer, a fawning, duplicitous Spanish mountebank, and a puritanical spinster are but three examples—these and other central characters (with the exception of Detective Inspector Cockrill) reduce the other members of the tour to contemptuous nicknames (Brand 12, 18, 103). As in earlier examples of the Golden Age microcosm, all the characters harbor secrets; all present false fronts to their peers. Human relations, stripped of clear class markers partly as a result of the make-believe personas fostered by the participants, are nonetheless primarily economic, but in an anonymous mélange brought about by the package tour melting pot of post–World War II social leveling. Here is the democratic age of middle-class mediocrity rising ascendant, confronting a freakish throwback to absolutism in the form of the tiny island nation of San Juan el Pirata, a throwback, however, whose primary aim is economic stability through catering to this selfsame middle class.

The Locked Room

The locked-room mystery requires special attention within the larger scope of the Classical and Golden Age genres in that it consciously intensifies spatiotemporal closure. Scaggs reads the form as "reassurance" during the Interwar period, "reducing the world ... to self-contained, enclosed, manageable proportions and dimensions" (52), though this would hardly explain its presence in Poe, Doyle, or Futrelle.[5] Reassurance, in fact, is a quality of most earlier detective works, a restoration of the "crystal sphere" which Kathleen Hulley regards as characteristic of the fiction preceding Hammett, and whose "metaphysic rested on the assumption that time and space have continuity and coherence, that events are not merely contiguous but filled with cause and direction" (113). Herzel understands the locked room to represent the constant tension between the rational-scientific world of the detective and the intrusion of vestigial supernatural elements into that world (for example, in *The Hound of the Baskervilles*). The fundamental problem concerns the conflict between the prosaic world of experience and a parallel universe unresponsive to and inexplicable by the dictates of logic. Herzel concludes that the detective "destroy[s] the miraculous world by explaining the impossible situation in terms of the practical world" (70). This conclusion is only warranted, though, if we accept the latter to possess an objective substrate of reality, and not itself to be a construction whose aim is authoritative meaning. Geherin more cautiously recognizes that Holmes's method, whether in the case of locked rooms or otherwise, "rests upon the belief that everything in the universe obeys the laws of logic and is therefore knowable" (4)—Geherin does not contest this point, nor does he emphasize the operative word *belief*; he only uses it in contrast to the chaotic situations characterizing other genres such as the hard-boiled tale.

The locked room as a metaphorical or ideological condition is attributed to Poe's first effort by Cook, whose book-length treatment *Narratives of Enclosure in Detective Fiction: The Locked Room Mystery* pursues this problem in great depth and through a wide range of textual examples. For Cook, "the locked room mystery is a form which not only gives the fullest expression to the elements of closure and enclosure, but allows the greatest possible impact of ratiocination on a plot as perplexing, seemingly impossible, as it is absurd" (6). Detection itself becomes a metaphor for the ordering of signs, mastered from outside, and the

---

[5] Nor would it explain the international appeal of this subgenre. See the dated but still useful index compiled by Robert Adey, *Locked Room Murders and Other Impossible Crimes*, or John Pugmire's website *A Locked Room Library*.

guarantee of their containment and stable meaning or integration into "plausible" narratives to establish an objective substrate of reality (6). Taking these ideas on their own, only a fragment of Cook's larger thesis, we are compelled to examine the effect the detective has on the system, since we cannot assume that the clues are simply part of some objective given, to be sorted into true and false leads and subsequently assembled into a form demanding consensus. A level of self-awareness is achieved in Carr in that the topos is undermined ("burlesque" according to Cook) by the infamous locked-room lecture in *The Three Coffins* (1935); the comic intrusion of metatextual commentary from Dr. Fell accentuates the constructedness of this most artificial of artificial forms (90–91). Although self-awareness may suggest ironic theatricalization, for Cook, Carr employs self-consciousness to examine the formal bases of narrative construction rather than to expose ideological constraints.

The ideological aspect concerns the engagement of the detective with the enclosure, with the problem of determining what constitutes the enclosure or frame, and subsequently, the relations between inside and outside. Initially, the locked room mystery defines a miraculous space that refuses to obey the dictates of prosaic normalcy. The event that erupts within this enclosure is neutralized by the operations of detective analysis, but the question of how the enclosure is demarcated is typically taken as given. If the spatial parameters are manipulated, this typically occurs within the process of the detective's investigation, possibly leading to an explanatory reconfiguration of space and time that corresponds to the "normal" universe. If we concede that spatial and temporal barriers are simply there or brought into alignment with given laws, the detective's analysis may appear to be a metalinguistic sleight of hand. The detective's corrective demystifies the world, returning us to a plottable Cartesian homogeneity. We arrive at this position by the reduction of description (narrator, witness, and evidence) to background noise, gibberish which is inadequate to the objects (traces, modes of egress, dead bodies) that confront us in the miraculous space. Poe establishes this scenario as a self-thematizing problem from the very start in the language mix-up from "Murders in the Rue Morgue." The cacophony of language is the breakdown of attempts at classification in that each witness believes a different language is spoken in the death room. Dupin eventually establishes that the problem of language itself is misread. Cook, I think, errs slightly on this point in claiming that Poe indicates "the power [language] possesses to misrepresent and confuse" (106). In fact, language is shown not to signify at all—unless we take non-signification as a type of signification—and no representation takes place. The detective's task from the start is to step in and literally make nonsense of it all, and this is one reason that Poe's story is remarkable, since he gives Dupin the opportunity to enact or perform this rite, to reconfigure what seems to be an incontestable limit. Dupin establishes a grounding principle by which the law of correspondence, or economically speaking, convertability, can be set right by first determining the very basis of sense.

The locked room, however, is never an entirely closed system, protected from entropy by insuperable barriers (its literal, physical closure) or the need to "read" and find correspondences through its submission to detective analysis. Copjec remarks that "the detective ... is not ... on the side of metalanguage, or the reparation of the signifier's default. He is, instead, on the side of the failure of metalanguage, he represents the always open possibility of one signifier more" (177), though in practice this potentially infinite sequence is brought to an end. Copjec's take on this displacement is apt, but Golden Age texts do not actually function this way, mostly because audiences don't want their narratives to function this way—such a surfeit of freedom in fact undermines closure and certainty (for instance, as we find it in postmodern works like *The Name of the Rose*, *The Erasers*, or *City of Glass*). Here we find the link to the earlier discussion in which social boundaries are "logically" purified and reduced to an unproblematic exclusion of uncomfortable side issues like class or authority. The detective, in the case of the locked room, is then free to overlook, in sociologist Alvin Gouldner's phrase, how propositions of truth "are always generated within the shaping perspective of speakers' social positions" (*Against* 241).

By gathering together the threads which artificially negate social difference, the detective achieves a transcendental power whose nearest relative is theology—specifically the theology of the miraculous. The detective's power to dispel the supernatural or inexplicable is ironic, given his or her own magical capacities, but the conjoining of the social and the theological is overlooked, given that it takes place within a secularized and politicized figure. This figure does not entirely renounce the aura of transcendental status. Knight argues that the roots of the Classic and Golden Age detective's extralegal status are found in earlier crime tales, where "divine guidance lies behind the revealing of guilt" (*Crime* 4; see also Kayman 42; Rowland 10). The new godhead, however, is very much flesh and blood in that "[detective fiction] deifies the authority of reason or the imagination" (Roth 61). The point is well illustrated by a text positioned at the margins, and thus self-consciously partaking of both worlds. In Chesterton's "The Hammer of God" (1911) the theological dimension of absolute framing finds its surrogate in a mere mortal; Father Brown's mediating function, whereby the taboo of contact with sin and the sacred is disarmed, steps in to correct our vision. When this power is transferred to the "extra-human" authority of positivist science, it is no less magical, clear enough in the technologically mediated successes of contemporary forensic detective television series. In an added theological feature, the detective frequently establishes contact with evil (transgression, taboo), the neutralization of which precedes the reestablishment of boundaries through plausible rituals. Kestner's characterization of Holmes as "representative and exceptional" as well as "extra-legal" (*Sherlock's Men* 38) is astute. But his representative quality is tellingly linked to class commitments, accentuated by support for patriarchy and bourgeois standards of moral, economic, and political conduct; his exceptional status, and that which divorces him from the common herd, is a set of semibohemian vices (from clutter to cocaine), ascetic tendencies, and inhuman, dispassionate rationality—to this we could add arcane knowledge. Finally, his extralegal status is manifest in his willingness to engage in actions that are technically criminal or to suppress evidence or solutions when it suits him. To suggest, as Bargainnier does (41–42), that the detective is a neutral outsider to class who is given the power to judge between good and evil is, therefore, an exaggeration. The radical enclosure of the locked room is the stage upon which the detective-magus can conjure up a vision of social order, but like any drama, it transpires within a stage space that is conventionally and ideologically determined.

"'Me lord,' he went on, 'there's a Judas window in nearly every door, if you just come to think of it.'" (Dickson, *Judas* 166)

The Three Coffins is frequently cited as the exemplary locked-room murder, probably because of the systematic, self-thematizing gesture of "The Locked Room Lecture." In terms of epistemology, institutional power, and the authority of individuals in determining what constitutes knowledge and truth, Carr's *The Judas Window* (1938) and *The Problem of the Green Capsule* (1939) better serve my purpose. The theoretical potential of the former lies not only in its agonistic qualities (brought out in part by the courtroom setting), but also in the juxtaposition of different institutional levels (for instance, the courts, the police, forensic and medical experts, psychologists) and the conflict between public and private institutions (marriage and the family).

The plot of *The Judas Window* is both complicated and implausible. James Answell intends to wed Mary Hume; however, the marriage hangs in question because she is being blackmailed by Answell's cousin Reginald Answell, whose mistress she was some time prior to her engagement. Her father, Avory Hume, having neither met nor seen either man, agrees to discuss terms with Reginald; through a case of mistaken identity in a phone conversation he ends up inviting and meeting James, whom he believes to be his daughter's persecutor. His intention, worked out with his brother Dr. Spencer Hume, is to engineer a feigned attack on himself by Reginald (after giving him drugged whisky) and to threaten the man with confinement to a mental institution through his brother's medical authority and the testimony of reliable witnesses not in on the plot but useful to substantiating what they believe to have happened. The actual plan is known only to his brother and to his confidential secretary, Amelia Jordan, who promptly uses her knowledge to murder her employer and place the blame upon the man she believes to be Reginald (whom she also thinks a blackmailer). Her motive to commit murder is a combination of spurned love from Avory, a widower who never transferred his affections to her, and the imminent loss of a legacy through Avory's intention to alter his will after his daughter's wedding. The locked-room element arises partly through the complicity of the victim, who bolts the door on the inside, the windows having been secured and firmly shuttered to hide the interview from prying eyes. Through the removal of the doorknob, an aperture (judas) appears which is sufficiently large to admit the murder weapon, an arrow fired from a crossbow. This arrow, originally inside the room, is fired back into the room by Amelia, piercing the heart of the victim and killing him instantly. The apparent perpetrator wakes from his stupor to find his host dead, the incriminating whisky removed, his own fingerprints on the arrow, which apparently has been used as a dagger, and a pistol planted on his person. The room appears sealed off from the outside world; incredibly, the manipulation of the door raises no questions from the police, apparently competent in every other respect. Even if the timing could have been worked out, the preposterous idea that an arrow fired blindly could reach its target stretches belief far beyond the breaking point.

The presiding judge's courtroom is compared to a chessboard, where, according to Dickson's detective, H.M., the facts and factors are "all goin' to be on the table all the time" (Dickson, *Judas* 47). The known quantity metaphor (the "rules" by which any fact is known) is problematic in that the facts depend on the preexisting regularity of the board's grid. Nonetheless, as in many stories, a struggle arises over who can determine how this frame operates; reframing alters the perception of pieces on the board as well as their value. Their interpretative significance is dependent upon their arrangement in space and time, but this seems unproblematic as long as we understand the space to be sealed. Competing frames of reference, placed within the agreed-upon parameters of the timeline, are construed differently within those limits. Hence, two complex timetables appear in the novel in double columns: one table represents agreed-upon facts derived from the investigation, interviews, and other disclosures; a parallel table raises doubts about how these points are to be understood or possibly contested in the context of a battle with witnesses and prosecuting attorneys. The outsider perspective which brings the uncontested space into a regulative relation is well represented by the idea of the Judas window, a one-way device in a door that allows outsiders to observe the contents of a room unbeknownst to its occupants—a device associated explicitly in the novel with prisons or disciplinary spaces. This apparatus is universalized so that all enclosures are potentially brought within its purview, a point indicated by H.M. himself: "The room [in which the murder took place] is just like any other room. You've got a Judas window in your own room at home; there's one in this room, and there's one in every courtroom in the Old Bailey. The trouble is that so few people ever notice it" (Dickson, *Judas* 48). The relation is not just that of authority surveilling private space; the narrator is a mechanism like the Judas window, whose function opens that space to, but also constructs it for, the reader as a field of vision. To claim that the narrator is ideologically neutral would be farfetched—the mediation of a window in a door or a narrator is a perspective-thinking which entails ordering, empowerment, and the projection of values. H.M.'s benevolence, his Father Christmas persona, obscures his dangerous intellect and disarms criticism. His mastery is expressed directly by the narrator at the novel's close: "He had wanted to be the old maestro; and, by all the gods, you had to admit he was" (Dickson, *Judas* 192). A greater challenge arises, however, when the evidence entails an ostensibly unshakable objective basis whose placing into question draws attention to the constructed nature of all reference points and frames.

The Problem of the Green Capsule brings together these concerns with an added twist. First, along the lines of the discussion so far, the story demonstrates the proclivity for Golden Age texts to define events within boundaries to fix positive knowledge. These boundaries consist of frames that close off the site in terms of space, time, agency, and ideology. Second, Carr engages in the self-conscious dramatization of crime, a point returned to in more detail in my Conclusion. The locked room is commonly a stage space—artificial and highly conventionalized. The criminal performance draws attention to the represented quality of crime and its aestheticization. Carr's novel opens in Italy, where a group of travelers are observed by the vacationing Inspector Andrew Elliot. The travelers, consisting of the wealthy Marcus Chesney, his niece Marjorie Wills, Marjorie's fiancé, George Harding, Marcus's brother Dr. Joe Chesney, his estate manager, Wilbur Emmet, and psychologist Professor Ingram, comprise the core characters of the novel. Elliot later becomes involved in the case, at which point he learns that the Italian trip was an attempt to remove Marjorie from Sodbury Cross, where the family resides, in order to escape the public hostility directed towards her. Local residents believe that Marjorie has willfully introduced poisoned chocolates into a confectioner's candy bin, resulting in a child's death. Marcus is convinced of his niece's innocence, and in his generally abrasive way, dismisses the "evidence" by asserting the worthlessness of witness testimony. Having made up his own mind about how the crime was committed, he literally stages a demonstration for an assembled audience—Marjorie, George, and Professor Ingram—which they are to watch carefully before responding to a questionnaire. The performance is filmed by George and enlists the aid of Wilbur as a supporting actor. George's film will serve as an objective record to supplement memory and establish the truth once the questionnaires have been completed. During the performance Marcus is murdered, ostensibly because he reveals the M.O. for the crime; but the truth of what happened (and his own solution to the first crime) is obscured by the pitfalls constructed by the victim to confuse the testimony of the witnesses. Elliot, unable to cast light on the case, calls in Dr. Fell, who helps the police to a solution.

Because the crimes appear linked, the first task of the investigators is to grapple with the parameters of the site since the original crime, involving the poisoned chocolates, seems a senseless, random act. The absence of a motive in the small community, coupled with the volume of outsider automobile traffic through the town, prompts the police (unlike the locals) to view the shop as an open site. Any visitor could distract the proprietress of the confectionary and drop the poisoned sweets into a box (Carr, *Green Capsule* 12). The open site is challenged by evidence that Marjorie is connected with the poisoned candy under incriminating circumstances, though her motive remains obscure. The second crime, connected to the first by the use of poison, undermines attempts to keep the site open, given the authorities' reluctance to accuse members of Marcus's socially prominent household. The near impossibility of an outsider being involved in the second crime leads the investigators to conclude that someone close to Marcus is responsible (Carr, *Green Capsule* 36, 70), and that the murderer's purpose was self-protection. The triangulation of time, space, and character (class, as it turns out) are necessary to pinpoint guilt; establishing a frame of vision for these categories circumscribes a determinable body of fact, constructed through the intervention of the detective.

The first attempt at stabilization concerns space. Ingram, the psychologist, asserts that most experiential boundaries conjoining perception and understanding are porous. Marcus's questionnaire, designed to undermine eyewitness reliability, contains traps to accentuate these weaknesses. For instance, when Marcus asks about what was said during the performance, his question is taken by Marjorie and George to mean what the actors said; Ingram, however, understands the question to include anything said during the performance that could be heard by all, and both Marjorie and George make audible comments. Although Ingram's intention is to supply alibis for the pair (to quell the suggestion that one of them might have impersonated Emmet in the performance), his observations end up reconfiguring space. The performance space, which is the apparently contained site of the murder, is extended to enclose the audience members within the range of suspects, since the detectives are subsequently able to explain how the illusion of being in the audience while actually committing the murder was managed.

The second enclosure, time, is also brought under scrutiny in a literalized way. The performance space contains a clock, which for the demonstration is contrived to deceive the witnesses; the deception also defeats alibis and throws the timeframe into doubt. The idea of absolute time divorced from perception is initially dismissed outright by Professor Ingram: "if [Marcus] gives us a clock to judge by, the only way we can judge time is BY that clock. I regarded that as in the agreement. I can tell you the various times when things happened by that clock. But I can't tell you whether it had the correct time to start with" (Carr, *Green Capsule* 52). Of course, how some absolutely correct time could be established remains unexplained. Ingram's apparently reasonable statement also comes to nothing. When the film is shown, close observation reveals that Marcus had removed the minute hand from the clock for the performance so that the shadow cast on the clock face by the hour hand by a strong light indicated a different time to each observer, depending upon where he or she sat. The "authority" of the clock collapses, since only the slow-moving hour hand was affixed. Looking to a mechanical device is potentially no more objective than depending upon eyewitness reports. After closing the doors to conclude the show, Marcus replaced the minute hand and all appeared normal. Later, we learn that two films were made, which intensifies the idea that the representation of space vis-à-vis time can be manipulated—the objectivity of technologically mediated evidence is susceptible to revision after all.

The final boundary, agency, which we have discussed in its class dimension, refers in this case to the actors in the narrative. The killer turns out to be George, a satisfactory outcome in that the audience applauds the removal of obstacles to the budding romance between the likable Elliot and Marjorie. Furthermore, Marjorie, a prime suspect up to the end, is exonerated. George Harding, Marjorie's fiancé, is depicted as a social climber and fortune-hunter who attempted to force his way into the good graces of a local family, partly to advance his own goals as a research chemist. After being convinced of his criminal acts, Major Crow exclaims, "the idea of this fellow living among us—!" (Carr, *Green Capsule* 135–36). His remark is ironic given the locals' animosity towards Marjorie when they believed she was the culprit. The removal of George reestablishes the class equilibrium which he threatened.

The second major concern pertaining to enclosure is made more complex by the filming of the crime. Although two films of the "same" performance were made, the performances differ in detail, and the substitution of one demonstrates the effects of human manipulation. Machine-generated evidence is placed in doubt and Fell's judgment is the ultimate measure of truth, though our sympathies are directed to understand such judgment as rational rather than merely subjectivist.[6] We overlook Fell's power to establish frames of reference, since the truth is discovered after the film's tricks are brought to light. Whether or not the facts are juggled, the film only appears to document an objective reality; as it turns out, the parameters of the crime scene are no more secured by a film record than by subjective human judgments. This shift of focus is clear later on when the audience, unknowingly part of the stage action (the murder) during the fateful night of violence, later becomes the focus of attention at the "reconstruction" enabled by the film screening (Carr, *Green Capsule* 146–47). The re-creation of the crime involves a restaging that in fact draws up new parameters to encompass the guilty party, the man once thought to be outside the frame of action. That this relation was already present in the film suggests that limits are perceptual and that perception is not a matter of irreducibly objective records.

The film literalizes what we find in a metaphorical form, both elsewhere in the novel and in Golden Age fiction generally, namely that stage space is potentially indeterminate. The literalized aspect of Carr's novel relates to a self-conscious theatricalization, a theme introduced in the preliminary parts set in Pompeii, where the reader and Inspector Elliot comprise the audience. The parameters of the performance, however, are in flux—Elliot's status shifts from audience member in Italy to actor in the English sequel of the investigation, where the village itself becomes a place of intense watching and surveillance by the hidden but observant populace. In the Italian segment of the novel, the opening paragraph, Marjorie Wills stands amongst the principal male characters (also observed by Elliot) "as though in the midst of a group of masks" (Carr, *Green Capsule* 1). This image is later reinforced: "Four pairs of sun-glasses were turned towards the girl, as though she stood inside a ring of masks. Sunlight gleamed on the glasses, making them as opaque and sinister as masks" (Carr, *Green Capsule* 4). The theatrical performance and its setting, allusive to Classical drama, are ambiguous. Marjorie's potential status as a tragic heroine associates her with criminal excess but also transforms that excess into an aesthetic experience.

---

6   This idea is developed in Joshi's chapter on the supernatural in Carr (114).

Knowledge, too, is regarded by Marcus as something that is both staged (susceptible to the manipulations of clever people) and customarily misapprehended by the average person. He writes in a letter to Fell: "All witnesses, metaphorically, wear black spectacles. They can neither see clearly, nor interpret what they see in the proper colours. They do not know what goes on on the stage, still less what goes on in the audience" (Carr, *Green Capsule* 142). The superimposition of spaces at the end is an interesting form of reconstruction—not a reconstruction from the participation of living audience members, but of dead ones, since the actors in the film, depicted on a screen hung in a doorway to give the illusion of the actual drama taking place in the same space, are two men who have been murdered. Their performance, however, reveals a truth subtending the business of the detective, namely, that there is a misalignment between their actions and the memories of two witnesses, Marjorie and Professor Ingram.

Homogeneity and Totalitarianism

A shift of emphasis from property crimes in the Classical period to murder in the Golden Age suggests a changing understanding of the exceptional event. The taking of life under normal circumstances usurps the State monopoly on violence, but the intrusion of the detective, who interferes with the official organs of society, in Roth's pointed, but accurate language, "authorizes authoritarianism for the individual, for society, and for the bourgeois state" (61). When society is understood to mean homogeneous, productive society, we find decision-making power collected into the hands of an individual serving the interests of productive homogeneity. To be sure, some critics would reject this characterization. For Symons, Holmes's exteriority to the law is necessary for its validation and represents a desirable external confirmation of limits: "[Holmes] was a kind of saviour of society, somebody who did illegal things for the right reasons" (69). Moreover, we might read this structural principle in a nonpolitical way, such that the reader's attempt to construct evidence meaningfully entails, in McCann's phrase, "a transcendent ... vantage not finally determined by circumstances," that is, our "epistemological and moral agency" (220) extends beyond the limits imposed by normal institutions in unexceptional times. These alternatives deserve contextualization in that they may not entirely do justice to the instability of the Interwar years, whose socioeconomic problems were played out in striking political ways. Nicholas Atkin characterizes the Interwar situation in Britain and France as "hardly propitious ... for liberal democracy," both for everyday citizens and for their leaders (244). That fascism was avoided in these countries was not a given, but depended, in Atkin's view, upon the combined effect of several factors: "a strong sense of national self-worth, stemming from the 1918 victory; resilient state structures; the willingness of mainstream political parties to defend parliamentary democracy, even though this was acknowledged to possess shortcomings; the failure of extremist movements to seize their moment; and an underlying social stability" (245). Still, a few critics have raised the question whether detective fiction, though strongly associated with pluralistic democracies, is nonetheless implicated in a totalitarian fantasy.

An early and yet still cogent example is William Aydelotte's essay "The Detective Story as a Historical Source" (1949), which assesses the Golden Age detective story's political orientations in regard to readers' acquiescence in the detective's potentially authoritarian role. Aydelotte finds in these tales tolerance of, if not preference for, quasifascist methods to achieve social order despite the fact that detective fiction attained prominence in western capitalist countries which avoided fascism. In the modern period, capitalism was initially associated with a revolutionary bourgeoisie intent on overthrowing feudal economic restraints. The success of this struggle inaugurated an era of chaotic competition, which finally led to the hegemony of the big bourgeoisie and the consolidations of monopoly capitalism in the late nineteenth and early twentieth centuries. The detective genre first appears in developed form at the interstices of change in the 1840s, when challenges were beginning to arise for the propertied small producer.[7] The crisis of the small entrepreneur deepened in the Progressive era in the United States. At the acme of the Golden Age in the 1930s, monopoly capitalism had achieved consolidation. Transformed notions of labor concomitant with these economic changes are the subject of Chapter 5. For now, we will focus on the overlap of Golden Age structural tendencies with totalitarianism, beginning with a brief review of the political options.

A number of Marxist social historians of the 1930s understood the "choice" between fascism and Communism actually to be a choice between capitalism and Communism. The argument in Lewis Corey's *The Crisis of the Middle Class* (1935), a work which gives some insights into the readership of both Golden Age and hard-boiled texts, as well as Daniel Guérin's *Fascism and Big Business* (1936) is that monopoly capitalism can rescue itself from the specters of overproduction, falling rates of profit, and legal redress from exploited groups most easily by radicalizing State capitalism's coddling of industry through a fascist seizure of the system. Through an ideological appeal to the disgruntled petty bourgeoisie, traditionally the shock troops of middle class revolutions, fascism gained broad popular support to legitimize political control (Guérin 46). Wealthy owners of industry, having ceded political power to fascist politicians, became their public scapegoats while actually conspiring behind the scenes with their "enemies" to intensify the exploitation of the middle and laboring classes; these agreements entailed the naked application of State violence to dissent, a response which was

---

[7]   Two decades before the appearance of "The Murders in the Rue Morgue" property ownership in the US stood at about 80 percent (Corey, *Crisis* 113), a figure confirmed by Mills (*Power* 260). By the 1840s property as the primary source of income began to decline. In 1927, entrepreneurialism, in terms of the middle classes, had declined to 30 percent and "over two-thirds of the middle class were dependent salaried employees" (Corey, *Crisis* 141), lower than the figure found in England for the same period (Corey, *Crisis* 154–55).

no longer restrained by any semblance of democratic intervention or uncoerced public discourse (Corey, *Crisis* 219). Corey's concern over the self-delusions of the American wage earner and his contention that such workers could be the vehicle of social change resonate with later radical historians and sociologists. We find his imprint on *White Collar* and *The Power Elite* by C. Wright Mills in the 1950s, the cautious predictions of Alvin Gouldner in *The Future of Intellectuals*, and the reconstructive work of Michael Denning in *The Popular Front*.

The notion that liberal democracy and capitalist markets comprised necessary preconditions for detective fiction is compelling, given that private property, the dynamics of wealth and, not unimportantly, bourgeois norms of conduct are intimately connected to criminality in many narratives. Aydelotte's attack on the "daydream" qualities induced by detective fiction is directed towards the politically irresponsible fantasies it gives rise to, a complaint made less insistently by Marshall McLuhan a few years earlier (620). Both derive from what Dollard and his coauthors characterized as "substitute response" in their 1939 work *Frustration and Aggression*. Their hypothesis—that frustrations give rise to psychological substitutes as a coping strategy—leads consumers of popular culture "[to read] romantic stories when real romance is unavailable" (Dollard, et al. 9). If detective fiction plots are substitutes, the implied psychological consequence for Dollard and his coauthors suggests the displacement of aggression, within certain limits. A weakness in this idea is the individualized nature of reading and the necessarily collective social aspect of political movements. The atomization of twentieth-century reading habits compels the authors to adopt a position towards the individual, namely that "any given frustrating condition may occur to several individuals simultaneously. In such a case, a 'group' is viewed distributively rather than as a collective thing" (Dollard, et al. 13). The impulse to read pulp magazines serves as a means "to flee from frustrations by seeking an approved channel through which aggression may be expressed and substitute responses developed" (Dollard, et al. 160). Aydelotte describes the other side of this equation by postulating the origins of those frustrations in the "enormous demand for gratification" and the "basic drives which apparently cannot be satisfied in our western society on the level of ordinary reality"; such unrequited desires entail fantasies "going rather beyond democratic institutions" (80).

The desire for control is satisfied in fantasy through a detective authority who extralegally transcends the system. But this ceding of power is not simply egotistical self-gratification; it is also granted to counteract the nightmare of a Hobbesian war of all against all, a fear contemporaneously preoccupying theorists like Carl Schmitt in *Political Theology* (1922). The *bellum omnium contra omnes* is in fact an ideological cornerstone of the Golden Age, given that real political decisions are not played out at the level of individuals as they are represented in fictional texts. This atomized warfare is buttressed by universal suspicion and extended to the mechanisms of justice supported by a supposedly neutral State— though typically reduced to the level of corrupted individual representatives of larger institutional interests. As what can only be termed strange bedfellows,

Aydelotte and Mandel are close when the former remarks: "The criminal is a fantasy developing out of a competitive, uncohesive society" (80), though I would revise this to a fantasy society of uncohesiveness, since the controlling interests in monopoly capitalism are in fact no longer in competition with each other. Lest we seem to be getting too far away from textual examples, we can consider this remarkable passage from Mitchell's *The Rising of the Moon* (1945), in which Mrs. Bradley advises the young protagonists, two boys helping her with a serial killing case: "Bring me your conclusions to-morrow at seven o'clock. Avoid lonely places. Avoid everybody with whom you are acquainted, saving only your own relations and Christina, and, possibly myself and the inspector. Be watchful and suspicious. Trust no one. Do not loiter. Do not go or remain out of the house after seven o'clock in the evening" (189). Although somewhat late in our period, and therefore prone to comic interpretation in Mrs. Bradley's insistent and somewhat ironic tone, the question of trust is reduced in scope to very narrow parameters.

And yet, Mrs. Bradley's request is self-contradictory, because if we are only *perhaps* to trust the detective figure, then the very instructions should be cast aside for a more trustworthy self-reliance. Aydelotte recognizes in this contradiction the "modern political leader or agitator" (80), who is able to smooth out social contradiction in the satisfying narrative of the denouement, but who, at the same time, is ambiguously situated in terms of the official structure of social authority. Mrs. Bradley's vague association with the Home Office follows no perceptible protocol, requires no regular reports or recognition of bureaucratic hierarchies. In *The Rising of the Moon* her presence grates upon the sensibilities of the local inspector, with whom we are not allowed to sympathize. From the other side of the fence, we see much the same thing going on in Chief Inspector Parker's mind in his admiration and resentment towards Wimsey (for example, in *Unnatural Death* [177–78]), whose freedom of movement and from bureaucratic restraints produce ambivalence. Mrs. Bradley and Lord Peter, despite their charm and comic bonhomie, represent threats to democratic society. The "ordered universe" of the detective hero "is not that of the police or other regular authorities, but an order that is discovered and imposed by him" (Aydelotte 81)—or so it seems to the reader, who is subject to the narrative power commanded by the detective's ability to order signs. As a dictatorial force who, except in the subversive parodies of writers like Anthony Berkeley or possibly Edmund Crispin, remains largely uncontested, the detective is represented as "the extra-legal superman who is called in to accomplish by extraordinary measures what is impossible within the traditional organization of society" (Aydelotte 81).

In Gladys Mitchell's second novel, *The Mystery of a Butcher's Shop* (1930), Mrs. Bradley remarks on her role of "stage manager" in clearing up mysteries (173). Her manipulation exceeds what the term *manager* normally implies; her exceptional status is literalized in her open violation of the murder taboo (in her first novel, *Speedy Death*), which instigates many detective investigations. In later books, she unrepentantly condones murder, dispensing with the casuist salve of Holmes's mock trial in "The Abbey Grange." The tendency to uncompromising (and violent) absolutism, however, loses momentum by the 1940s, curiously about the time the war commences. Indeed, despite Mrs. Bradley's medical qualification, she seems selective about how the Hippocratic Oath should be applied, especially frightening in the decade of Hitler's rise to power. In 1930: "We must always have the moral courage to release from life those who are not fitted to bear life's burdens. Social morality, consisting, as it so largely does, in refraining from action, is to some minds an unachievable ideal, and to others simply nonsense" (Mitchell, *Saltmarsh* 127; see also Mitchell, *Saltmarsh* 287). Of one murderer, whose actions she approves, Mrs. Bradley remarks: "He's a perverted philanthropist, a kind of a-moral public benefactor. In short, he's God. Most artists are! It's the effect of the creative instinct on undisciplined intelligences" (Mitchell, *Death* 246). Later, she sums up her feelings: "The murder was a gesture. 'Away with incompetents!' she said. 'Let us have the thing done as it might be done by the angels'" (Mitchell, *Death* 255). Even as late as 1941, we get this chilling advocacy for a brutal eugenics:

> Mrs. Bradley, among other psychologists, had been called into consultation, but her simple suggestion was that delinquent children, who, like delinquent adults, can be divided into those brands which can be snatched from the burning and those which, unfortunately, cannot, should (literally) be killed or cured. The former treatment was to be painless, the latter drastic. This view was received without enthusiasm by the authorities and was treated, even by the Press, with reserve. (Mitchell, *When* 8)

In addition to these scattered comments, the murderers in *The Mystery of a Butcher's Shop* and *Death at the Opera* are allowed to go free in that they are respectable bourgeois property owners or professionals. In the former novel, the blame is shunted onto a suicide, who, though innocent of the crime, was deemed mad by Mrs. Bradley. In the latter a psychopathic serial killer, who clearly is a sick man, is brought to justice—the extenuating circumstances of insanity are no grounds for mercy. This is the authority in whose hands we are asked to place ourselves.

Ceding power to the external force of the detective, however justified, nonetheless *is* fantasy, just as the preponderance of murder—the truly exceptional situation—has little to do with real cases of homicide. Although genre-based explanations for the shift to murder from fraud and property crimes are plausible (Maugham 96–97; Knight, *Crime* xiii, 67), these earlier transgressions had little power in themselves to suspend normative codes or to conjure up a state of exception. They may invoke the threat of State violence to insure restitution, but these crimes do not mandate a capital charge and therefore do not bring us to the extreme limit. Murder is necessary since it is this exception that self-evidently justifies the suspension of the social order, which figures most literally in the power to indefinitely detain suspects and thus curtail their constitutional liberties. Within this structure, the detective is a dictatorial figure who seduces the reader through the dismantling of options "logically" attained through the valuation or dismissal of evidence.

This is not to say that murder is an obvious crime. Some stories are premised on the detective's capacity to demonstrate that murder has actually occurred—Gladys Mitchell's *The Devil at Saxon Wall*, Ellery Queen's *The Greek Coffin Case* and "The Lamp of God," Henry Wade's *The Duke of York's Steps*, Sayers's *Murder Must Advertise* and *The Five Red Herrings*, Christie's "Four and Twenty Blackbirds," Freeman's *The Mystery of 31 New Inn*, or Van Gulik's *The Emperor's Pearl*, for instance[8]—but beyond this relatively uncommon narrative device, the definition of murder as the willful killing of one person by another is woefully inadequate, or it is a special case that stands apart from such acts that are legitimized (wars, self-defense, execution of criminals) or which are the byproducts of capitalist exploitation. Murder, as it appears in its complex fictional form, tends to be the exception that stands in for the political exception. Its exceptionalism is made possible through the closed site of the Golden Age puzzle and the universal consensus that unjustified murder was committed (construed as an attack on the corporate social body). The representatives of generally ineffective institutions are willing to cede power or to cooperate with extra-institutional figures. Institutional representatives are, moreover, willing to suspend the authority invested in them and to acknowledge the authority of the detective. The usurpation of the monopoly on violence, generally understood to be the perquisite of a narrow band of officials, is softened by the detective's veneer of personal charisma or nonthreatening eccentricity. His or her application of reason or penetrating common sense serves the purpose of restoring health to the social body, and thus could be objected to only on irrational grounds.

Whatever its lack of historical specificity, Aydelotte's remark that "the detective story is no monument to the strength of democracy but rather a symptom revealing its weaknesses," particularly in "the insupportable burdens it places on the individual" in his or her "yearning for order" (81), is apt. More suspicious is his conclusion that the problem is reducible to psychology or questions of character instead of the dialectic between the individual and institutions which have demonstrated unconcern for liberty and equality, a situation that was evident to critics writing in the Interwar period. Envisioning the social framework as a static set of principles, the reader can nonetheless adhere to an ideology that stands in direct contradiction to the preconditions of social reality. The detective story nonetheless hints at a vague suspicion of powerlessness which resists the negative aspects of collectivism's potential psychological alienation instead of viewing its economic potential as a promise of liberation from scarcity.[9]

---

[8]   This device is found in hard-boiled stories as well, for instance in Frederick Nebel's "Doors in the Dark" and "A Couple of Quick Ones" and Raoul Whitfield's "Enough Rope."

[9]   Marx articulates this problem in the *Grundrisse* when he refers to "the absolute mutual dependence of individuals, who are indifferent to one another" (*Economic* 28: 94). This frightful loss of identity to an abstraction prompts the "regression" to fantasies of simpler social relations in the past.

"'Oh, for the eye of a bird.'" (Berkeley, et al. 203)

Certain examples of detective fiction thematize fascism directly, suggesting in these cases possible democratic responses to this threat and, of greater interest to us here, the detective's role vis-à-vis its eruption. A first kind of work is satisfied with a straightforward oppositional relation integrated into the plot itself whereby a totalitarian menace, embodied in an individual villain or small group of miscreants, is investigated and brought to heel by the detective. A second and rarer type finds the totalitarian threat embedded within the institutions nominally opposed to fascist ideology. Sometimes this second type enacts this more complex situation as a function of its very structure in metafictional terms, specifically the exposure of how detectives go about their detecting—we will return to this second type in the cooperatively authored novel *Ask a Policeman*.

Anthony Boucher, writing as H.H. Holmes, produces the first kind of work in *Nine Times Nine* (1940). The book draws together disparate elements, fusing them into a representation of American life at the tail end of the Depression and anticipating direct American intervention in the war.[10] Lacking the studied ironic distance of Latimer's *Red Gardenias* with its ambivalence towards a future of promise, Boucher's novel expresses faith in the combined efforts of an enlightened police force, religiously anchored values, and American working class perspicacity. Lt. Terence Marshall is part of a burgeoning middle-middle class or New Class, college trained, and as such represents a professionalization of the investigator (though, given his American context, he lacks Roderick Alleyn's ties to the pedigreed, moneyed elite). Matt Duncan, his unofficial partner, is class conscious, educated, and linked to journalism and the WPA. A third important character, Sister Ursula, balances Marshall; unlike his secularly defined power, her authority is derived from her spiritual principles and commitments. Her self-determined poverty also completes the triumvirate, linking middle-middle class professionals with struggling skilled workers whose economic status depends upon factors outside their control.

Wolfe Harrigan, a member of a wealthy Los Angeles family, dedicates himself to exposing and undermining phony religions by demonstrating the fraudulent practices of their leaders. We meet Harrigan's family, consisting of son Arthur, daughter Mary (or Concha), sister Emily, and brother R. Joseph, after Matt foils an attempt on Wolfe's life by the leader of the suspicious Temple of Light cult. Wolfe

---

[10] An example with a British focus is Nicholas Blake's *The Smiler with the Knife* (1939), a hybrid clue-puzzle and thriller. The fascist threat is represented here as a powerful secret society composed of stock characters: the amoral scientist, the General, the wayward and bored aristocratic daughter, foreigners, and stereotyped figures from the world of high finance. Interestingly, the detective is unable to infiltrate this inner circle—instead, the government relies upon an explorer (Nigel's wife), a society gossip journalist, and an athlete. These individuals, and what they represent, operate covertly under the guidance of a paternalistic hierarchy of aristocratic-leaning moderate democrats who condescend to support the working lower middle class.

is later murdered in a locked-room mystery, the solution of which implicates his brother, Joseph. Near the novel's end, we learn that Joseph is the mastermind behind the Temple, which he intended to use to achieve totalitarian political aims. Wolfe discovered this connection and was on the point of exposing it, necessitating his death. As the mystery is brought to a successful conclusion, secular legal institutions are aligned with spiritualized transcendental ones. This double framing relies upon both Sister Ursula and Lt. Marshall, so the dual nature of the investigator's transcendent capacity for determining truth is compartmentalized but neatly preserved and aligned. The conjunction of spiritual and secular in the bogus Temple of Light cult negatively parallels the unified front of Church and State. Ironically, both structures involve a convergence of interests which neutralize class differences. In its positive form this is achieved metaphorically in the marriage between the semiproletarianized petty bourgeois (Matt) and an heiress (Wolfe's daughter Concha). In its negative guise, fascist idolatry levels social differences while extracting resources from its economically-marginalized supporters and subverting democratic practices through the mystical fusion with a transcendent leader.

The romantic solution joining the happy lovers, despite its frequency in detective fiction, is somewhat less convincing than the fascist one. The management functions of institutions (secular State authority and established religious moral authority), combined with the intervention of a "disinterested," paternalistic, and scholarly upper crust (Wolfe), are important to a successful outcome. Matt functions as a liaison who is taken on by Wolfe as a popularizer, since Wolfe admits that his own prose style is best suited to academic audiences. Indeed, he is convinced that a popular appeal must be made: Wolfe's political attitudes emphasize the relative importance of the masses, by which he means the lower middle classes, who, after the decade of the 1930s, find themselves, like Matt, in the shadow of proletarianization. Throughout the novel, however, the target group is displayed as naïve and manipulable; whether the message is fascism or democracy, charismatic delivery carries the day. This tendency is clear by the novel's end, when a lecture on democratic tolerance is delivered through the same mouthpiece which was spouting totalitarian propaganda the night before.

Sister Ursula's participation in the investigation also deserves comment, given the uncertain boundary between politics and religion. According to the novel, fascist politics are not founded upon genuine principles but upon charismatic presence, or, as Wolfe explains to Matt: "all it needs is a leader with a good personality, a sense of stage effect, and a few catch phrases." Matt responds: "I think I see. [Religion] is the same set-up as the political world—a leader and a slogan and you're set" (Holmes 42). The power of inspired speech is underlined in Joseph Harrigan's effect on the hardheaded Matt, who is presented to us as balanced, informed, and cognizant of the spectrum of American political views (Holmes 147–48). Matt recognizes Joseph as a right-wing ideologue, but he confesses that the man's talk ... was honestly worth listening to. You can disagree completely with a speaker's position, and still enjoy and respect the acuteness with which he presents it. So Matt felt now. Most of Joseph's opinion he would have dismissed, coming from another, as sheer reactionary drivel; but he sensed in this exponent a certain rockbound integrity which impressed him. (Holmes 61)

The passage subtly suggests that the undermining of constitutional freedoms stems in part from the very nature of those freedoms. Freedom of belief and expression, religious practices, rights to assembly, and political activity, whether or not their promise of liberty is fulfilled, allow for movements that threaten the very system that establishes their condition of possibility.

Crises are to be expected, though, when abstract freedoms come up against real material conditions. And so, a curious tension arises between specific socioeconomic and historical developments and vague claims about human nature. The historical conditions necessary to mass movements like the Temple of Light are plain to see. Indeed, the novel opens with Matt doing research for a WPA project from which he is about to be "released" due to insufficient funding. His college education, talent as a writer, and willingness to work have produced little more than a string of jobs which he holds briefly before being let go due to layoffs or nepotism. Though disheartened by these challenges and self-comparisons to wealthy former acquaintances who have evaded his plight, his relative youth still serves as an antidote to despondency and a search for ideological solutions outside his own intellectual and physical capacities. Not so with the audience Matt observes when attending a Temple of Light service, which consists of men and women over the age of 40, the age group which as adults had longer experience with the final victory of monopoly capitalism in the Progressive Era and the crippling effects of the Depression on career development. Matt's direct link with the cult, Fred Simmons, an impoverished "retired grocer from Sioux City, Iowa," is representative—a man characterized as possessing a "mixture of kindliness and hoss sense" (Holmes 45) who is living out his life quietly on a very restricted budget; he represents precisely the type of small-time entrepreneur who has been crushed by powerful economic cartels.

Against these material conditions, the cult encourages the renunciation of individuality and merger into a mass force ready to endorse violence. Matt's first reaction to the audience is dismissive: "The proceedings here might be strange, grotesque, ludicrous; but there could be nothing dangerous about them when they rested on a congregation of ordinary, wholesome, salt-of-the-earth Fred Simmonses" (Holmes 47). His attitude changes after the hypnotic power of the leader is unleashed upon them: "They were no ordinary Southern Californians now. They were participants in a mystery of hate—eyes burning, lips parted, teeth gleaming. ... Matt could no longer smile at the ritual, no matter how absurd, that could transform plain and good people into the vessels of mad hatred" (Holmes 52). This perception, though, is tempered by Matt's ultimately unfounded belief in these "harmless people" who are "such poor innocents" (Holmes 78)—they are "good people" who, given the difficult circumstances of economic life, are ripe for manipulation.

Employing a totalitarian theme is not the same as its incorporation into the narrative structure as an economic principle; as a component of structure, its ideological distinctness fades from view at the margins, becoming a textual blind spot which apperceptively orders the world of the text. An engaging and critically neglected exploration of this sort, that is, as a structuring principle as well as in content, is the satirical *Ask a Policeman* (1933), authored collectively by Anthony Berkeley, Milward Kennedy, Gladys Mitchell, John Rhode, Dorothy Sayers, and Helen Simpson. The limits of composite authorship might have weakened this novel, had it not been for the clever device of asking each author to compose his or her section using another author's series detective—the result sits astride pastiche and parody and highlights detective "constructedness." Lord Comstock, a ruthless and unsympathetic newspaper magnate, is murdered in his home surrounded by a host of people who despise him: servants and secretaries, but also, less probably, an archbishop (the victim's former public school headmaster), a government whip, an assistant commissioner of police, and allegedly the Home Secretary himself. These representatives of various classes and institutions have reason to dislike Comstock, a cad in private life who manipulates the masses with "stunts" and muckraking campaigns aimed at, among other things, Christianity, the government, and Scotland Yard. The novel, though denouncing the totalitarian propaganda potentially harnessed by powerful interests behind the press, by implication has little good to say about its readers. As with the lower middle class audiences in *Nine Times Nine*, any message presented in a sensationalistic way will be digested and forgotten—but for its brief life, it will be believed. In the end, the amateur detectives close ranks to protect vested interests that correspond to their own vision of stability, but they don't give much credit to the groups which consume a diet of ideological tripe. Despite the farcical situation of implicating major institutional representatives in a murder, the problem of a transcendent outside is introduced and justified in the name of "fair play"—ironic, given the conflict of interests that arise. To prevent a potential cover-up, the Home Secretary announces that "Instead of you [Scotland Yard], the outside experts are to be called in, allowed forty-eight hours to make their reports" (Berkeley, et al. 62).

The Home Secretary's power in this instance is the singling out of the event as exceptional ("the death of a man like Comstock is not an everyday event," he remarks [Berkeley, et al. 4]). The exceptional position given the Comstock murder indicates his status as a foe who must be neutralized, since he threatens to usurp the State's power. The Commissioner of Police logically enough reflects that "the newspapers controlled by the millionaire journalist exerted an influence out of all proportion to their real value. Inspired by Comstock himself, they claimed at frequent intervals to be the real arbiters of the nation's destiny at home and abroad." He continues this line of thought: "Lord Comstock's policy was not concerned with the welfare of the State, or of anyone else but himself" (Berkeley, et al. 5). Comstock's links to totalitarianism are explicit in his current "Back to

Paganism!" campaign—not just a dismissal of Christian ethics, but, according to his newspaper, the *Daily Bugle*, the only means by which "the existing economic depression could be finally cured" (Berkeley, et al. 6). Later in the book, he is linked to German "ways of thinking" (Berkeley, et al. 167), making the connection to Hitler more or less obvious. The point is further suggested by Mrs. Bradley's psychological portrait of the man (Berkeley, et al. 84), as well as his rise from obscurity and the missing story of his "intervening years" (Berkeley, et al. 8) before he bursts onto the public scene.

Nonetheless, the antitotalitarian message paradoxically implicates its own middle-class audience. The inflexibility of the value system and the social hierarchy insures control and plays with truth and justice along socially defined lines that defend the existing, unequal system as a better alternative to the unequal ones it combats. Decision-making cannot be entrusted to the masses, who are simply dupes manipulated by media organs whose purpose is either gain or the satisfaction of its executors' complexes (Scotland Yard A.C.: "the bone-heads that make up the great mass of the British public" [Berkeley, et al. 138]). Murder does not conform to its everyday denotative meaning, in that any number of justifications are offered—retaliation for blackmail, protection of friends in high places, defense of social institutions (church, political party, or police)—fewer excuses are offered, if any, for unsympathetically portrayed chauffeurs, private secretaries, or butlers, who are either of questionable character or simply out for revenge. When the culprit turns out to be, we are assured, someone who can hardly be dealt with as an adult in terms of moral culpability, the ranks close—this is the very accusation leveled by the media to start with. If Lord Comstock represents a fascist leader's underhanded methods for achieving success (successful because the masses respond favorably to stunts), then we are also shown how he is *not* defeated—not by ineffectual representatives of the various classes: aristocrat (Lord Peter), professional (Mrs. Bradley), artist (Sir John Saumarez), or rentier (Mr. Sheringham), most of whom are willing to protect their own prime suspects. Lord Comstock is felled by a contingent event (a 14-year-old boy with an air rifle). The arbitrariness of the shooting corresponds to an impossibility that must, at any cost, be brought within the scope of a meaningful plan, or, as Dr. Fell confidently declares in *Death Watch* when too many coincidences crowd around a mysterious death, "It wasn't accident. Therefore it was design" (242).

This being a parody and satire, we are aware of the tension between being inside and outside the problem at the same time. The desperate attempt to establish a boundary in which the value of specific players' actions can be established is refocalized at the end, as we learn that the State's shadow forces have all along been surreptitiously collecting data, sometimes employing theft, fraud, and covert surveillance to do so. In spite of these efforts to contain space and time, the attempt to plug the holes opened by several lines of inquiry is unsuccessful. The obsessive concern with timeframes, in the form of three timetables (63, 184, 254) and an examination of the actions of the participants to the minute, if not the second, threatens to annoy the reader, particularly at the end, where these minutiae are discussed interminably. The means by which correct values are established are overwhelmed by the inclusion of too many reference points, which threatens to debunk any claim to transcendental truth value. The inability to submit to any single authority, and the conclusions that suggest total guilt, lead, bizarrely enough, to the idea of no guilt. The event happened—a man is killed—but the efforts of 300 pages cannot adequately regularize the spatial and temporal frames to establish convincing relationships. The final blow to this structure is struck when the solution that we are left with exceeds the frame—the shot is fired, for our purposes, from off the map (literally, the map that precedes the commencement of the narrative); none of the detectives save Wimsey adequately establishes the proper frame of reference, and so the crime appears to be a contingent eruption of violence. The politicizing of institutions in *Ask a Policeman* illustrates the danger of rendering sovereign decisions ambiguous, the reduction of a set of competing forces within society, any of which might entail cooperation, but all of which might as well take oppositional stands—without the possibility of locating some ultimate authority.

Chapter 3
Expenditure and Discursive Recuperation

Boundaries and the Bataillian *Crochet*

Despite the shift of emphasis in setting, theme, and character, the contiguity of the hard-boiled genre with the Golden Age clue-puzzle is manifest in patterns of narrative development. The structural boundaries are thematized for Hilgart in terms of the chess games which Marlowe plays over (385–86)—games whose outcome is not in doubt, since the attrition of chessmen generates a narrative whose shape is determined independently of any pair of players.[1] Marlowe differs from his Golden Age counterparts in that his participation in cycles of violence, social disorder, and criminality does not ultimately take the form of Mrs. Bradley's stage management. He does not personally establish boundaries through which the space of homogeneous productive relations is guaranteed. If such relations coincide with his efforts, Marlowe remains insufficiently aligned with or empowered by dominant institutional interests to register an investment in outcomes.

The site begins to open, literally, with the abandonment of the bounded and isolated community as defined in the Golden Age clue-puzzle in favor of the confused social milieu of urban conglomerations. The event erupts unpredictably in violence that cannot be brought to heel through the sanctioned extralegal agency of the detective. The detective's outsider status is not a position of visionary mastery in defining the exception, partly because his or her legitimacy is not usually institutionally endorsed. If the social fabric comes undone, the detective is unable or unwilling to patch it up, since from the start, "social values, communal mores, have no real value" (Knight, *Crime* 112). In Nebel's Donahue stories, the job comes first. If, in a case like "Rough Justice," the agency's objectives are accomplished, everything else, including a murderer, can take care of itself. For more introspective men like the Op, Marlowe, and Archer, the tough detective potentially becomes a ridiculous, sentimental figure whose language no longer suffices to reorder society; rather, this function is the mandate of institutions and their representatives whose own interests do not project the illusion of Golden Age justice. Because the detective's actions may make little measurable social difference, "the detective [is] forced to define his own concept of morality and justice" (Cawelti, *Adventure* 143), or, in Horsley's words, the Golden Age's "consolatory, potentially redemptive myth no longer seems viable" (*Twentieth-Century* 69).

---

[1]   This reference to the limits of chess is expressed by detectives as diverse as Futrelle's Thinking Machine in "The Problem of Dressing Room A" (12–15) and "Kidnapped Baby Blake, Millionaire" (12) and Van Gulik's Judge Dee in *The Chinese Maze Murders* (42).

This standard description of the hard-boiled dilemma—the compulsion to act (or labor) without the promise of a satisfying resolution or reward—nonetheless demands critical examination. The representation of criminal conflict entails a concern with frame, discourse, and authority. This last word, *authority*, is complicated by in-text authorship, which comes to the fore in first-person hard-boiled narratives. The contradictions between criminal and society are at least *superficially* unproblematic in the Golden Age if we understand the contradiction to be within the scope of Hegel's conceptual antagonisms, a dialectic that operates within an authoritative notion of sameness to insure the detective's primacy. For the Golden Age, the staging of crime within a theatrical space managed by the detective entails a scripted mock dialectic between detective and opponent. In contrast, the grounded perspectivism of the hard-boiled operative, caught up in dynamic flows of action, problematizes the determination of value, since anchored points of reference outside the play seem precluded. The hard-boiled detective's range of vision is thus limited in contrast to the elevated view enjoyed by the Golden Age detective; the texts dispense with maps, since the visual no longer promises mastery. Rather, hard-boiled space is epitomized by Marlowe's tortured eavesdropping on Harry Jones's murder at the hands of Canino in Raymond Chandler's *The Big Sleep* (1939): the helplessness of an ineffectual director who stands in the wings, unable to put a stop to the eruption of evil within the true arena of action. This disturbing scene entails a cutting off of the visual which is necessarily driven into an imaginative internal space of representation.

To apply Bataille's terms, Golden Age narratives take the homogenous field of productive relations as both primary and desirable—useful knowledge is that which excises heterogeneous disruptions from the social body. In contrast, the hard-boiled detective is closer to the abjection and criminality of the heterogeneous. The texts frequently bring us into contact with a narrative voice removed from calculating society and bourgeois propriety; the gap is underscored by encounters with forms of knowledge (gambling, bootlegging, street fighting, safe-breaking, pimping) possessing no "proper" usefulness. Eruptions of violence, delivered up close and sometimes directed against helpless opponents, pepper the pages:

> He picked her up by the front of her dress and slapped her in the face—quick, sharp slaps that rocked her head back and forth. (Norbert Davis, "Red Goose" 172)

> He returned to the divan and struck the girl again—with the gun. He planted a knee on her stomach and went on striking her. He did not look mad, merely interested in his work. (Nebel, "Red-Hots" 16)

> A squint-eyed Portuguese slashed at my neck with a knife that spoiled my necktie. I caught him over the ear with the side of my gun before he could get away, saw the ear tear loose. (Hammett, "Big Knockover" 383)

The distance required for a "proper" perspective on these events is collapsed, sometimes in the case of first-person utterances to a pressing immediacy that blocks reflection. And yet the text arrives. Does the detective's voice, anterior to this proximity, presumably arising from a calm-inducing distance in time, nonetheless guarantee the resumption of productive relations in the act of writing? How should we read the apparent discursive reduction of the detective text, given that the first-person narrative demands the survival of the detective?

For answers, we turn to Bataille and to his interest in communication that blocks or leads to the discursive reduction of experience. These experiences occur at the limit and preclude the mediation of the written word, save as a recuperative gesture. The detective's limit-experience—death or absorption into the immediacy of violence—should insure silence or inarticulateness, and yet experience is *worked* into narrative form, placing the detective's voice outside the action. The narrative voice depends upon a hook [*crochet*], a term introduced by Georges Bataille in *Guilty* (1944) to deal with apparently paradoxical relations that conjoin immediacy and discursive relations:

> On a roof I saw large, sturdy hooks [*crochets*] placed halfway up. Suppose someone falls from a rooftop ... couldn't he maybe *catch hold* of one of those hooks with an arm or leg? If I fell from a rooftop, I'd plummet to the ground. But if a hook was there, I'd come to a stop halfway down!
>
> Just a little later I might say to myself: "Once an architect planned this hook, and without it I'd be dead. I should be dead, but I'm not at all—in fact, I'm alive. A hook was put there." ....
>
> I understand now—picturing the momentum of falling—that there's nothing in this world unless it meets up with a *hook*.
>
> Usually we avoid seeing a hook. We confer an aspect of necessity on ourselves, on the universe, on the earth, on people.
>
> With a hook arranging the universe, I plunged into an infinite play of mirrors [Le crochet ordonnant l'univers, je me suis abîmé dans un jeu de miroir infini]. This play had the same principle as a fall blocked by a hook. (Bataille, *Guilty* 74; Bataille, *Oeuvres* 5: 316)

I will refer to the hook as a *crochet* in order to emphasize its specifically Bataillian usage. The *crochet* points up a discursive problem central to many hard-boiled texts. The fall from the roof is a literal slip or Bataillian slippage (*glisser*) in which the subject loses his footing and falls to death and silence. The immediacy of experience defies communication. But the subject is suspended, and the death limit becomes accessible to language. Writing it down, again to literalize this metaphor, means a descent, groundedness, and the loss of immediacy. The recuperation of language is the accident of a *crochet*, which "hooks" the I, suspending it while also escaping this I's range of vision. Knowledge of things and their transmission, at least in an everyday sense, appears contingent with this *crochet* ("nothing in this world unless ..."), the discursive net whose ideological mesh remains invisible most of the time ("usually we avoid seeing a hook").

Death potentially functions this way in the Golden Age narrative, but this death very rarely touches the narrative voice or the detective. Indeed, the invulnerability of the Classical detective is demonstrated by the relative ease of Holmes's resurrection. Rather, the dead body of the victim is the center of gravity which draws the suspects into orbit around it; Žižek, in one of his few astute comments on detective fiction, states that "the corpse is an object which functions as a binder, a tie for a group of subjects" (39). The detective miraculously reanimates this corpse, which is made to speak the circumstances of its demise and to declare "Thou art the man!" The Golden Age detective self-consciously takes on the role of the *crochet* upon which our hopes depend. Or, we could say the detective is a *crochet* who prevents tableaux from falling, who insures that they remain suspended, but invisibly so.[2]

The detective intercedes in a Godless universe. Foucault's phrase "the now-constant space of our experience" (71) from "A Preface to Transgression" acknowledges the challenge posed by the death of God and the collapse of exteriority. The spatialization metaphor is central to his essay with its evocation of boundary, shape, inside, and outside, though space is not a container of objects determined by coordinates. Foucault writes: "Transgression … is not related to the limit as black to white, the prohibited to the lawful, the outside to the inside, or as the open areas of a building to its enclosed spaces. Rather, their relationship takes the form of a spiral that no simple infraction can exhaust" ("Preface" 73–74). The hard-boiled operative seems aptly described by such a spiral. Taking up a position at any point allows little more than a glimpse of coming attractions and the risk of turning back on oneself.

The hard-boiled detective's limited range of vision, which we experience with a tenuous promise of resolution, tentatively dispenses with claims to exteriority and only resolves itself in decline. Decline, in its Bataillian sense from *On Nietzsche* (1945), is the discursive recuperation that, *a fortiori*, posits an architect and a purpose. It should not be read as a statement of value implying loss, but, rather, the conditioning counterweight to Bataille's notion of the summit. The summit evokes an outpouring of energy and the disappearance of limits, particularly those which underpin homogeneous productive relations; the latter suggests the return to a bounded ego which recuperates itself after exhaustion, which reconstitutes itself through the labor of writing (again, in its first-person dimension). The decline is the restoration of productivity in its everyday sense.[3] The summit risks

---

    [2]   Paralleling this idea, the detective is the keystone which "prevent[s] systems (whether political, philosophical, or scientific) from collapsing" (Hollier, *Against* 32). In another text Hollier links the keystone to God and heterogeneity, which "serves as much to close the profane world as to open it" ("Dualist" 133), that is, the tension irreducible to dialectics. See also 132 of his "The Dualist Materialism of Georges Bataille."

    [3]   And hence to forms of knowledge that are not sovereign: "To know is always to strive, to work; it is always a servile operation, indefinitely resumed, indefinitely repeated. Knowledge is never sovereign: to be *sovereign* it would have to occur in a moment. But the moment remains outside, short of or beyond, all knowledge" (Bataille, *Sovereignty* 202).

the integrity of the self in that it thoughtlessly gambles or wagers the self (and meaning); it loses sight of the self. These boundaries, the limits that comprise discrete identity, are reformed in decline (Bataille, *On Nietzsche* 17). Bataille is aware that "to structure and explain the summit morality assumes the decline" and "the fact of 'speaking' of a summit morality itself belongs to a decline of morality" (*On Nietzsche* 37), morality here taken as our attitude towards limits, not a table of proscriptions or precepts. The hard-boiled detective's brush with death, attested in numerous examples from Daly to Spillane, is the summit "where life is pushed to an impossible limit," but also which is necessarily a decline in that we know anything about it (Bataille, *On Nietzsche* 39).

A final theoretical consideration is the relation of death to the terms considered so far—homogeneous, heterogeneous, *crochet*, summit, and decline. Libertson notes how Bataille's thought shifts between the 1920s and the 1940s, from obsessions with abjection, taboo, and violence to the mysticism of the *Atheological Summa*. Libertson traces the movement from a set of economic relations related to conservation, limits on expenditure, and the primacy of productive relations to an epistemology concerned with the same subject areas. For a conservationist epistemological model, in which knowledge informs practices favoring production, science takes on the role of gatekeeper. Science is alternately conceived as "both a *function* and a *foundation* of the homogeneous world" (Libertson 673)—in its former role, it polices the homogeneous field of productive relations; in the latter role, it confronts the mutually defining Other of nonproductive expenditure. The recurring "critical gesture" in Bataille, whereby "two terms which apparently exclude each other violently are placed in a relationship of mutual conditioning" (677), has a definite literary dimension, since motivated approaches to the heterogeneous suggest attempts at neutralization. The confrontation with expenditure that tests the limits of rational calculation, excess of all sorts in which the loss of the subject and therefore of meaning becomes possible, is nonetheless reduced in the transmission of such experience through discourse.

The subject, whose apprehension and knowledge of objects is premised upon the containment of homogeneous particles, is nonetheless open to heterogeneity, since the subject's boundaries are but "mal fermée." The "being of the subject," Bataille's direct concern in later works, "is described as an illusory integrity whose closure is in reality not complete, or whose 'unity' is 'imperfect'" (Libertson 681). The intimate relation of homogeneity and heterogeneity, shifting to continuity and discontinuity within the imperfect boundaries of the subject, points to the literary representation of death: death is not simply the break that interrupts and terminates the living continuity of beings. It is *the* profound entry into continuity that shuts down knowledge and communication. The association of excess with the continuous poses a problematic relation to the discontinuous world, whose beings are certainly aware of the losses construed by eroticism and death, but which stave off violent eruptions in the interests of self-preservation: "This contact is paradoxical, because discontinuity opposes the violence of continuity, in the struggle for survival, but at the same time *incarnates* and expresses that violence through its very desire to survive. Continuity is excess. Survival is a paradoxical mobilization of excess in the direction of self-conservation" (Libertson 686–87). This survival reminds us of the discursive recuperations of the hard-boiled detective, particularly those who are their own narrators. Their confrontations with violence and death motivate their own excesses in the name of survival, which then becomes a precondition for the text. And yet, hard-boiled labor tends towards loss, or "perte sans profit," unlike the Golden Age investigator whose object is the stabilization of a system premised on unproblematic accumulation. Moreover, hard-boiled detectives tend towards death in ways that their Golden Age counterparts do not, and thus they place themselves in positions where death serves as a different sort of limit—not one to be contained through becoming the object of knowledge, scientific or otherwise (the corpse as problematic Other), but rather as the challenge to communication premised upon the obvious need to survive the ordeal. "Communication 'en-deçà de la mort' or, in a sense, 'communication unto death', will be the actual subject of [Bataille's later] system" (Libertson 691), as it will be for Hammett and Chandler in their most innovative work.

The textual analyses in the remaining parts of this chapter illustrate how knowledge and homogeneous relations are framed and events are determined in a range of authors associated with hard-boiled fiction. George Harmon Coxe literalizes the problem in his photographer-investigators Flash Casey and Kent Murdock. Casey and Murdock are incapable of guaranteeing the truth value of events as individuals. Yet they function as human agents controlling the technically mediated apparatus by which final truths are established. Jonathan Latimer's Bill Crane stories from the 1930s are the second focus, especially his exemplary first installment, *Murder in the Madhouse*, in which neither detective nor institutional formation can serve as a defining boundary. Finally, we turn to Whitfield, Nebel, Hammett, and Chandler, in which radical perspectivalism, haptic or disoriented notions of space, and the internal contest between experience and discourse reach their most developed forms.

"Stories could be faked but to get a picture you had to be there." (Coxe, *Silent* 193)

Although the Golden Age detective sometimes suppresses the "true" truth to protect favored interests, this suppression typically entails no irresolvable breach between audience and social institutions. The hard-boiled detective's greater distance from official truth organs—greater or lesser depending upon the detective's relation to the police, D.A., or judicial system—heightens awareness of the distance between private and public truth in which competing interests are invested. When the detective works officially within institutional boundaries, the conflict is internalized, leading sometimes to a crisis of faith and commitment (found earlier in some of Chandler's sympathetic cops, but more common to the procedurals of Ed McBain, Reginald Hill, and Ian Rankin). In hard-boiled fiction originating in the thirties and forties, our detective not uncommonly has left the official force as a consequence of this conflict (for instance, Donahue, Cardigan, Marlowe, or Archer).

The dispirited police officer is not the only institutional representative sworn to serve the public weal who can feel powerlessness in the face of entrenched interests. The manipulations and obfuscations of the power elite are also registered by the journalist. By the 1920s and 1930s the servility of the press to business interests was well documented, for example, in James Rorty's *Our Master's Voice* (1934) and parts of Douglas Waples's *Reading in the Depression* (1937) (116–25). Journalist-narrators, a not infrequent sidekick, join the detective in exuding ambivalence towards a press frequently regarded in a negative light: news media are often disparaged as weak on analysis (the language contradictions reported in "The Murders in the Rue Morgue"), subject to manipulation (Holmes's planting of clues in "The Six Napoleons"), entrapment (MacBride's strategy in "The Law Laughs Last"), of dubious veracity (*Ask a Policeman*), or downright criminal (Lester Dent's colorful "The Tank Terror").

Unlike the Watson role, the journalist-detective is something of a rarity; the best examples are probably found in George Harmon Coxe's Kent Murdock and Flash Casey novels and stories.[4] The weighting of Coxe's stories towards action over intellectual investigations places him closer to the Hammett tradition thematically and stylistically. In terms of how boundaries are established, however, the socially marginal characters, urban settings, hard drinking, and fisticuffs resemble hard-boiled embroidery on a Golden Age–leaning structuring of knowledge. Murdock and Casey's use of photography, in fact, offers a new approach to the closed site. The time-space limit in Coxe is mechanically mediated through the manipulation of the photograph's widely believed truth function. And thus, the clue value that the picture takes on illustrates the power exerted by its claims to objectivity. That pictures should function this way—when they could as easily be manipulated or doctored to concoct a "truth" serving some narrow interest, such as we find in the blackmail shots of Imlay in Chandler's "Spanish Blood"—is softened by the overstated integrity of Casey and Murdock, men who live for their jobs.

In Coxe the photograph frames the event in a way that *seems* detached from the personality of authority figures. To be sure, Murdock and Casey are behind the camera, but their role is ambiguous, not only their faith in the superior eye of the camera but also their ultimate deference to their newspapers' hierarchical structures. Though they do not possess independent authority, our photographers, motivated by fair play, loyalty, and a truth-seeking impulse, nonetheless become vehicles for fixing boundaries. The mechanical means employed to record truth obscure the underlying ideological influences in that the signs they produce ostensibly correspond with objective reality. Such assumptions fade in postmodern detective fiction, where the arbitrariness of the sign seriously compromises stable

---

[4] An obvious and early exception is Leroux's Rouletabille. The journalist sidekick, however, is relatively common—for example, Walter Jameson, Hutchinson Hatch, Jeff Marle, Nigel Bathgate, and Ross Harte.

meanings and knowledge (Cohen 129; see also Laura Marcus 254 and Rowen 224). Neither the Classic/Golden Age nor the hard-boiled modes demand much skepticism towards the event, only the ways in which events are managed and to what end. The notion of intrinsic value is problematic in the postmodern tale, given the epistemological uncertainty directed towards the event itself, coupled with the opacity of the clue and the calculated "deviation" from detective story narrative conventions. The postmodern clue is but a token whose value is determined by an unstable, floating rate of exchange.

A brief investigation of photographs in relatively early examples of detective fiction reveals that as clues or motives, they often pass unquestioned as objects of redeemable value. In their evidential role, photographs figure prominently and from the start in Thorndyke's cases. Moreover, the photograph, employed by antagonists, promises tangible social consequences. In "A Scandal in Bohemia" we conclude that Irene Adler's intention to block the King's wedding by turning over the compromising photograph to the bride's family is no empty threat. Sordid blackmail functions this way in Sayers's "The Unprincipled Affair of the Practical Joker," Mitchell's *Come Away, Death*, and Chandler's *The High Window*. As we approach the height of the hard-boiled period, noticeable changes occur. A burgeoning token economy of dematerialized objects is traceable in photography clues running from Chandler (*The Big Sleep*) to Ross Macdonald (*The Galton Case*) to Paul Auster (*City of Glass*). The immateriality of the photo-clue arises from its technologically mediated infinite reproducibility and its signifying instability in time vis-à-vis its referent. In *The Big Sleep*, the problem of Carmen's picture retains a negotiated market value, though one that makes no pretense to intrinsic worth, since it is regarded as pornography.

Macdonald's and Auster's use of the photograph, however, have more overtly philosophical underpinnings in that attempts are made to use the photographic sign to establish identity (correspondence) and, in Macdonald's case, value. These attempts differ from Thorndyke's scientific applications in texts like *The Red Thumb-Mark* (1907) because they cannot appeal to absolute or universal standards of external truth—Thorndyke's use of photography and the scientific manipulation of photographic evidence only serve to shatter the human dimension of testimony in favor of an indisputably factual demonstration. Certainties of this sort are worlds away from *The Galton Case* (1959), which employs a common Macdonald device—a missing person and a complex backstory. Archer's search begins with a photograph of a father whose image, Archer hopes, will allow him to identify the son, but the photograph turns out to be more confusing than helpful. Although Archer locates the right person, certainty is constantly undermined by the young man's mutation under a series of aliases. Macdonald thereby subtly suggests the arbitrariness of any attribution of value in a nominalist world. Instead of establishing truth, the photograph questions convertabilty in a breach between the sign and its referent. In *City of Glass* (1987), again, a photograph from the past is used for identification purposes, this time to spot the "same" man in the present, Peter Stillman, Sr. In an even more radical move, Quinn, the bearer of the photograph, matches the picture to two Stillmans, who simultaneously appear at the train station where Quinn expects him to alight. Signification literally breaks down into aggressive polysemy. Quinn, whose job is to shadow Stillman, must make a choice, but "whatever choice he made ... would be arbitrary, a submission to chance" (Auster 68). In Auster, we have reached an open expression of anxiety vis-à-vis the sign in which the detective is himself traumatized by his inability to establish any ground of certainty.

The problems raised by Chandler, Macdonald, and Auster are not anticipated by the work of George Harmon Coxe's photographer protagonists; nonetheless, the use of pictures in Coxe's novels point up an epistemological dimension to the camera's role in the investigative process. The truth-generating potential of the camera is not wasted on his series characters Flash Casey and Kent Murdock. These men, at least dimly, perceive the ethical consequences of a photographic "reality" and the serious social consequences this reality may give rise to. Nonetheless, Coxe's protagonists tend to view truth as awaiting discovery; the evidence construed by the camera in fact demonstrates guilt independently of the photographer's act of pressing the shutter. Casey muses over this situation in *Silent Are the Dead* (1941), in which the establishment of a "true" truth involves the manipulation of the image. In two instances, the protagonist literally masks photographs in order to construct images that favor specific outcomes (Coxe, *Silent* 114, 173). Because truth is displayed by the photograph's objective correspondence to reality, a character's ostensibly incriminating presence at a crime scene can only be dealt with by a literal cover-up—language is insufficient to explain away such strong evidence. Ironically, a masking rather than an unmasking enables the "truth" to be established.

Casey nonetheless persists in the belief that the photographer as truth-producer is at the same time a truth-establisher, that his labor uncovers incontrovertible evidence. In displaying this faith in the image's relation to an objective world, he participates in William Little's "fantasy of matching signifier to signified, clue to crime," remaining "confident that signs conform to a classical economy of representation" (138). Despite this mode of thought in Coxe's stories, irrational motives and interpretative practices draw attention to the class status of the participants and the power of truth-generating institutions. Ultimately, the relatively powerless hero finds reassurance in traditional hierarchies and, importantly, his fusion with technology as a means to establish certainty. These concerns are already well developed in the Kent Murdock novel *The Camera Clue* (1937).

The Camera Clue opens with the murder of Jerry Carter, a blackmailer, who may have been killed by Nora Pendleton. Carter threatens to block Nora's approaching wedding with compromising letters unless she grants him sexual favors. Nora visits Carter's office to intimidate him with her father's gun, which she fires; believing that she has killed Carter, she takes refuge with her friend Joyce Murdock, Kent's wife. Kent's loyalties in the case are divided between friendship, maintaining good relations with the police, and his professional impulse to view the murder as an exclusive story. The ensuing investigation reveals a complicated web of relations which display the universality of guilt in a society motivated by self-interest. The idea that anyone, including the blue-blooded and hyperfeminine Nora, is incapable of crime is dismissed by Murdock: "Murdock tried to think reasonably [about Nora's confession] while reaction came to him on two conflicting thoughts. The first said, *It's absurd. She couldn't do it*. The second said, *She could do it*. It was this second thought that stuck" (Coxe, *Camera* 6).

The solid New Class professionalism of Murdock, a technician with marketable skills (Coxe, *Camera* 13; see also Coxe, "Murder Mix-up" 223), raises a challenge to ideological blocks that close the site. Curiously, he is willing to place his career in jeopardy by supporting Nora, a decision in which "he double-crossed the police or he double-crossed Nora Pendleton—and he had already committed himself [to Nora]" (Coxe, *Camera* 13). He is prompted to act by his wife, whose society status is described in the first Murdock novel, *Murder with Pictures* (1935), and elaborated in *Murdock's Acid Test* (1936). In both *Murder with Pictures* (Coxe 190) and *The Camera Clue* (Coxe 151), Joyce lauds middle-class professionalism, emphasizing the importance of work and the hollowness of society. Yet Murdock is willing to put this career at risk to protect the interests of a class definitely not his own. Nora's description hints at their different orbits: "sitting there in an overstuffed chair, her eyes steady and direct as she watched him, there was a poise and assurance to the set of her head and neck that was a heritage of class and breeding." Her appeal, however, raises contradictions: "Mixed with the anxiety in her glance was approval. Murdock knew she was depending on him" (Coxe, *Camera* 11). Nora's anxiety arises not so much from having committed murder, which she basically feels was justified, but from the reaction of her fiancé's haughty family, to whom she is still an "outsider," even though later, when she is proven not to have committed the killing, we are told that "with luck and her father's influence, Nora Pendleton's name would not reach the newspapers" (Coxe, *Camera* 69). Membership in this class is not simply a question of money; Nora subsequently describes her fiancé's photograph as possessing "a sort of patrician flare to the nostrils of the straight nose" and eyes that are "hard and superior" (Coxe, *Camera* 33), and Kent reflects on Roger Spalding's career from Groton to Harvard to "a junior partner in a socially prominent firm" (Coxe, *Camera* 119). Moreover, Spalding's involvement in the case warrants his detention, but Superintendent Dolan candidly tells him that his "family and position" save him from this indignity (Coxe, *Camera* 122).

Murdock's social position, education, and relative powerlessness vis-à-vis official social organs are blocks to outsider omniscience. His empowerment is achieved through the technological mediation of the camera and its ability to fix space and time—the collapse of identity between man and machine is in fact emphasized in that he and his fellow photographers refer to themselves as "cameras." Murdock acknowledges his peripheral status by refusing to hand over a photograph upon demand: "I have nothing to do with publishing pictures. I just take them" (Coxe, *Camera* 15); authority depends upon his merger with the machine so that his own human subjectivity is indistinguishable from its technical operations. We note the continuities: "Acting almost before he thought, he adjusted the shutter and focus and put the camera to his shoulder," an act followed by a description of the world through the camera: "As he pressed the shutter-release he noticed several things through the wire rim of his finder that had so far escaped him" (Coxe, *Camera* 14; see also Coxe, *Camera* 17). This formula recurs, stressing that the camera is an appendage that comes into play without the self-conscious mediation of the human agent who operates it. Subsequently, what the camera sees—that which escapes the man who took the picture—constitutes significant evidence. And yet, the problem of Carter's murder is but one facet of the apparent truth-bearing value of Murdock's picture. A total of six men in *The Camera Clue* are threatened by the picture he takes: two for adulterous relationships, one for establishing the identity of an embezzler, one for a private domestic matter, one for blackmail, and one for a revenge motive. The camera records truth detached from subjective perspectivism; as a measure of guilt, it dehumanizes the role formally reserved for the omniscient detective. Ironically, Murdock's picture, which seems to be the impetus behind two subsequent killings, is not the vital piece of evidence and does not point to the murderer in Nora's case. The significance of photographic evidence is understood by the characters' relentless attempts to obtain pictures that incriminate them, never doubting that they do. Throughout *The Camera Clue*, until the solution is revealed in the last couple of chapters, we are made to think that these men are desperate enough to kill in order to possess a monopoly on this truth value.

"He suffers from delusions. He has a fixation that he's a great detective. He becomes quite violent when he is doubted." (Latimer 155)

Although better known today for his film and television screenplays, particularly the television dramatization of Perry Mason, Jonathan Latimer had already achieved a measure of success with his William Crane series in the 1930s. Two sinister novels frame the series—*Murder in the Madhouse* (1935) and *Red Gardenias* (1939). Crane launches his investigations in these first and last works under cover, which he does not do in the three middle novels. In the first novel, his imposture takes the reader by surprise—we are one-third of the way through the book before we get dependable confirmation of his identity. From our vantage, we might dismiss this "doubt" as nitpicking, given our familiarity with the protagonist from subsequent novels—but we must recall that this is the first novel in a series by a then-unknown author; readers had no other texts by which to establish Crane's persona. The suppression of Crane's identity disappears from *Red Gardenias*, in which his, his coworkers', and his client's positions are clarified within the first two chapters. Although Bill Brubaker correctly assesses *Red Gardenias* as the most stylistically fluid and economically plotted novel of the series, *Murder in the Madhouse* is more germane to this study. In addition to satirizing contemporaneous America and representing the first station on Crane's journey as a Depression-era anti-Everyman, the novel offers a complex commentary on the framing device of detective fiction in which neither detective nor institutional boundaries are able to stabilize meaning.

Brubaker, in his monograph on Latimer's fiction, *Stewards of the House*, develops the economic background of the 1930s vis-à-vis Latimer's career (both as government employee and novelist) in some detail. He rightly notes how "class distinction [in the novels] defines character and manifests itself through the politics of personality, in the social comedy of an elitism based upon taste and consumption, and by often shockingly abrupt and grotesque acts of violence." He goes on to remark upon "the theme of pervasive social corruption central to the series" and the acute anxiety affecting many of the characters, "the fear of life without money" (22). Crane is prone to these fears and fetishes. He tolerates unreasonable demands from his boss, Colonel Black, in the labor buyer's market of 1935, but he also expresses his "normal" attraction to enormous wealth, stating: "The key that would give its possessor eight hundred thousand extra dollars. Who wouldn't murder for that?" (Latimer 287). This is a sentiment that is unexceptional in both *Murder in the Madhouse* and the subsequent Crane novels. Given the instability of Depression-era America, Crane's quest is not simply to conduct the investigation to a solution, which he manages despite his reckless appetites, but to achieve solvency along the way.

The plot of *Murder in the Madhouse* is relatively simple. Private detective William Crane poses as an inmate in a private asylum for wealthy mental patients. His object is to recover a box containing a fortune in securities which has been stolen from one of the patients, Miss Van Kamp, the sister of his client. In tracing the movements of the box, an array of people, including staff members and the detective himself, are implicated. In terms of character, theme, and setting, *Murder in the Madhouse* is a hybrid text; Brubaker notes the transposed aspects of the Golden Age clue-puzzle: the isolated country house and wealthy closed community, which he slightly exaggerates as "a microcosm of history and social organization" (26). At the same time, the novel exhibits hard-boiled qualities: tough characters, violence, and Roth's "crime surplus," resulting in four killings and several murderous attacks.

The universe represented by Latimer holds little redemptive potential, and certainly none arising from beneficent individuals or institutions. Because the psychiatric treatment is expensive, the inmates derive from a wealthy social caste. Moreover, Miss Van Kamp's considerable fortune does not represent the sweat of her brow, innate talent, or laboriously developed professional skill—the jewelry and bonds are acquired through inheritance and investment profits. As she is an old, unmarried woman, her wealth is sterile, destined neither to find its way to her subsequently murdered paid companion, Miss Paxton, nor to be used by its owner, since, we are told, she will be dead a year hence. Yet her chief obsession is a fortune which she cannot use (the inmates are not allowed to have money) and which she originally intends to will to the sanitarium, an institution which is questionable not only in terms of its murderous, promiscuous, drunken, and venal staff, but also in its class bias. Though Miss Van Kamp appears to be the only true representative of the idle rich, most of the others are linked solidly to the professions or are the wives of such men. In contrast, the servants and attendants cover a range of underclass positions: the gang member thug, the Holy Roller, the ex-con, and the marginalized black cooks. Between these extremes we have, at the top, the professions represented by the doctors, then the sheriff and his staff, and the nurses; somewhere in this mix is Crane. Placing him, though, is no easy task, even retrospectively from the end of the series with the promise of marriage into money in *Red Gardenias* (Brubaker 24). This social range is interesting in terms of whose interests are served, how sympathy is or is not placed, and who is victimized and blamed.

Crane's ambiguous status is in part a quality of the general difficulty in defining detective labor—a subject developed in Chapter 5. Crane's comic declaration that he is C. Auguste Dupin, an approximation of the truth inasmuch as he is a detective, is ostensibly a symptom of his ill-defined neurosis (Latimer 144, 155). But his affinity with Dupin is limited. Though propertyless and possessed of observation skills from which he can make quick inferences, Crane is far from being an impoverished aristocrat whose pursuit of truth satisfies some intellectual impulse, much less an ethical higher calling. His intelligence is harnessed like that of the New Class technician in the service of the moneyed elite to shore up or protect their wealth from threatening incursions.[5] What he gains, he gains under duress, faced with the dire reality of Depression-era unemployment. Although institutions—medicine and law enforcement, for instance—come in for much criticism, the four murder victims are basically inoffensive, if not sympathetic, people who are in the wrong place at the wrong time. None of the victims is threatening except as a source of potential information that might implicate the real criminals. Despite being well disposed to Nurse Clayton and the as-yet-unmurdered Mr. Penny, Crane offensively declares: "I might as well tell you that the only reason that I came here was to serve Miss Van Kamp and her brother. She wanted her securities back, and I got them for her. The murders were only incidental" (Latimer 298). Unlike Coxe, whose hard-boiled figures slip into sentimentality instead of irony, Latimer "has it both ways: he masters the style he mocks" (Collins n. pag.). Moreover, as a detective, Crane is something of a failure. His deductions are farcical parodies of a Sherlock Holmes–type investigation, and instead of solving the crimes through the thoughtful analysis of clues, he acquires his knowledge by snooping and eavesdropping (tinged with voyeurism in his surveillance of Miss Evans with her paramours). Crane resembles the putdown Vivian Regan dishes out at her first meeting with Marlowe, referring to private detectives as "greasy little men snooping around hotels" (Chandler, *Big Sleep* 600). Indeed, Crane's search for the box and his actions arguably create more violence than they prevent—though he remains indifferent to the resulting mayhem. And despite offering us

---

[5]   Latimer's theme was pertinent, given sociological models of changes in Depression-era reading. See Waples's summary of Lasswell's research (22).

a narrative denouement, his evidence is either bluff or built upon analysis by his boss, the distant Colonel Black. Until the end, he is suspected of one or more of the crimes, and in fact commits a few en route to the solution. We come to suspect that the better detective is the enigmatic and mute Mr. Penny, whose chain of logical inference leads to his death. Mr. Penny's charming inoffensiveness is bizarre, given the confidence with which the narrator "reads" the signs of his behavior (in that he does not speak). Winks, gestures, and facial expressions are a language legible to the narrator, and less convincingly to Crane. At one point, Penny enters Crane's room and has a "conversation"—half-written, half-spoken—about the crime; Penny outlines his thoughts and indicates the box's hiding place. Later, another note to Crane suggests that he has further information to impart, though he is killed before this comes off. "Real" detectives in this book are speechless, self-effacing types (reminiscent of Anthony Berkeley's Mr. Chitterwick or Mr. Todhunter) or distant, godlike figures who occasionally deign to favor the human world with a pointer.

Latimer's innovation resides in the relentless lack of reference points, and this absence persists well into the work, particularly in respect to the detective. Despite its gesture towards the closed site of the country house, the novel does not create a contained homogeneous space within bounds established by detective or institutional authority. There is no establishment of uncontested rationality in a general or institutional sense, and the detective does not serve as a clear point of reference by which a monopoly on truth is stabilized. Categories like sane/insane or criminal/noncriminal are demonstrably unstable in the novel. Institutional controls are placed upon inmates in codified rules, but the rule makers, Dr. Livermore and Dr. Eastman, display neurotic and violent behavior. Their staff consists of gangsters, ex-convicts, and religious fanatics whose abuse of power oversteps reasonable levels of restraint. The assumption that class status is proportionate to power is overturned in that the inmates, though wealthy, are bound by rules that curtail their movement and impose disciplinary constraints on behavior, such as a ban on money or liquor. Crane, as a detective, enters on the same level as those confined within it, and he is, moreover, immediately suspected by several people of being the criminal, since the murders commence with his arrival. Our own initial uncertainties confirm that he does not possess that exteriority (represented, for instance, by literal freedom of movement) by which to recognize events, isolate them, and establish truth.

"Several things happened—and in *one* of them you were right." (Whitfield, "Caleso" 102)

Latimer's novels are self-destablizing as a function of their comic self-referentiality; they therefore serve as a hard-boiled correlate to extreme Golden Age texts like *The Poisoned Chocolates Case* or *Ask a Policeman*. A less self-conscious figure is featured in Raoul Whitfield's Jo Gar series. Although the stories are perhaps more interesting for the local color of their settings—the Philippines, Hawai'i, or Japan—than any pretense to tight plot constructions, a handful of the stories approximate the beads-on-a-string structure that is given more masterful treatment in Hammett and Chandler. "The Caleso Murders" (1930), with its strong forward momentum and its abandonment of clue-puzzle conventions, represents the best example. The story contains breaches in logic and constant gaps in information that require "leaps" of action without the benefit of tangible clues or reasoned cause-and-effect chains.[6] Beginning *in medias res*, we pursue people we know little about, who seem dedicated to committing crimes which we don't fully understand and for reasons that are poorly explained. These are not plot defects, but rather the convergence of incomplete data, uncertainty in the minds of the pursuers, and inconsistent behavior amongst the criminals themselves. Although an unknown relationship later comes to light to help establish causal connections, the explanation cannot be reasonably predicted by mastering the information we are given (even keeping in mind the less-than-fair-play standards of most Golden Age texts). Instead, we dash through a series of vignettes, each ostensibly related to the same event, that function together like pieces from different jigsaw puzzles. The promise that a unified picture will emerge is deferred, and the force required to mesh together the disparate fragments violates the assumption that truth exists independently of the investigator.

The action opens with news of a dangerous escaped criminal, whose precise relationship with Lt. Arragon of the Manila police and Gar is unknown. Apparently, the escapee, Palerdo, is determined to murder his former employer's wife. Although more than one motive is hinted at, none is sufficient to explain his actions. Señor Mantiro, Palerdo's former employer and victim, was knifed after he had beaten his wife, but the criminal is given a life sentence after the intervention of Señora Mantiro. Confusingly, Palerdo is intent on killing the woman he apparently was defending and who was his benefactor after the murder. Bit by bit, expository material accrues, though the information is plagued by gaps and gleaned from untrustworthy sources. The case proceeds through fits and starts and involves a distorted time element. After Palerdo's escape he manages, in broad daylight and with all of Manila's police force looking for him, to commit murder. Moreover, he locates and kills Señora Mantiro and her driver without raising an alarm, only to disappear again immediately. Soon afterwards, Palerdo's hiding place is discovered by Gar's chance pick-up of a suspicious-looking man who just happens to lead him to the hideout. After Gar locates Palerdo, he tells him that he believes him innocent of the killings, though we are uncertain whether this is mere bluff. If Gar is truthful, we would have to accept a very unlikely coincidence, namely, that someone else happened to choose the time of Palerdo's escape to commit the crimes, either to put suspicion on Palerdo or, by chance, to act upon motives which we cannot guess at since we have no other suspects.

---

[6] Whitfield rarely engages in fair play, so answers are often produced magically by Gar on the penultimate page. Hagemann recognizes this quality, for him a weakness, in the stories (xxxii).

As in many of the Jo Gar stories, violence erupts without warning, but the detective is equal to it. A feature Gar shares with Spade is his willingness to resort to subterfuge, threats, and double-dealing to achieve results. He shoots at Palerdo after he is attacked with a knife, though he does him no injury. Gar knows that Palerdo is not dead, and therefore still dangerous: "'You are not hit,' he said grimly, 'but now—I shall kill you. I shall kill you, Palerdo, and say that you resisted arrest—'" (Whitfield, "Caleso" 150). Given that he kills a number of people in the series, we cannot be sure whether this is bluff. Palerdo commits suicide, but not before he gives the name of the woman he claims to be the killer—a claim summarily dismissed by Gar, though not aloud, since he intends to trick Palerdo's accomplice into a betrayal of the true killer's identity. The woman Palerdo accuses turns up dead, killed in a sampan "accident" before Palerdo has even escaped. As bodies pile up, each one defers the promise of meaning to the next, yet the motive in producing one corpse relies upon finding a motive for a second or third killing.

Following the accomplice Santos Costios, who originally led Gar to Palerdo and whom Gar has persuaded Arragon to release provisionally in hopes that he will lead them to some answers, Gar finds himself at the scene of the Malay woman's "accident." At a tense moment on the boat, Gar thinks out loud: "'The Malay woman—sold nuts—to sampan men,' he breathed softly. 'Perhaps Palerdo—'" (Whitfield, "Caleso" 153). Typical of this story, we get no further, and the connection forming in Gar's brain is deferred. In these circumstances, though, more is slowly revealed, so that we realize that the knowledge to sort the relationships has been withheld by the authorities from Gar (and us) because Gar's own relationship to the criminal was not fully known; at a late point in the text, we learn Palerdo was led on by Señora Mantiro, who hoped that he would kill her husband so that she could openly consummate an affair with her Dutch lover. The climactic point is not only a climax of action but also one of irony in this thoroughly ambiguous story: as Arragon and Gar lie low in a sampan, listening in on a conversation between Costios and an unknown man in a language they do not understand, Gar remarks: "Under the roof of this sampan we will find the murderer of Señora Mantiro and the *caleso* driver. We will learn why Palerdo lied even as he was about to kill himself" (Whitfield, "Caleso" 156). Seconds later, an explosion blows the sampan to splinters and deposits everyone, dead or injured, into the Pasig River. After a rescue, Gar deceitfully convinces Costios he is going to die in order to extract the truth—Palerdo has in fact killed Señora Mantiro, just not in the place where the body was found. The general scheme is expressed well by Gar's closing comment to the lieutenant. "'You did very well,' [Gar] said, 'under all the circumstances. Several things happened—and in *one* of them you were right'" (Whitfield, "Caleso" 159). The framing of the event is beyond the immediate grasp of the participants, and the chain of events is so unlikely that we look skeptically upon this forced closure.

Whitfield's habits of composition have been attested to as hurried (Nolan 132), and despite comparisons to Hammett, his detective writing only occasionally achieves Hammett's level of control and integration. What he appears to owe most to Hammett, and this is true of the best Jo Gar stories (like "Silence House" and "Climbing Death"), is the beads-on-a-string structure, a genuinely new form with interesting epistemological consequences. This structure, reaching polished development in many Hammett texts and consistently present in Chandler's novels, was approximated by other writers with some success, for instance in certain Donahue and Cardigan stories by Frederick Nebel ("Red Pavement" and "Hell's Pay-Check" are exemplary) and Norbert Davis's *Sally's in the Alley*. It is to this structure in its most developed form that we now turn.

"[O]ne place was still as good as another." (Hammett, "Dead Yellow Women" 207)

Dashiell Hammett's reputation as an innovator is well deserved, though his Continental Op and Sam Spade stories and novels are irreducible to a consistent vision or subgenre orientation. This fragmentation is partly the result of Hammett's inhabitation of diverse narrative structures—the caper, the clue-puzzle, the thriller, the satire—but also the western and the Gothic novel. Hammett is not a "pure" exponent of the hard-boiled tale; in many of his short stories, we discern thematic elements associated with hard-boiled writing grafted onto a clue-puzzle epistemological model and Golden Age tendencies. Stories like "Arson Plus," "The Gatewood Caper," "One Hour," "Tom, Dick, or Harry," and the first Spade short, "A Man Called Spade," exhibit this pattern; these stories are not grouped into any one period, but span Hammett's entire writing career. Structurally, such works conform to a ratiocinative focus (sometimes presenting a closed world of suspects in a physically bounded site),[7] despite incorporating the familiar trappings of hard-boiled fiction: underworld characters, the urban milieu, and unpredictable intrusions of violence. Though ratiocinative approaches may be played down, they are commonly present and sometimes decisive. The absence of armchair deduction in the pursuit of a solution does not mean that our frame of knowledge is represented in a substantially different way. Hammett's radical contribution is discernible when he goes about giving us access to knowledge apprehended within a *dynamic* frame of reference. Coupled with misapprehension, this structure in flux blocks the detective (and us) from fully assimilating what he or she perceives. As readers, we are equally hampered by the detective's limited range of vision.

This problem has been apprehended differently by others. Sinda Gregory, for instance, understands Hammett's detectives to operate in a world without the presupposition of a preexisting order. The consequences of this presupposition for knowledge are pursued by Gary Day, who investigates the ways that truth values are established and clues are read vis-à-vis the narrative voice/authority of the Op. Day questions the possibility of establishing a frame for meaning in the Op stories, despite the fact that these texts "are concerned with 'knowing,' which

---

[7]   The suspension of the narrative, during which the Op makes comments on detective work, is analogous to the metafictional devices of the Golden Age narrative. Several stories contain such remarks on shadowing ("Zigzags" 102), shooting ("Zigzags" 117), the quality of witnesses ("Tom, Dick, or Harry" 246), and fighting ("Whosis Kid" 210).

is to be established through a pattern of loss and recovery" (41). A sequence of deferred meanings fails to yield certainty, so that "even the criminal is a substitute, a signifier pointing to a signified which becomes another signifier" (41). Again, though these assertions apply to some stories and novels, this "pattern" is not present in all of Hammett's work.

To be sure, no matter how deferred meaning becomes, the event still dominates the development of the narrative, so that a basis of comparison does exist between hard-boiled narratives and the clue-puzzle. Despite the relative social weakness of the detective, the cause-and-effect relations that knit clues into narrative are typically the mastery of the detective's isolation of events and the neutralization of counter-voices, especially those of criminals. In Hammett and Chandler, this structure is certainly undercut in that the criminals speak; detective and criminal inhabit the same world and are sometimes indistinguishable. The detective, far from mastering the gestalt of the case, is reduced to perspective and hapticity, and in several exemplary cases they are only certain of disorientation until the final moments. Paradoxically and perhaps counterintuitively, disorientation can serve as a reference point and a resource which must be conserved for the narrative to be transmitted. The consequence of a shift to first-person narrative, and the suppression or elimination of the perplexed but trustworthy sidekick, is a limiting gesture which tends to favor episodic development and creates obstacles to simultaneity of action.

"Bodies Piled Up," also known as "House Dick"—both titles are suggestive— is a breakthrough text for Hammett, one which structures its problems consciously to achieve a new direction in detective fiction. This impulse develops contemporaneously with the Golden Age; its publication date in December 1923 places this form near the start of Christie's career and before Dorothy Sayers, Margery Allingham, Ellery Queen, John Dickson Carr, or S.S. Van Dine had published a mystery of any kind. Hammett's structural innovation involves the introduction of uncertainties that threaten the transmission of the narrative. The detective's restricted range of vision—sometimes literalized in confusing spaces like those in "Dead Yellow Women"—places his level of knowledge below that of other characters. Although this relation is common to much Golden Age fiction, given the sidekick narrator's weak grasp of the detective's insights, in this case the detective lacks such insight. More radical still, ambiguities arise around the recuperation of any meaning in the metaphorical death of the detective. Such devices are present in "Bodies Piled Up" and in stories like "The House in Turk Street," "The Whosis Kid," "Dead Yellow Women," and "The Big Knockover." Indeed, the *Black Mask* title, "Bodies Piled Up," is suggestive of a new direction—a "violation" of Maugham's demand that a single murder anchor the textual conflict and that any subsequent violence be a direct consequence of that primary act (97). The title also shockingly suggests mass production—corpses as stockpiled inventory which a sluggish economy cannot dispose of.[8] In this vein McCann

---

[8]   Hammett may be making ironic reference to the depression of the previous year, 1922.

notes that "hard-boiled crime fiction seemed driven to produce a surplus of corpses" (77), what Roth terms a "crime surplus" (32). Taking an historical view, the 1920s was a period of growing disemployment in which worker productivity and increasing investment in capital goods demonstrated how the system could work against itself—overproduction of commodities and fewer wage earners generating the income to purchase them. Crime is a productive industry which also has succumbed to capitalist contradiction in which production overruns itself. This surplus, however, is also a function of discourse, a verbal deluge in which violence is presented but not present. Violence, in fact, cannot be present since that would effectively shut down talking about it, or, as Christianson rightly points out, "the toughest talk is really no talk at all"; "violence requires no lengthy verbal prolegomena, its exercise is swift and nonverbal among those who practice it seriously and for genuine reasons" (153).[9]

The second title, "House Dick," used when the story was anthologized, conveys the idea of space, the boundaries implied by a house, though this impression is challenged by its specific usage. The house in this case is not economic in the sense of the *oikos* or a corporate body; rather, it is a hotel, a property. The hotel, unlike the country house or other bounded Golden Age site, epitomizes porosity, especially in that it is typically situated in an urban context and unable to regulate the flows within it (the Op's basically hopeless job). Classes of hotel are frequently mentioned in Hammett's and other authors' works (we are informed, ironically enough, that "the Montgomery is a quiet hotel of the better sort" [Hammett, "House" 42]), but this obstacle is easily circumvented by the duplicitous characters inhabiting Hammett's world. One of the victims, Homer Ansley, present in another's (Vincent Develyn's) hotel room, is not a resident of the hotel, though he "had been seen [in the hotel] in Develyn's company frequently" (Hammett, "House" 44). The Op, reflecting on the timeframe of the killings, opines that "the murderer could have left the room, closing the door behind him, and walked away secure in the knowledge that at noon a man in the corridors of the Montgomery would attract little attention" (Hammett, "House" 45). Thus, we have a generally open site.

From the start we are impressed by a number of impostures, substitutions, and misapprehensions in the story. The Op himself is a temporary substitute, taking over from a hotel detective who was fired for drunkenness—he anticipates, erroneously, little trouble in his stint at "hotel coppering." The investigation begins after three corpses are found tumbled into a wardrobe in one of the rooms—three men whose personal lives and relationship to each other give no clue to why they were murdered. The examination of selected residents' lives and effects reveals some murky antecedents, undermining the initial claims to "quiet" and "better

---

[9]   This point is developed by Richard Hofstadter in his anthology *American Violence*, where he remarks that those "who preach violence know very little about it, and sometimes prove pitifully ineffectual in trying to use it." They are destined, instead, "to become its chief victims ..., especially when their own romanticism carries them from the word to the deed" (Hofstadter and Wallace 30).

sort"—for instance, one of the dead men, Ingraham, is found to possess rigged gambling paraphernalia and later is determined to have been scouting around to open a gambling den. Ingraham, who seems the most promising suspect, nonetheless cannot be linked to the other victims, but the absence of a relation or a motive does not faze the reader, who is accustomed to this indistinct terrain—we are confident that everything will be brought into sharp focus when viewed through the detective's lens. Yet the promise of ratiocinative fireworks is not fulfilled, and after floundering on the question of motive, new tactics are employed: "We now dropped that [motive] angle and settled down to the detail-studying, patience-taxing grind of picking up the murderer's trail. From any crime to its author there is a trail. It may be—as in this case—obscure; but, since matter cannot move without disturbing other matter along its path, there always is—there must be—a trail of some sort" (Hammett, "House" 46).

The break, though, turns out to be a confusing relation rather than definite evidence of criminal activity. A man named Ross Orrett, also using the name B.T. Quinn, appears suspicious, not for any clear connection to the murders (save that he was a resident in the hotel at the time) but because of his search for a known criminal, Guy Cudner. As it happens, Orrett is not guilty of the murders, but his pursuit leads to Cudner in an accidental chain of events spurred by information from an untrustworthy informant. At this point, none of the facts are sufficient to explain the killings, which seem to run parallel to the activities of the characters in a separate universe—we are led to believe, like the detectives, that "Cudner wasn't in on the murders" (Hammett, "House" 49) since we believe him to have no relation to the Montgomery. Later we learn that the killings were "errors" committed by Cudner—for all practical purposes, contingencies arising from the misreading of a room number, the mental substitution of one numeral for another. The reading of the characters' relations, though, is also misconstrued by the Op, who is as confused as we about what motivates the players. Like us, he remains in the dark until the last possible moment, when it is revealed that they are playing against each other instead of working together.

The Op's attempt to bring on the crisis involves another substitution in which he impersonates a criminal (unbeknownst to him, the killer). By inscribing himself with Cudner's telltale scar, the Op hopes that Orrett will "misread" him as Cudner and then reveal evidence linking him unmistakably to the killings. Although the detective's willingness to step into the criminal's role is not unknown to the Classic and Golden Age story,[10] such cases lack the willingness to impersonate that role to the point of actual criminal behavior—which is certainly what transpires in the shootout at the end, as well as in the orgy of violence erupting in tales like "The Big Knockover." The projected endpoint of the Op's logical deductions not only

---

[10]   Sherlock Holmes plays this role in "Charles Augustus Milverton." Poirot does so in "The Veiled Lady." Lord Peter takes on criminal personas in "The Adventurous Exploit of the Cave of Ali Baba" and *Murder Must Advertise*.

departs sharply from the Golden Age but also suggests a *mise en jeu* of narrative itself, in which the integrity of the narrative I is at risk.

The shootout is climactic primarily in the sense of action. In the midst of it, the Op reflects: "Just what there was between them [Cudner and Orrett] and what bearing it had on the Montgomery murders was a mystery to me, but I didn't try to solve it now" (Hammett, "House" 52). And it might well have remained a mystery, except for the somewhat lame episode of the dying Cudner's confession and the inadvisable willingness of Orrett to give information about himself. From a Golden Age perspective Hammett has painted himself into a corner, whereby the knowledge demands as defined by Dove reappear as a limit that usurps the writer's independence—only through a sort of parody or conscious stretching of disbelief is this limit challenged. The key to explaining the hotel murders comes from the most unlikely source—a man described as "the most dangerous bird on the Coast, if not in the country" (Hammett, "House" 48), a man, therefore, very unlikely to apologize for his crimes with words like "sorry" and "mistake" in his melodramatic dying message (Hammett, "House" 53). Later, the Op approaches Orrett, who had tried to kill him a week earlier, on more or less friendly terms in the hospital, again emphasizing the lack of sharp distinctions between the pair. The Op admits that he doesn't know what happened, and Orrett, conscious of his need to be cautious about himself, relates a narrative that constructs a frame around the events, the history of an error. And yet, in doing so, Orrett's story reveals the error of his own actions—since it turns out that Cudner was not in fact his true enemy. His closing remarks to the Op, that upon returning to New York he intends to take care of the man who set him on Cudner, is a "promise" that compels "belief." The backstory, then, far from giving meaning to the events, reveals a history of misapprehension and substitution that leads to four deaths, with the promise of more in the future. The idea of a return to order is mocked in that there was no order—not in the sense that there was disorder—but that there was only chance. The worlds of the criminal and the detective protagonist overlap to the degree that we barely distinguish them—at times they are adversaries, at other times they impersonate each other, at others they are chummy—and to finish off, the hardened criminal not only escapes punishment, but garners some measure of sympathy from the reader and usurps the Golden Age detective's role as mouthpiece for the truth. Of the 31 Op and Spade stories, only a handful approximate this degree of framing uncertainty, though many are intermediary and most have some affinity with this structure. Even when Hammett seems most emulative of Classical or Golden Age conventions, we may well be suspicious.

The murders in "Bodies Piled Up," as well as the massacre in the culminating scenes of "The House on Turk Street," to which I return in the Conclusion, arise from misreading and misapprehension. In other stories, the role of chance is foregrounded. The Op's surveillance of the Whosis Kid in the story of the same title is prompted by the offhand remark of a colleague eight years earlier and a handful of statistics:

> So far as I knew, the Whosis Kid wasn't wanted anywhere—not by the Continental, anyway—and if he had been a pickpocket, or a con man, or a member of any of the criminal trades in which we are only occasionally interested, I would have let him alone. But stick-ups are always in demand. The Continental's most important clients are insurance companies of one sort or another, and robbery policies make up a good percentage of the insurance business these days. (Hammett, "Whosis Kid" 183)

The identification is correct, but the impetus is still hazy, especially given a nine-hour stakeout in a car watching an apartment entryway. Even after some time on the job, during which he witnesses the attempted murder of the Kid, the Op doesn't do much but watch, and we are still no closer to what it all means: "Between bites [of dinner] I turned the day's events over in my mind. I didn't think hard enough to spoil my appetite. There wasn't that much to think about" (Hammett, "Whosis Kid" 192). His matter-of-fact remark is followed by half a page of unanswerable questions. When violence again erupts, the Op, like the reader, remains a detached bystander: "This party had the shape of a war between gunmen. It would be a private one as far as I was concerned. My hope was that by hovering on the fringes until somebody won, I could pick up a little profit for the Continental, in the form of a wanted crook or two among the survivors" (Hammett, "Whosis Kid" 194).

The jumble escalates as others join the fray, and we realize that we have read 15 pages without much notion of what is going on—no relations have been established that point to the shadow of a solution: "So far, so good. I had started with the Whosis Kid, dropped him to take Maurois, and now let him go to see who this woman was. I didn't know what this confusion was all about, but I seemed to be learning *who* it was all about" (Hammett, "Whosis Kid" 196). The string of substitutions moves to a woman's apartment which "looked like the scene of the next action" (Hammett, "Whosis Kid" 204–5), but what that might be is deferred, even after the woman's erstwhile bodyguard, Billie, arrives and engages in a comic brawl with the Op. One by one, all the players (Ines Almad, Billie, Maurois, Big Chin, and the Whosis Kid) assemble in this space—basically, what the Op is hoping for since, he reflects, "if everybody got together here, maybe whatever was going on would come out where I could see it and understand it" (Hammett, "Whosis Kid" 216). At the moment when relations are clarified, disorientation literally returns as the lights are extinguished, prompting a chaotic shootout: "My head filled up with funny notions. There wasn't any room. There wasn't any darkness. There wasn't anything ...," the Op thinks as he slips into unconsciousness (Hammett, "Whosis Kid" 235). As in "Bodies Piled Up," this climactic moment could be read as the Op's death—though of course he is resurrected (unlike, curiously, the Kid, "arms spread in a crucified position" [Hammett, "Whosis Kid" 236]); he returns to life and satisfactorily provides the missing exposition in the last two pages of a tale of nearly 60.

The ambiguous, even surreal qualities of space where "something was going to happen" (Hammett, "Whosis Kid" 218) is bizarrely revisited in "Dead Yellow Women" (1925), published later in the same year as "The Whosis Kid." As it does in "Bodies Piled Up" and "The Whosis Kid," violence erupts spontaneously and remains unexplained until considerably later in the text. Although some fuller attempt at a framing exposition is provided in the Op's preliminary description of two murders and an assault, the wealthy client, Lillian Shan, is not especially cooperative. The link between the tales lies in the disconcerting representation of space, which becomes a metaphor for the Op's inability to establish a comprehensive vision of the investigation. Whereas Ines Almad's overcrowded apartment contains the players but offers no coherent reference point for determining their relations, Chang's house in "Dead Yellow Women" involves bizarre spatial dislocation—the byzantine plot is spatialized as the Op meanders up, down, and around, meeting characters out of a hard-boiled Lewis Carroll—the weird little Chinese "doll," Chang's wizened lieutenant, the gang members, and Dummy Uhl, the junkie—all preparatory to the bodyguards and the audience with the chief crook, who is also, in this instance, an ally. He is an ally if for no other reason that the client, Lillian Shan, turns out herself to be allied with this man.

Architecture becomes the principal metaphor by which points of reference are denied to the Op and, by extension, to us. In his first visit to Chang's residence, he is led through an endless sequence of halls and rooms:

> This running upstairs and downstairs, turning to the right and turning to the left, seemed harmless enough. If he got any fun out of confusing me, he was welcome. I was confused enough now, so far as the directions were concerned. I hadn't the least idea where I might be. But that didn't disturb me so much. If I was going to be cut down, a knowledge of my geographical position wouldn't make it any more pleasant. If I was going to come out all right, one place was still as good as another. (Hammett, "Dead Yellow Women" 207)[11]

This weird spatial dislocation is again evident during the stakeout in the dark Shan house. Because he cannot risk tipping off the intruders, the Op sits in the dark in a state of sensory deprivation, which eventually is interrupted by a chaotic barrage of men (which we later learn to be the landing of illegal Chinese immigrants). When vision is shut down, knowledge necessarily becomes dependent upon other senses—olfactory, aural, and haptic—none of which compensates for the lost ordering power of sight, and all of which make the Op seem more vulnerable. Instead of taking a position anterior to the action, a coign of vantage from which discrete elements in the visual field are weighed, given significance, and molded into a coherent narrative, the narrative itself engulfs the detective, who becomes indistinguishable from its components: "I was one of a struggling, tearing, grunting and groaning mob of invisibles. An eddy of them swept me toward the kitchen. Hitting, kicking, butting, I went along" (Hammett, "Dead Yellow Women" 217–18). The Golden Age detective is an autonomous individual; the Op literally hopes to evade such a distinction; he dismisses the idea of using his gun, since anything

---

[11]   These descriptions resemble the equally confused space during the climactic scenes at the cult house in "The Scorched Face" (Hammett 101–5).

that would lift him out of the chaotic jumble would also give the crowd "something tangible to tear apart" (Hammett, "Dead Yellow Women" 218).

Hammett's contribution has an epistemologically destabilizing dimension entailing the shutdown of conduits of knowledge characteristic of the Classical and Golden Age narrative. No doubt, deconstructive readings of Golden Age texts would identify gaps and fissures in which knowledge is undercut, but Hammett foregrounds these fissures in ways that is only approached in the Golden Age through self-referential parody. Hammett is able to expand this model in two novels with great effectiveness, namely *Red Harvest* (1928) and *The Dain Curse* (1929). Similar to Carr's *The Problem of the Green Capsule* and the parody *Ask a Policeman*, Hammett's texts also tend to dramatize the very problems that they foreground. We will examine how this functions later in this chapter after a look at Chandler's *The Big Sleep*, a novel that emulates in its narrative structure the spatial dislocations characteristic of some of Hammett's oeuvre.

"Fate stage-managed the whole thing." (Chandler, *Big Sleep* 727)

In a chapter on Chandler, Sean McCann discusses the widespread belief in the 1930s that economic development had reached its natural limits. This belief is discernible in Franklin Roosevelt's policies and recovery plan, the New Deal notion of "economic maturity" (McCann 165); however, this limit did not simply signify the definitive closing of the frontier: it was a limit intrinsic to capitalism itself. In the early 1930s, this position was given statistical teeth by radicals like Lewis Corey, who predicted in *The Decline of American Capitalism* (1934) that the "automatic principle" would come to dominate labor, reducing the worker who retained employment to a "technician who repairs, controls, and directs" (266). Indeed, the paradox of increasing productivity and decreasing purchasing power through disemployment restricted already saturated markets. In Chandler's vision of this social trend, General Sternwood's declining health serves as a metaphor. His wizened body signifies the exhausted resources of the extractive industries that enabled him to achieve his social position. At the other end of the social spectrum, the crooks populating the pages of the novel illustrate this principle by attacking and feeding on each other as they compete for "an inherently limited stock of money" (McCann 167).

This critical vision of Chandler's writing, positioned above and outside, is conditioned by our historical perspective on the era. To complement this reading, we must enter the confusion on the ground. From the restricted perspective of the novel's moving I, we are forced into haptic relations. This collapse of omniscience bolsters the charge of "poor" plotting evident in Chandler's own self-criticism, for instance in a letter from 1951: "I have never plotted anything on paper. I do my plotting in my head as I go along and have to do it all over again. ... With me plots are not made, they grow" (Gardiner and Walker 92). His organic notion of plot rejects conventional finished forms of omniscient storytelling and significantly restricts our range of vision, and thereby of knowledge. Chandler radicalizes this idea, in the sense of taking it to its end, by embracing such uncertainty in practice, not just as an author creating the appearance of uncertainty. Structural disunity also arises from Chandler's practice of suturing together previously independent stories, producing in *The Big Sleep* a "double-humped" narrative in which the investigation continues long after the initial inquiry is finished. This structure is itself fragmented and episodic—though short, the novel is divided into 32 sections. Chandler's undermining of a teleological principle in his fiction is innovative in its "violation" of the certainties we expect from the genre. We move with Marlowe, the text's dynamic keystone, whose perspective constantly reconstitutes meaning without, however, possessing authoritative omniscience. Marlowe lacks the capacity to frame a static, homogeneous space as a totality. This kind of (discursive) knowing is precluded in *The Big Sleep* because no single corpse can serve as a point around which the detective can construct stable boundaries. The exceptional is not so easily contained, nor does the detective possess the authority to enforce his reading on others.

Frederic Jameson recognizes this structural peculiarity in his essay "On Raymond Chandler." In contrast to Golden Age homicide, murder in the hard-boiled story is an excuse to start a flow of language which doesn't guarantee meaning. On the one hand, the detective's function as guarantor through the rights of authoritative explanation is seriously compromised; on the other, no single body has the capacity to organize the community of hard-boiled fiction: "Chandler's demystification involves the removal of purpose from the murder event. The classical detective story always invests murder with purpose by its very formal perspective. The murder is ... a kind of abstract point which is made to bear meaning and significance by the convergence of all lines upon it" (Jameson, "Raymond Chandler" 146). Murder upon murder in *The Big Sleep*, and by more than one killer, confirms that no single body forms a privileged point in time or space. The exception cannot remain exceptional when it is sequentialized, but neither can Marlowe convert this dynamic trajectory into a meaningful, discursively framed crime that encloses the others. In Jameson's words, "the empty, decorative event of the murder serves as a way of organizing essentially plotless material into an illusion of movement" ("Raymond Chandler" 124). That illusion is premised upon the promise of closure which, at least in *The Big Sleep*, is at best fragmentary due to the transformation of and limitations on the narrator.

The novel commences with the blackmail of General Sternwood, Marlowe's dying millionaire client; the problem apparently stems from his psychotic younger daughter, Carmen, who has amassed gambling debts and whose propensity to be blackmailed is high in light of her deviant behavior. Marlowe is called in to settle the business, which leads him to uncover Carmen's involvement with a pornographer, Arthur Geiger, a man subsequently murdered by Carmen's jealous ex-boyfriend during a nude photo shoot at Geiger's house. The pictures disappear, ending up in the hands of Joe Brody, a former lover of Carmen's who has also blackmailed her father. Brody muscles in on Geiger's book trade, only to be murdered himself by Geiger's gay lover, who believes Brody is guilty of the first killing. In the meantime, Geiger's actual killer has ended up dead in a car "accident," the exact circumstances of which remain mysterious. These events comprise the first half of the novel; in the next sequence, several characters who appeared in the first half come to the fore. Although the preliminary business is concluded to General Sternwood's satisfaction, closure is elusive—Carmen's criminal behavior is not punished, murders are not publicly brought home to the right people (the perpetrators being conveniently dead), and the cover-up of the porn ring (run with police knowledge) protects the guilty.

Now the focus shifts to Rusty Regan, errant husband of the General's older daughter, Vivian, and to Vivian's association with big-shot gambler Eddie Mars. The General is worried about the likable Rusty's abrupt disappearance; the rumor is that Rusty has eloped with Eddie's wife, though the police missing person bureau cannot or will not confirm this charge. Again, the complicity of the police and other official organs, like the D.A., with criminals and their special treatment of the rich is obvious. After dodging dangers set up by Mars, Marlowe locates Mrs. Mars, determines that she did not run away with Rusty, and further, gives some compelling evidence that Carmen shot Rusty after he rebuffed her erotic advances. Vivian, desperate to protect her sister, had enlisted the aid of Mars and his gunman, Canino, to dispose of the body, giving Mars a powerful reason to blackmail Vivian. None of these criminals pay for their crimes, with the exception, perhaps, of the killer Canino, who is shot to death by Marlowe. Mars is undeterred; Carmen is institutionalized; Vivian still has the specter of blackmail hanging over her; and, presumably, the General dies soon thereafter.

This quick overview does not do credit to the novel's complexity, especially in the richness of its manipulation of economic frames of reference and "legitimacy" in terms of both class and profession. Conflicting economic systems are thematized in the clash between Marlowe's feudal daydreams, the pressures of capitalist reality, and the threats posed by both the bureaucratic institutions administering justice and the sinister representatives of the shadow economy. Marlowe is doubtless aware that his chivalrous fantasy is misplaced from the start—not only in the ironic foreshadowing of the stained glass window in the Sternwood home that culminates, chapters later, in his throwing the deranged Carmen out of his apartment, but also in the indeterminacy of the cavalry pennants on the wall of the entry hall, his uncertainty as to whether they are "bullet-torn or moth-eaten" (Chandler, *Big Sleep* 590).

I will confine my remarks here, however, to the problem of transmission, since, like Hammett's "Bodies Piled Up" and "The Whosis Kid," the novel enters the locus of death itself—the death of the narrator, who, in fact, is able to convey this moment of death. The relation to death is complicated by its reduction to work—it would be hard to find a more Bataillian paradox. Near the end of the novel, Marlowe has been captured by Canino and restrained in the house where Mona Mars has been in hiding. Mona, knowing that Marlowe will be killed by the ruthless Canino, helps Marlowe escape his bonds (but not his handcuffs, since Canino possesses the key) and conspires to give him a chance against the gunman. Marlowe's plan involves feigning death to put Canino off his guard:

Flame spouted from [Canino's gun] abruptly, the blended roar of three swift shots. Glass starred in the coupe. I yelled with agony. The yell went off into a wailing groan. The groan became a wet gurgle, choked with blood. I let the gurgle die sickeningly, on a choked gasp. It was nice work. I liked it. Canino liked it very much. I heard him laugh. It was a large booming laugh, not at all like the purr of his speaking voice. (Chandler, *Big Sleep* 741)[12]

The word *work*, used to describe the detective's death, is striking—he dies using the language of a job description; his labor brings us up against that limit. The scene is merely play acting, though; it establishes a conventional fictional limit which entails no gambling with the ego and sufficient narrative distance for the stage props and lighting effects to be completely within the reader's view. The penultimate chapter gives us something different.

Near the end of the text, we are granted insight into Rusty's disappearance. Our immediate attention, however, is occupied by the detective's first-person death. As the detective prepares to cross that boundary, he engages in (Bataillian) laughter:

I laughed at her [Carmen]. I started to walk towards her. I saw her small finger tighten on the trigger and grow white at the tip. I was about six feet away from her when she started to shoot.

The sound of the gun made a sharp slap, without body, a brittle crack in the sunlight. I didn't see any smoke. I stopped again and grinned at her.

She fired twice more, very quickly. I don't think any of the shots would have missed. There were five in the little gun. She had fired four. I rushed her.

I didn't want the last one in my face, so I swerved to one side. She gave it to me quite carefully, not worried at all. I think I felt the hot breath of the powder blast a little. (Chandler, *Big Sleep* 755)

At first, this remarkable passage is confusing. Caught up in the action, we must get our heads around being shot point blank. As a fitting climax to the novel, Chandler takes Hammett's evocation of death from the short stories a little further, in that the terse sentences do not overwhelm us with descriptive effects; rather, we get concise, matter-of-fact statements. The *crochet*, which is brought into vision by Marlowe's ruse, does not suspend us at the limit for long, and ultimately, given Carmen's inability to sway the detective, Marlowe retains his composure and identity. Structurally, this gesture is appropriately situated at the end. A more sustained and complex approach to the limit is achieved in Hammett's *Red Harvest* and *The Dain Curse*, with which we conclude this chapter. Hammett's detective oscillates between economic modes in which this core of identity is threatened

---

[12]   Marlowe laughs (inappropriately) in Brody's apartment when Carmen is about to shoot Joe (Chandler, *Big Sleep* 654) and after Canino's death (Chandler, *Big Sleep* 742).

with dissolution far more serious than the situation in *The Big Sleep* or Hammett's shorter fiction.

"I've framed my millions and nothing's happened to me." (Hammett, *Red* 116)

Red Harvest is Hammett's most complex engagement with frames of reference, perspectivism, and determinations of value. Even on the level of genre, as Carl Freedman and Christopher Kendrick note, the novel refuses to be bracketed: there is the unwritten but implied proletarian novel of the failed strike, whose protagonist is labor leader Bill Quint, and whose action has ended in failure before the Op appears on the scene; there is the more or less ratiocinative closed-site mystery concerning Donald Willsson's murder; finally, there is the gangster novel which comprises most of the book (Freedman and Kendrick 26). The action opens in Personville, a mining town of 40,000 in the American West. The Continental Detective Agency has been brought in by newspaperman Donald Willsson, son of the city's mining magnate Elihu Willsson, possibly in connection with Donald's anticorruption campaign—ironically, corruption that implicates his father as well as the crooks he had some years earlier brought to Personville to deal with striking mineworkers. Donald is murdered hours after the Op arrives, though speculation that he had been killed in retaliation for his campaign and possibly with the complicity of his own father turns out to be misguided—he is shot by a jealous ex-lover of Dinah Brand, a woman Donald was visiting to secure information about political corruption.

The Op makes a short job of finding the killer, but in the meantime he encounters characters who both complicate his efforts and threaten his safety. In response, he takes a commission from Elihu Willsson to clean up Personville. On the one hand, his task is to neutralize the forces which have wrested power from and now threaten Elihu; on the other, the Op is out to wreak personal vengeance, whose outcome is to stimulate escalating cycles of violence. Christopher Bentley, using the description of Personville's situation between two ugly mountains in an "ugly notch" and its generally polluted appearance, equates the town with America's "arsehole" (62). In Bataillian terms, the anus is an appropriate emblem of the abject antiproduction that characterizes the place, expenditure which cannot be assimilated under the aegis of productive relations and which exceeds the boundaries of the economy even though it is a product of that economy. Also appropriate is the antigovernment in place, a collection of hoods who run illicit monopolies in a demented parody of "legitimate" capitalist practices. The gangster novel, which follows the solving of Donald Willsson's murder, takes up most of the book. Its development entails the Op's efforts to widen breaches within an already shaky structure governed by the major players: gamblers, bootleggers, racketeers, and a corrupt police force. These men are set against each other by the Op's clever manipulations so that mutual destruction ensues.

One engaging feature of the novel is its tendency to offer unstable ideological frames. Much detective fiction tacitly posits a narrative frame in which a shift of perspective rearranges the elements in the investigative field, revalues or devalues their relative significance, reestablishes relations of cause and effect, and unmasks duplicitous characters. However, the ideological premise grounding the narrative's validity usually remains unquestioned. Bill Quint's labor history of the region (Hammett, *Red* 10–11) brings the fragility of these ideological assumptions into focus in the first pages of *Red Harvest*. His exposition orders events, places them within an objective frame of causality, heavily influences our sympathies—and yet, recounted by the Op, these events are openly acknowledged to be *a* story, one which no doubt will be told by others in different ways. To illustrate, Quint explains Donald Willsson's murder as city politics by other means, a mere addendum to his tale of violence. The journalistic establishment, headed by Donald, offers its own version: the editor implies complicity between the police and the killers—both Quint and the editor turn out to be wrong. Chief of Police Noonan has his own story, which implicates Dinah Brand (Hammett, *Red* 22); he is closer to the truth, but he is still motivated by his own interest in heading off his opponent, Max Thaler. A contest arises over the very facts of the case, whose outward appearance seems solid enough. The ways the lines of cause and effect, crime and culpability are drawn generate narratives.

When Dennis Porter writes that detective fiction "is a genre committed to an act of recovery," he refers to the forging of causal chains organized around points of uncontested meaning (*Pursuit* 29–30). Contestation does not extend to the ground of meaning itself, only to the characters granted voice. The Op's violent escapades in *Red Harvest* are, paradoxically, communicated to us in ways that diverge from his discursive reductions (reports) manufactured for the benefit of the Agency (personified by the Old Man), reports which we don't read. As McCann perceptively writes, the dynamics of violence are arrested by "submitting to the labor of writing" (110). This reduction is required by the Old Man, whose telegram demands an explanation of the Op's activities in Personville—a discursive interruption which fixes and interprets the flux of events (Hammett, *Red* 125). The deferral of the reports, which the Op's worried assistants remind him need to be posted (Hammett, *Red* 102–3), points towards a Bataillian dilemma. The disruption of homogeneous productive relations, whose discursive aspect has already been discussed, does not yield a synthesis. Rather, as Scott Shershow remarks, "the [Bataillian] restricted and general economies … exist only in the form of an absolutely irreducible ontological relation" (108). The Op must find some way to mediate his interaction within two incommensurable economic modes of being. The threat of the Op's disappearance into a sovereign forgetting of self in his cooptation by the violent world of Personville is his participation in a radical expenditure characterized by death, drugs, and the war of all against all. These states contrast with his "decline" from the summit, his problematic reintegration into communicable modes of bourgeois "normalcy." Such modes include the reestablishment of "order" by which the State exercises its monopoly on violence and the isolation and explanation of events. The novel ends on a grimly amusing note, that this labor is so much busy work which smoothes over an antilabor out of synch with the conventions of the opening project. A further irony: the nature of this project is never communicated to him or to us, since Willsson dies before he meets the Op. And yet the Op's text—not his report—arrives, and its narrative presents his labor as a product in the text we consume. Should we characterize this outcome as a form of Cartesian anchoring by which "the self-hood of the detective becomes a sign which is essential, secure, stable, the last grounded sign, the sole entity present to itself" (Malmgren, *Anatomy* 104)? Or are we confronted with Derrida's characterization of sublation as an *"economy of sacrifice* that keeps what it gives up" (*Gift* 8)?

The Op's willingness to put himself in harm's way—into circulation, as it were—is a wager often enough premised on bluff and the value of the narratives he can mint to keep the economy of violence moving in an inflationary spiral. His life is the ante which other players see. The Op's mobility, again his fluid convertability at most of the major established points (Willsson, Thaler, Reno, Noonan, Pete the Finn, and possibly Dinah Brand), demonstrates his value relative to all stakes, his true exteriority to none of them. The parody of a parley at the so-called Peace Conference, at least one of whose members is present by virtue of a murder committed earlier that day, is destined to break down due to the nature of the "gangster power structure" which "makes for a permanent state of anarchic emergency" (Freedman and Kendrick 14), one which, unlike the oligarchic calculation of interests beyond individual moments of loss, can never displace the chaotic competition of (literally) cutthroat tactics. Amusingly, the conference reaches a climax as Pete the Finn, the town's top bootlegger, addresses the general assembly of criminals: "You've got no brains to know what is best for yourselves. So I'll tell you. This busting the town open is no good for business. You be nice boys or I'll make you" (Hammett, *Red* 131). Monopoly capitalism enforced at the end of a gun. The failure of parliamentarian politics feared by political theorists of the 1920s is parodied in that the political exception (Carl Schmitt's *Ausnahmezustand*) cannot be contained. No sovereign intervenes to reinstate homogeneous relations or, in this case, ironically enough, stable heterogeneous ones. Thus, unsurprisingly, all the players, with the exception of Elihu Willsson and the Op, have been rubbed out by each other at the end of the day. As Freedman and Kendrick correctly ascertain, this survival on Elihu's part is the acquiescence of the State to acceptable forms of exploitation, which ultimately we are asked to read as preferable to the "anarchic and Hobbesian" state of affairs governing hitherto (24).

What comes to the fore is the way that narratives and meanings are fluid or sliding, so that the fixity of meaning is denied, especially as it emerges within the flux of events. The stories told by Bill Quint, the newspapers, and Dinah Brand in her transparently self-serving attempts to press her advantage are examples. To this we add the Peace Conference, the Op's unsuccessful attempt to give a story to Helen Albury, sister of the bank teller who shot Donald, and his vision of Personville's future for Elihu at their last meeting. Finally, there is the story that the Op gets from the dying Reno about Dinah Brand's death, which the Op believes he may have committed in a laudanum-induced stupor. To be sure, the Op, like most detective-centers, is barred from absolute ignorance by genre conventions. A detective completely lacking in knowledge belongs in comedy (for instance, in Norbert Davis's *Sally's in the Alley*), and in fact this overturning of the convention is used as comic relief in *Red Harvest* in relation to Mickey Linehan, an operative called in to assist. Upon arrival he declares: "I don't want to brag about how dumb I am, but this job is plain as astronomy to me. I understand everything about it except what you have done and why, and what you're trying to do and how" (Hammett, *Red* 103). Fifty pages later, we get: "Don't tell me anything that's going on—I'm only working with you" (Hammett, *Red* 151). Near the end of the novel, when a warrant is out for the Op's arrest, Mickey is apprehended to supply information about his whereabouts; he later reports to the Op: "I didn't know anything, couldn't guess anything, didn't have any idea of what you were working on, just happened to hit town and meet you" (Hammett, *Red* 178). We could argue that the Op is not much better off, indicated by the much-cited passage about "stirring things up"—which Dinah Brand scoffs at as amateurish (Hammett, *Red* 75). But the fact of his survival is precisely that which displaces the knowledge conveyed by words, and it is this irreducibility that creates a major internal division in the Op's consciousness concerning whether he murdered Dinah. Reno's convenient and contrived confession to Dinah's killing, and his implausible description of subsequent events, influences our assessment of this complex novel—the first impulse might be that Hammett would have been better off omitting it altogether, not just because of its artificiality (of which the entire work could be accused), but because it seems to conventionalize the novel within a set of expectations; not just the blamelessness of the investigator, but the need to know. Perhaps it is the contrivance of the dying man's confession which illustrates the fleeting nature of all knowledge; death absolutizes enunciations that the promise of life might twist to fit grounded interests. In this light, the novel's closing remarks—"I spent most of my week in Ogden trying to fix up my reports so they would not read as if I had broken as many Agency rules, state laws and human bones as I had" (Hammett, *Red* 186)—resonates as yet another in a chain of competing narratives, one which does not fool the critical reader (the Old Man in this case). One of the great achievements of *Red Harvest* is to bend the exterior and interior relations that are so well marked in Golden Age fiction into the form of a Möbius strip.

"'Fairly plausible,' I conceded, 'but it doesn't hang together right.'" (Hammett, *Dain* 241)

The Dain Curse, Hammett's most tortuous work, has three parts; each offers a promise of closure. The novel is well suited to summing up the concerns of this chapter in its peculiar approach to a narrative that threatens to exceed all attempts at framing. The text is only brought to heel through violence against a narrative-creating competitor to the detective's voice. This "solution" to shutting down or privileging narrative transmission resides in a complex doubling gesture in which in-story authorship is split between complementary characters—the detective (the Op) and a novelist (Owen Fitzstephan). In the first part the Op is called in to investigate the theft of several diamonds which scientist Edgar Leggett is experimenting upon. The inquiry opens the door to a byzantine plot that eventually brings to light Leggett's sordid past. Leggett, an alias for Maurice de Mayenne, had been condemned to penal servitude for a crime committed years earlier in France. His wife, Alice, is the sister of the victim, Mayenne's first wife, who was murdered under mysterious circumstances. Crooked private detectives follow up Mayenne's trail. Both are killed in the process, drawing attention to inconsistencies in Mayenne's story that threaten exposure. Sorting out these facts is made difficult by the unreliability of our sources—before his apparent suicide, Leggett/Mayenne writes to the police, explaining his background and the roles played by Alice and his daughter Gabrielle. The story, which the Op reads simply as a letter, is pressed into service as a suicide note by Alice, who hopes to mask her own criminal involvement. The Op's impromptu speech in the "suicide" room before the assembled characters, a parody of the Golden Age denouement, demolishes the letter's credibility as exonerating Mayenne's wife; instead, the Op shifts the blame for his and her sister's murder onto Alice. She promptly confesses but is killed in an escape bid before further facts can be extracted. During this part of the investigation the Op renews a friendship with Fitzstephan, who takes a keen interest in the proceedings, partly because of his acquaintanceship with the Leggetts. The section ends with the musings of the Op and Fitzstephan over what "really" happened; the case appears to be closed.

In the second part the Op is recalled to watch over Gabrielle by her lawyer, Madison Andrews, who is concerned about her connections with a religious cult called the Temple. The Temple is operated by Joseph and Aaronia Haldorn, and despite suspicions of charlatanism, seems to have a calming effect on the distraught Gabrielle. The Op's protection job is complicated by his need simultaneously to manage Andrews, Gabrielle's annoying boyfriend, Eric Collinson, her physician, Dr. Riese, and her overprotective maid, Minnie Hershey. Although the Temple turns out to be a financial scam, the real threat to Gabrielle takes the form of Joseph Haldorn, a crazed egomaniac who believes he should have exclusive possession of her. Gabrielle's own state of mind does not help matters, given that she spends most of her time on a morphine jag. The Op is drugged and subjected to a "ghost" show concocted for residents by effects specialist Tom Fink, but he successfully rescues Gabrielle from the insane Joseph. By the end of the second section, a couple more murders have been tallied up, and Gabrielle appears to be free of any direct threat (the curse of the title). Echoing the close of the first section, the Op dines with Fitzstephan to ponder these confusing events, but expresses dismay at finding an explanation: "I hope you're not trying to keep this nonsense straight in your mind. You know damned well all this didn't happen" (Hammett, *Dain* 284).

The case is reopened in the third section, this time at the instigation of Eric Collinson. Over the objections of Andrews, Collinson had taken advantage of Gabrielle's confusion to marry her. Contacting the agency from Quesada, the newlyweds' honeymoon retreat, Collinson demands that the Op hurry out to investigate an unspecified threat. Soon after arriving, the Op discovers Collinson's corpse; Gabrielle has disappeared. Hampered in his investigative efforts by bickering local law enforcement and the posturing of government officials, the Op finally discovers Gabrielle's whereabouts. Her kidnapping is explained, but something (the curse?) lurks behind the bare facts to block satisfying closure—the Op senses a mind directing these bizarre events despite the skepticism of Andrews (Hammett, *Dain* 306) and Fitzstephan (Hammett, *Dain* 331). His suspicions seem to be confirmed when an attempt is made on the detective's life with a hand grenade; although the Op emerges relatively unhurt, Fitzstephan, who had come out to the small town with information for the officials, is nearly killed. Near the end of the novel the Op visits the wreckage of Fitzstephan in the hospital, where he reveals the writer's central role in an impressive string of murders. Fitzstephan, spurned by Gabrielle and unwilling to cede her to another man, had engineered the complex sequence of events. The grenade had been an attack on Fitzstephan by Fink, who believed his recklessness was endangering everyone involved.

This bare summary indicates the novel's labyrinthine and essentially Gothic qualities; the Op's allusion to Tad's Blind Man ("a blind man in a dark room hunting for a black hat that wasn't there" [Hammett, *Dain* 256]) to describe the confusion of his investigation sometimes applies to our own position as reader. New characters and angles are constantly feeding into the text so that the "solution" amounts to a shutting down of narrative, as the Op forces Fitzstephan to doubt the foundations of his own story-generating capacity. But the I-narrator of the detective novel, in fact, is doing the same thing in that his real work is the creation of the work we read. Nonetheless, the novel operates within the structure described in Chandler—restrictions that reduce the detective to a haptic relation to his object of inquiry. The novel may be differentiated from Chandler in its self-recognition of this problem, particularly in the doubling of the Op and Fitzstephan. The Op's eventual claims to mastery—his exposure of the vanquished Other who had for most of the novel occupied this hidden but privileged position—is undercut by a lack of conviction, in both senses of the word.

The double function of the Op and Fitzstephan is recognized by several critics. The interconnection of the characters usually refers to their capacity to generate narratives, though this commonality brings them into conflict. Both men are intent on "locking away" or "fixing" the object of their interests; however, the Op declares, "I do mine with the object of putting people in jail," whereas Fitzstephan rejoins, "I do mine with the object of putting people in books" (Hammett, *Dain* 210). Although both men are storytellers, they operate in different modes. Fitzstephan's speculative approach holds little interest or value for the Op—it lacks a fact-based, cause-and-effect structure, in short a necessary materiality. The Op desires a text without lacunae, and yet his failure to offer a coherent narrative structure is obvious at the end of the first section. The Op's attempt to define events and to reduce them to a series of connected, logical, and factual sequences is contested by Fitzstephan, who complains: "It's fellows like you that take all the color out of life. … Doesn't Gabrielle's being made the tool of her mother's murder convince you of the necessity—at least the poetic necessity—of the curse?" (Hammett, *Dain* 247). "Taking the color out of life" ironically means to arrest the creative impulses of his interlocutor, or, if this is a psychological aspect of himself, to resist these in favor of a rational, interlocking explanatory structure. This tension points towards the unique way in which Hammett contrives to represent the death of the author.

As remarked, the death of the first-person narrator threatens transmission. The doubling of the Op and Fitzstephan—their complementarity, which also draws in Hammett as split personality (former operative, now storyteller)—is a means to survive the destruction of the self. The detective remains, now as a storyteller, and one who is master of the field since Fitzstephan is put out of commission; the contest is resolved in that victory belongs to the one who commits the text to paper. Subjected for much of the novel to Fitzstephan's behind-the-scenes machinations, the Op turns the narratological tables by excluding Fitzstephan's voice on the grounds of insanity; in McCann's apt phrase, he thereby "renarrates Fitzstephan's fable … so that Fitzstephan becomes, as Gabrielle previously was, not the author, but merely the vessel of his own tales of degeneracy" (116). In another irony, Gabrielle is successfully controlled by the Op where Fitzstephan's efforts end in failure.[13]

Gatenby argues that *The Dain Curse* entails "a battle of competing 'truths'" (between the Op and Fitzstephan) which highlights "the 'hocus pocus' of the modernist belief in interpretation" (57). I would argue that hocus pocus is a prominent trait in much detective fiction—so much so that the Great Merlini, Diamondstone, and the Green Lama are accomplished magicians as well as detectives.[14] The sleight of hand is a given; the real question concerns how misdirection works to support interests. The curious ability of the detective to inspire this confidence in the Golden Age is the issue at stake, since the detective is central to establishing the truth-limits of the investigation (the detective as "the legitimator of knowledge" whose transcendental status is "a guarantor of legitimacy" [Gatenby 56]). Gatenby's criticisms of Gregory should be taken in light of what the detective does ideologically; if, as he claims, she reads the detective as "an embodiment of the modernist belief in an a priori subject" (Gatenby 58), the focus should be on the word *belief*. Unsurprisingly, Gatenby finds in Hammett "a loss of faith" (56) in respect to the efficacy of detective fiction to bring problems to a close. *The Dain Curse* in particular threatens the dissolution of the genre

---

[13]   Robert Parker's claim that the Op represents Gabrielle's "salvation" (36) is more accurately described by McCann, who understands the Op to "[manipulate] Gabrielle Leggett into domestic happiness" (138).

[14]   Will Murray, in his introduction to the Diamondstone collection, remarks on the interest in magicians in the pulps, listing a number of sources (n. pag.).

premised on the established reference point of the detective ego—Hammett posits the primacy of the crime and not the detective, so that the Op's subject position is generated "by the crime he 'reads'" (Gatenby 58), and a transcendental guarantor simply does not compel belief.

Ironically, Fitzstephan, the non-worker (not value-producing, since no one buys his books) is a constant source of work (narrative raw material) for the Op. But the Op's aggressive closure also plays into Fitzstephan's critique. He takes the ironic posture—which we see more clearly in a second reading—by suggesting that detectives pronounce their quarries insane when they reach a certain level of criminal excess. This "solution" is a means of dealing with their own lack of imagination (Hammett, *Dain* 330). The dissatisfaction of the insane criminal is, superficially, the undermining of individual responsibility closely aligned with Golden Age ideology. Incapacitating Fitzstephan, which in part leads to a solution, also disables that element of the Op's character which is threatening to take the narrative to ever greater lengths and into cycles of expenditure that annihilate everyone. The pineapple is as good as a death, and the double economy is disabled so that narrative closure can be achieved. The spiral of development characterizing Derrida's reading of Hegel is thus set within boundaries.

Chapter 4
Clue, Value, and Counterfeit

Determining the Clue

Like gold deposited in the vault, the detective sometimes functions as security to demarcate a textual field of exchange, simultaneously acting as a medium by which the value of disparate elements in that textual field is established. These elements may take the form of clues, which are declared to measure up or lack intrinsic worth through the detective's authoritative role as general equivalent. To be sure, this gold standard, understood in its contemporary sense of an acknowledged universal measure, is not solely the province of the detective, since in many hard-boiled stories powerful institutions forcibly impose their own standards; competing modes of valuation can threaten the detective, who faces consequences for acting against these interests. In these cases, the detective's ability to guarantee a correspondence between language and reality collapses, giving rise to a floating mode of valuation. In its historical dimension, the thematization of this shift from the Golden Age to the hard-boiled is not entirely unrelated to the complete or partial abandonment of gold in several western countries, including the United States.[1] As we will see, particularly through Goux's work on the literature of the period, such instability parallels a shift in the detective's economic role, demonstrable in the isolation of clues and their value as evidence.

The clue should not be conflated with the event itself, of which it only constitutes a trace. To make a finer distinction, clues become metonymic through the intervention of the detective working within a defined field of inquiry, suggesting that the event itself must be circumscribed. Borrowing an idea from Goux, these clue signs "must undergo translation into the phonic signifiers of speech or the phonographic signifiers of alphabetic writing, which are now the general equivalents for the world's signs" (*Symbolic* 172). Whereas this sleight of hand may be convincing in the Golden Age due to the general in-text alignment of detective with institutional power and dominant cultural interests, once the institutional relation is severed or brought under strain, the detective can no longer work the magic. The illusion depended upon a noninterference pact, in which the competition between detective and criminal (or audience) never extended to the serious verbal disputation of the results. The link between detective and criminal is certainly evident from the beginning of the tradition in the potential conflation of Dupin and Minister D——.

---

[1]   Changes in the gold standard were well known to the public, even in the pulps. The government's attitude towards gold hoarding is a theme in Lester Dent's 1933 story "The Death Blast" (31). Specific reference to the Gold Reserve Act of 1934 appears in Frederick Davis's "Crucibles of the Damned" (154).

But there is no real exchange here or exchangeability as long as Dupin retains rights over the representation of reality via his narrator. The nature of exchange, possibly most acutely represented in the cryptic and truncated economic identity evident in the elliptical Holmes-Moriarty interview at Baker Street ("The Final Problem"), is not confined to some transaction in the limited terms of monetary instruments, but is in fact verbal. Verbal exchange, however, still needs some regulation or frame of reference for the value of signs to achieve stability.

The ratiocinative detective story associated with Doyle supports an ideology of value vis-à-vis the clue, a value whose guarantor is typically the detective-specialist. The more or less self-conscious need for this guarantee, whose correlates are skepticism and instability, deepens in the twentieth century and manifests itself under changing economic regimes. The shifting role of the detective within these economic formations affects relations of representation, equivalence, and convertibility as a function of evidence or, in Keller and Klein's words, the movement "from narrative to inferential reasoning of the explication" (56). The process of sorting, retaining, discarding, sequentializing, and encoding generates identifiable narrative types usually dependent upon the detective's presence. To be sure, in terms of the Golden Age, an objection may come to mind in Freeman: Thorndyke repeatedly emphasizes the indeterminate worth of any fact (though what constitutes a fact is never explained in depth) and hence the necessity of painstakingly minute description, since the position of any datum cannot be precisely apprehended until the totality is ascertained. All the same, Thorndyke's mantra that his interlocutors have all the information he has is naturally never taken seriously by the reader, who understands that the determination of meaningfulness and heft in the overall hypothesis is unquestionably Thorndyke's domain. Thorndyke is able to assert that "no such fact can be regarded as irrelevant, until all the data are assembled and collated, it is impossible to judge the bearing or value of any one of them" (Freeman, *Cat's* 57)—what is overlooked here is that the assembling and collating are not neutral; indeed, what passes for an acceptable truth is likewise something of a foregone conclusion.

The formal distinctions between the subgenres may be explained in conjunction with Jean-Joseph Goux's literary analyses pertaining to the loss of the gold standard in the early twentieth century. The loss of what Goux terms "gold language," and its replacement by the token, is discernible when texts are compared. For a protagonist like Holmes truth is presented as a matter of isolating discrete (linguistic) elements, the assembly of clues, and a consequent determination of value. In tandem with the post–World War I stress placed upon the gold standard, the detective operates in a system where truth itself is reduced to a commodity whose value is controlled by market forces. The timeline defined by these authors traces a progressive abstraction and immateriality pertaining to signs (or clues), which historically corresponds to the disappearance of convertibility. Circulating objects (commodities) come up against a problem of value which is either resolved or left unresolved by the detective protagonist. As would-be guarantors of convertibility, detectives seem less able to force the clue to signify in ways whereby an unmistakable core of value can be displayed.

In "The Locked-Room Lecture" from *The Three Coffins*, Fell proposes that "a great part of our liking for detective fiction is *based* on a liking for improbability," to which he adds, "There can be no such thing as any probability until the end of the story" (Carr, *Three Coffins* 160). Fell's statements lead us to ponder how to understand any discrete element within the total system in relation to the boundary-establishing function of the detective. Hühn is correct to state that the detective's "final explanation—disclosing the criminal's story as well as the history of his detection—closes the meaning of both texts effectively and thus collapses all levels of writing and reading, stabilizing the meaning of all signs" (458). As we saw at the end of Chapter 3 in the analysis of *The Dain Curse*, this is sometimes only accomplished through the detective's aggressive shutting down of the narrative spiral. In any case, the structural necessity of closure that results in positive knowledge is almost always dependent on the efforts of the detective and/or the institutions with which he or she is affiliated. Whether or not the public truth corresponds with our knowledge matters little—the offer of a system which has internal consistency is coincident with this detective- or institution-mediated closure. This point is tautological for most readers. Hard-boiled fiction, defined as haptic rather than visual, draws attention to a sequential unfolding that threatens both transmission and totality, or in which the detective's powerlessness (through social position or strained institutional relations) heightens epistemological uncertainty. We must also consider how clues are related in texts to the larger system. Clues may be understood as signs whose semantic polyvalence can be treated variously—as concrete determinations of value (true or false), as polyvocal, as guaranteed (gold language), or as floating tokens.

In Fell's picture of the world, the detective's role is not one of destroying probabilities; rather, the detective strives to convert the impossible into the improbable. As improbabilities they are subject to calculation, and subsequently to investment, return, rates of profit, and completion of cycles of circulation. This procedure is demonstrated in *The Three Coffins* in Fell's sorting out of the dying Professor Grimaud's words, in which Fell contests the meanings construed by the unimaginative Superintendent Hadley and the intellectually blasé Ted Rampole. In ascertaining the clue's genuineness, Fell's weight secures both meaning and value, adding ballast to floating signifiers so that they are securely anchored or serviceable as points for navigation. Extracting the gist of what the other men "heard," Fell ruminates and produces meanings that are readily agreed to by his interlocutors (Carr, *Three Coffins* 78–80). The object of his labors, certainly in line with Hadley, is to amass sufficient evidence to bring a murderer to justice. It is this notion of evidence which must occupy us first, since the facts in Fell's example are largely the product of the man's forceful personality. Subsequently, we will examine what happens when the detective no longer possesses authority, institutional support, or a fund of arcane knowledge.

Evidence

The idea of evidence, commonly understood to be a cornerstone of modern liberal democratic notions of law, is central to detective fiction, though its uses are typically more ideological than rigorous in a strictly legal sense. Panek and Bendel-Simso demonstrate that contemporary notions of evidence are tied directly to scientific transformations that profoundly influenced nineteenth-century medicolegal thought. They identify two especially important points: "Science ... called into question whether people can always understand or competently recall what they have witnessed, and science began to discover techniques and invent machines which could make the unseen world visible" (65). By the time we get to the detective narratives of the mid-twentieth century, the demand for material evidence is so pressing that Inspector Seabrook in Gladys Mitchell's *The Rising of the Moon* (1945) is willing to risk the lives of two boys to secure sufficient data to warrant an arrest (218). He is criticized by other characters for his lack of judgment, but only in regard to the ethics of his methods to obtain infallible proof; he is commended for the conviction itself. Lt. Terence Marshall in *Nine Times Nine* is praised for producing the types of evidence that pass muster in court (Holmes 64). In Carr's *The White Priory Murders* (1934), the innocent are so paranoid about the ways evidence might entrap them that they destroy physical clues that seem to implicate them—one character thereby *creates* a locked-room mystery in an attempt to misdirect how the evidence against him is read.

Evidence in the hard-boiled tale becomes more problematic, not in that it is rejected for the purpose of detaining suspects or securing convictions, but in that evidence is more overtly constructed to mean what institutional authorities and their representatives want it to mean—a situation that reaches a high point in the legal finagling of Perry Mason. Lt. Logan in Coxe's *Murder for Two* (1943) deems photographic evidence sufficient to get a conviction—images are objective facts (notwithstanding how they can be manipulated). More in line with hard-boiled conventions, Bill Delaney claims that Spade turns Brigid over in *The Maltese Falcon* because sufficient evidence exists to hang him despite his role in bringing the gang to justice (168–69). Goal-driven D.A. office lawyers will spin "evidence" to achieve the desired results, and Spade's activities can easily be inserted into a narrative that damns him as well as the others. The accusatory material, therefore, is true within its context, though our sympathies challenge that truth. Such polyvocalism describes the shifting value of the falcon, which turns out to be ephemeral and intrinsically worthless, but which nonetheless leads to real deaths. A number of stories reflect the ways in which narratives can be constructed or evidence can be thrown up against the protagonist. Daly's "The False Burton Combs" (1922) culminates with lawyers making a case against the hero for murder, which he only escapes through the unexpected testimony of an eyewitness. Lt. Delaguerra is framed by a game warden in Chandler's "Spanish Blood" (1935) to pull him off a case. Hammer's license is revoked based on the circumstantial evidence of his involvement in a murder at the beginning of Spillane's *Vengeance Is Mine!* (1950).

Taking a wide view, evidence comprises factual observations of phenomena, often the collection of significant material objects, traces, or residues, as well as properly documented or verifiable statements. Reflection leads us to view the isolation of objects and the notion of the factual itself as subject to the power of discourse, paradigmatically or methodologically limited procedures, and institutional interests which favor certain outcomes. Moreover, as Arthur Jellicoe, a lawyer (and as it turns out, criminal) in Freeman's *The Eye of Osiris* (1911), points out: "A court of law must decide according to the evidence which is before it; and that evidence is of the nature of sworn testimony" (88). A glaring example of the artificiality of evidence arises midway through Dickson's *The Judas Window*, in which the prisoner in the dock admits his guilt within the hearing of the judge, the lawyers, and assembled witnesses, jury, and onlookers—though only after the judge has closed the session. This "confession" is made in a chivalrous effort to spare his fiancée the need to make embarrassing disclosures in court, but it is not admissible as evidence. Had the declaration been made before the gavel descended, it would have concluded the trial, and it certainly prejudices the next day's procedures, but it must conform to juridical conventions to serve as evidence.

Evidence, whether integral to a solution or false evidence to be disproved or explained away, is sufficient to erect an invisible frame of meaning. Hühn notes that much of the so-called evidence that we are given would never hold up to scrutiny in the courtroom (an unfamiliar process to most), but its presence nonetheless presupposes "the absolute belief in the power and efficacy of the verbal construct of a story as such and in the very rationality or argumentation as the principle governing the process of narrative reconstruction" (456). Frequently, the institutionally aligned detective's oracular pronouncements are manufactured to satisfy the demands of a court whose interests are aligned with the State. Chandler's dozen "selected morons" ("Simple Art" 991) who compose the jury are so many obstacles to realizing justice, given their undeveloped deductive powers, a point comically but nonetheless poignantly suggested by H.M.'s disparaging address to his jury: "Well, my fatheads" (Dickson, *Judas* 17).[2] This denigration of an important feature of the Anglo-American judicial system is made explicit time and again by Sherlock Holmes, who is convinced of the correctness of his deductions—a reasoning process that Watson compares to intuition (Doyle, "Red" 307)—but who mistrusts the judgment of the "hard-headed British jury." The lawyer Thorndyke does not confine his concerns to juries: "To us [lawyers] the case looks complete. But how would it have looked to the police? or to a possibly unimaginative magistrate? or, especially to a jury of ordinary, and perhaps thick-headed, tradesmen and artisans? Juries like direct evidence, and that was what I

---

[2]   Golden Age writers' unwillingness to depict trial and punishment or the uneasiness it creates (for instance, Sayers's *Unnatural Death*) is read by Roth not entirely as a tacit distaste for such spectacles or as proof that knowledge of guilt is sufficient and all else is anticlimactic; rather, we are spared the trial and its aftermath because the kinds of evidence adduced in the solution would not be sufficient to achieve a conviction (29).

was trying to produce'" (Freeman, *Cat's* 257). As readers we time and again look on as detectives (Dr. Thorndyke, Miss Marple, Lord Peter, Mrs. Bradley, H.M., Prof. Fen, Ellery Queen, Inspector Alleyn, et al.) tell us that they are convinced of the culprit's identity, but that they prefer not to divulge their knowledge until they have amassed absolute proof (that is, sufficient evidence to convict). Naturally, one purpose of this device is to indicate that if we weren't so dense, we, too, would know the solution. But such declarations also bear a promise: that in fact a limited number of discrete clues, deductions, psychological typing, and isolated facts bring the whole enterprise home to the guilty party.

The strength of the narrative frame is often so pronounced that we make great concessions in linking evidence to truth.[3] In hard-boiled fiction the difficulty faced by the detective in converting clues into evidence becomes more pronounced, a point made by Keller and Klein (56). Keller and Klein tangentially suggest that at least the illusion of hard evidence—a fact-based, more or less positivist approach—reigns in the Classical and Golden Age, though this idea is compromised somewhat in Christie's "psychologists," particularly Miss Marple, whose hard-and-fast categories (for example, in *Murder in the Vicarage* [212]) cannot be quantified scientifically.[4] In the final Charlie Chan novel, *Keeper of the Keys*, Chan remarks to an inexperienced sheriff that clues may "[point] all ways at once"; however, "long experience shows ... that in time clues fall into place, false ones fade and wither, true ones cluster together in one unerring signboard" (Biggers 113–14). The distance between the private detective and institutional counterparts is simply too wide to make the easy transition from investigation to conviction. Thus, in *Red Harvest* the Op tells his colleagues that in Personville "there's no use taking anybody into court, no matter what you've got on them. They own the courts" (Hammett 104), a sentiment reflected in a representative passage from Frederick Nebel's MacBride-Kennedy series: "It doesn't matter what you believe; you have to produce evidence" ("Die-Hard" 79). Whatever form of law possessing legitimacy attracts the kinds of evidence (including blatant falsification) which functions within its sphere, and thus, the hard-boiled detective—given an often strained relation with law enforcement and the legal system—may have to dispense with evidence in its public forms (though not as a private means of arriving at conclusions).

Given this distinction, the question of evidence will be treated here as secondary to the question of value, though both terms move between the philosophical poles of absolutism and relativism as described at the end of Chapter 1. Indeed, the relation

---

[3]   Possibly the most blatant statement comes to us metafictionally on the first page of *The Three Coffins*: "The words 'according to the evidence' have been used. We must be very careful about the evidence when it is not given at first-hand. And in this case the reader must be told at the outset, to avoid useless confusion, on whose evidence he can absolutely rely. That is to say, it must be assumed that somebody is telling the truth—else there is no legitimate mystery, and, in fact, no story at all" (Carr 6).

[4]   The great dissenter is Father Brown, who states: "I attach a good deal of importance to vague ideas. All those things that 'aren't evidence' are what convince me. I think a moral impossibility the biggest of all impossibilities" (Chesterton, "Strange Crime" 232–33).

between value and clue is important, since the clue is typically closer to the detective as an agent in the narrative rather than the more anonymous institutionally linked idea of evidence. The clue is rendered visible, then ascribed value, though usually isolating the clue is conflated with the discovery of an intrinsic value. The core of value is blatantly dramatized in stories like "The Adventure of the Six Napoleons" (analyzed below), and is heavily dependent upon the detective-alchemist who converts dross into gold, or, to employ another metaphor, who discloses the clue to possess value as evidence, in short, that which passes muster for institutional definitions of guilt, justice, and proper, legally sanctioned punishment. Clues of themselves do not have this overarching function; rather, they are signs which are inscribed with value or determined to be valueless, but which in either case tend to point beyond themselves, or at least are *believed* to do so. Conventions sometimes create difficulties in the conversion of clues into evidence. As Keller and Klein note in the context of the Golden Age tale, the audience is "always faced with this need to translate from the language of observation to the language of evidence," which they rephrase as "the change in logic from narrative to the inferential reasoning of the explication" (56). These deduction-heavy stories demand "an exact equation between ... a knowledge never made completely explicit through the narration and ... solutions made valid through a chain of inference based on clues largely seen to be such through the detective's privileged knowledge" (Keller and Klein 57).

A ground subtends the work of generating correspondences; however, this ground remains outside the reader's immediate range of vision. Yet a necessarily stable frame of reference is the condition of possibility for value. In the context of detective fiction—specifically, the Classical analytic tale—this frame may be surreptitiously constructed by the detective (for instance, methodologically in the experiment or the reconstruction of the crime), though sometimes it is represented by lesser lights (Watson figures). Most commonly, it emanates from the detective like an aura, whose very presence in the clue-puzzle underwrites the possibility of a known totality. Within this frame of reference the detective thereby demands a faith "that all signs in a bounded space must be relatable" (Roth 185), even while claiming neutrality, objectivity, and deference to fact. The irrationality of this faith is obscured by successful outcomes—by the sympathetic detective who ultimately condones the institutional point of view, but this does not mean that the boundedness of the system is proven beyond the instrumentalization of knowledge—particularly in the hard-boiled. Cooper and Murphy suggest precisely the opposite to be demonstrated in a novel like *Red Harvest*, in which "the operations of the economy (or capital) as a stable, rational grid" are "undone" (152–53) and its ideological constructedness is laid bare.

The Gold Standard as Abstraction

Historically, the idealization of gold as a standard rests upon its intrinsic qualities: "portability, indestructibility, homogeneity, divisibility, and cognizability" (North 7). Nonetheless, there is nothing absolutely inherent in gold that establishes it in this role to the exclusion of anything else. Properly speaking, "the phrase 'gold standard' now denotes whichever commodity emerges as money from the free interplay of market forces" (Block 15), and gold is a commodity, though one that in the past was understood to possess a special relation to self (Marx, *Economic* 28: 71). Though the status of gold might at first seem an economic matter divorced from literature, the historical vicissitudes of the gold standard are of interest to us sociologically vis-à-vis the market instabilities coincident with the rise of Golden Age and hard-boiled fiction, both in the United States and Great Britain. During World War I and its immediate aftermath, the gold standard was generally abandoned; the United States stayed on gold but banned its export for a time (Bordo and MacDonald 5). Following the war, efforts were made to return to gold in Europe, and certain rules and guidelines were established internationally. Even severely damaged economies managed to go back on: Germany in 1924, Great Britain and its colonies in 1928, and France in 1928; however, the onset of the Great Depression led once more to collapse. The standard was again abandoned in the UK in 1931.

Goux's work helps us to make the transition from these economic developments to our texts. In his essay "Banking on Signs" Goux traces changes in sensibilities from the nineteenth to the twentieth centuries towards the concept of wealth and the "dematerialization" of value. The general scope of this change involves a shift in the way wealth was defined: from a grounded wealth possessed of weight, gravity, and immobility to wealth understood in the context of circulation, an abstraction whose value is progressively more symbolic (16). This abstraction could take the form of token money, but even greater degrees of abstraction were achieved in the "bundle of stocks" which suggests wealth "in its greatest liquidity and in its most extreme universality" (16).

Goux argues that this tendency to symbolic value is not confined to purely monetary relations; rather, parallels emerge in the arts, literature, philosophy, and social sciences, particularly in the avant-garde's plunge into abstraction: Goux's examples include Gide, Kandinsky, Mondrian, and Saussure. Theoretical and practical advances were followed immediately by an "economic system [that] dispensed with the gold standard, with the evident result of a generalized floating" (Goux, *Symbolic* 113). Abstraction is symptomatic of change, and in Goux's phrase it "demonstrates that the power of organization is no longer transcendentalized and fixed in any guarantee and that the agent (the subjective pole) no longer coincides with the existence of the individual subject, the cogito (monocentric perspective), but is now collective" (Goux, *Symbolic* 196). This collectivity is not, however, the economic collectivism that Corey and other socialists understood to be the basis of a new form of production; rather, it is more akin to Nietzschean perspectivalism or a Cubist "all-at-onceness" that oscillates nondialectically between the multivalent potential of the visual field and the restrictions imposed by point of view.

Classical detective fiction more or less resists the changes posed by abstract art. The perspectivism of reading, and thus the polyvocal potential of any text, is reduced to a master perspectivism in the idealized readership of the Golden

Age detective who transcends the "normal" reader and the system itself. A dialectic is affirmed by which the competing readings are dismissed, overcome by a hegemonic reading which confirms a ground of meaning that subtends the enterprise. In this context, deference to the detective's readership signifies faith in the guarantee of meaning and the overcoming of the text's threatened hermeticism (exemplified in the locked-room mystery). In the process the threatened grid of Cartesian space, enclosed and fixed, must be subjected to extreme skepticism for it to be reestablished, usually in highly implausible ways that tend more and more towards parody as the genre advances. By drawing into vision the grid as a grid, the coordinate system is potentially undermined along with the subject position, now self-conscious, that the grid's unproblematic acceptance allowed.

The myth-generating aura of the Golden Age, whose very name suggests Goux's conception of Realist "gold language," differs noticeably from the hard-boiled in our use of the term. This difference indicates a degree of consciousness about language, conceived as a referential system, and whose meaning derives from "the differential relationship of words among themselves." Goux continues in the context of literature:

> To a system of circulating gold-money (and of materialized value) would correspond language oriented to a referent and thus also a literature primarily concerned with the objective representation of reality. On the other hand, to the system of nominal money (that of tokens) would correspond a new conception of language and of literature, marked by the relationships among signifiers without the treasury of either a referent or a fixed standard of pre-established ideas anchoring this drift of relational play. ("Banking" 20)

In respect to detective fiction, Classical and Golden Age conservatism seems in part a reaction to the de-anchoring of absolute value, of a definitive, authoritative fund, and non-circulating base.[5] The demand for certainty expressed as visual proof is tenuously thematized by Doyle in "The Red-Headed League." Greater anxiety is expressed in "The Adventure of the Six Napoleons," in which a core of value is theatrically revealed to the public—Holmes serves in both mysteries as the guarantor of a fund whereby meaning is visibly disclosed. This is what Hilfer has in mind, I think, when he writes that "the modern anxiety of a world without symbolic depth, all signifiers with no signifieds, is at an opposite pole from the detective novel in which all signifiers, in the detective's resolution, transparently reveal their significations" (7). The Golden Age posits a prelapsarian (or perhaps pre-Babel) availability of meaning whose prescriptive language goes to the

---

[5]   Whalen remarks of Poe that "both reading and writing are here recast in terms of political economy. Given his experience of commerce and the concomitant crisis in literary production, it is no accident that Poe should draw a comparison between knowledge and gold, between information and self-expanding value or capital. During the crucial period in the cultural formation of Poe and the nation, information emerged for the first time as the form taken by capital in the signifying environment" (394).

essence of things. But in a fallen and fragmented world, the ascription of meaning lacks a guarantee, particularly after the death of God, the absolute, transcendental guarantor. The brokenness of language raises doubts about ascribing value generally, demonstrable in respect to the clue but even more so to narratives that ostensibly link meaningful clues in sequence.[6] The loss of the gold standard, in literary terms, is an epistemological shock by which meaning and things no longer have concrete and tangible relations. Without discernible boundaries of meaning, the possibility of defining actions as criminal and the assignment of individuals to categories becomes doubtful or subject to casuistry.

In the Golden Age, signs are conceded to be both meaningful and determinate; as we shift our focus to the hard-boiled, we necessarily move into areas of greater uncertainty. Carl Malmgren touches upon the major theoretical elements of this shift in the opening parts of his *Anatomy of a Murder*, where he makes an explicit equation of sign and clue and the claim that "mystery and its spin-offs constitute the semiotic genre *par excellence*" (10). A corollary to this claim is that mystery insists upon the non-arbitrary nature of the sign which fits into causal chains, illuminating "a necessary relation between signifier (clue, piece of evidence) and signified (deduction, interpretation)" (Malmgren, *Anatomy* 47), or what McCann calls "the right reading of signs" (89). Malmgren is cognizant of the leap involved in hard-boiled fiction, for instance in Hammett, where "one never knows for sure who one is or who will do what to whom or why" (Malmgren, *Anatomy* 74; see also Malmgren, "Crime" 382). How are we to understand this shift? Much of it has to do with the detective's relation to the gold standard, the authority to verify that the fund exists and to protect its integrity and, as a consequence, the interests of those who rely upon its security. In this vein, Holmes represents "the alchemical model of transformation" by which "base material" is converted to valuable clues, and furthermore, to guarantee these clues so that they "can never return to insignificance or reassume [their] old, false meaning" (Atkinson 102). The astuteness of this reading hinges upon the recognition of power by which our very frame of understanding the clue and its narrative emplotment—in short, its necessity to narrative cohesion—is irrevocably modified.

Counterfeiting

Disclosure of the counterfeit potentially brings every element in circulation under scrutiny, raising the question not only of the genuineness of those elements, but the authority by which the genuine is established. Horsley points out the centrality in detective fiction of "order and identity, related, respectively, to closure and disclosure" (*Twentieth-Century* 28). These two terms, *order* and *identity*, might refer to social membership (such as a class structure and its expectations) as much as to an economy in which intercourse is framed or ordered through visibility,

---

[6]   This idea is literalized in *City of Glass* in Peter Stillman, Sr.'s demented search for a new language of correspondence. See Nealon on this point (102).

identity, or value. In terms of characters in Golden Age fiction, the unmasking of the murderer frequently discloses a counterfeit who has been passing at face value. This unmasking undermines faith in nominal values; the detective's intervention, in these types of stories, is the identification and culling of impediments to the functioning of the economy, the reestablishment of confidence, and the stabilization of (social) exchange. Yet conscious intervention gives rise to doubts that can never be dispelled and perpetuates the fear of arbitrariness. We might view the threat of value becoming indeterminate to be a false problem in that the clue already promises meaning of some sort.[7] That less-gifted onlookers cannot read the clue and judge its value does not preclude its circulation and use. To cite an example, Christopher Metress gives attention to the troubling speculations made by Holmes at the end of Doyle's "The Adventure of the Cardboard Box" ("Thinking" 185), a story written at the time of *The Adventures of Sherlock Holmes* but not published until 1917. Holmes's interrogation of the conditions of meaning itself is too anxiety-ridden to remain comfortably within the Classical story's promise of reassurance, our expectation that the detective will not introduce any system-threatening form of skepticism. This is, however, precisely what happens at the end, as Holmes inquires of Watson: "What object is served by this circle of misery and violence and fear? It must tend to some end, or else our universe is ruled by chance, which is unthinkable. But what end?" (Doyle, "Cardboard" 496). Holmes's uncomfortable rhetorical flight never achieves sufficient self-consciousness to find specifically historically grounded answers.

In order to establish such a framework by which to discuss counterfeiting in detective fiction, we turn to Goux's compelling treatment of the subject in *The Coiners of Language*, an inquiry into the crisis of convertibility in its socioeconomic and literary dimensions. In the first part of his book, the part most applicable to this study, Goux examines André Gide's novel *The Counterfeiters* (1925).[8] One of the main threads in Gide's work follows the novelist-character Edouard's attempt to lay conceptual foundations for a novel which is itself titled *The Counterfeiters*. Edouard's intention to dispense with plot, with narrative, and in fact with faith in the very power of language to convey meaning beyond the evocation of a (crystalline) structure raises disbelief among other characters. On the level of Gide's novel, Goux demonstrates that the plot elements which do appear—doubts over paternity and doubts over the genuineness of literary language, like the passing of fake gold coins by the disreputable Strouvilhou—are figuratively if not literally connected to convertibility and to counterfeiting. For Goux, "the 'counterfeiting' of [Gide's] title reaches beyond monetary fraudulence

---

[7]   Marx proclaims in the *Grundrisse* that the circulation of a counterfeit makes little difference if its function is fulfilled, but this function is founded upon belief in a symbol; its token "serves only as the means of circulation ..., a fleeting mediation" (*Economic* 28: 145).

[8]   Coincidentally, Hammett's publisher, Alfred Knopf, published the first translation of Gide's novel in 1927. Gide admired Hammett, ranking him with William Faulkner (McGurl 706).

to broach the question of the ground upon which values and meaning are based: counterfeiting becomes the central metaphor for calling into question the role of *general equivalents*" (*Coiners* 3). This calling into question, which Gide employs as the central theme of his novel, is reflective of a social process. We witness a change from "a society founded on legitimation by representation" to "a society dominated by the incontrovertibility of signifiers"; these mere tokens possess "no standard or treasury to offer the guarantee of a transcendental signifier or referent" (Goux, *Coiners* 4).

Edouard's novel, which betrays a self-contradictory lack of faith in the very materials by which meaning is ostensibly transmitted, is Gide's rejection of gold language. Edouard's self-understanding of his project—to evoke "the rivalry between the real world and the representation of it which we make to ourselves" (Gide 205)—only pushes the point of view back a level; it does not twist out of the dilemma of representation. In the process, though, literary language must cease to possess intrinsic value (Goux, *Coiners* 10); this apperceptive displacement has an historical precedent: "the bankruptcy of a circulation of values based on gold money becomes a metaphor for the failure of the realist or representational system of language" (Goux, *Coiners* 13).[9] At the same time, the historical unfolding of this idea is concretized by the ironic displacement of stability in the novel—the novelist Gide creating a self-conscious narrator telling the story of a novelist who intends to write a novel bearing the title of Gide's own novel, and so on. Instead of a ground upon which to establish foundations, we find displacement and deferral.

The detective story, particularly the Golden Age story, is implicated in the collapse of the novel as Goux diagnoses the significance of its self-thematizing in *The Counterfeiters*. Many novels contain the elements identified by Goux which indicate such crisis. Goux isolates three points in Gide's work which are relevant to our discussion: "(1) the invasion of novelistic fiction by the economic metaphor, to the point that characters are replaced by economic abstractions; (2) the choice of the reflexive or specular structure ...; and (3) the decisive crisis of realist representation ... with the explicit ... aim of creating a literature that is 'pure' or 'abstract'" (*Coiners* 9). Whereas these elements are operative in a reasonably pronounced form in the Golden Age—as they are in the hard-boiled— it is the differences in how they are acknowledged, the level of anxiety that they produce, the polite deferral to an authority that reestablishes a fragile stability, and a submission to formal constraints that differentiate the subgenres. The detective's alignment with institutions as a guarantor of value is often the means by which the clue-token is declared valid and the solvency of the institutional frame secured— though we should note that, like Gide's villainous Strouvilhou, hard-boiled writers do not abandon the economic system itself, at least as metaphor. The second and

---

[9]   Derrida takes Goux to task for his unwarranted historical "pinpointing" in the opening paragraphs of *The Coiners of Language* (*Given* 110). Though I am working within Goux's understanding of the problem, I compensate for Derrida's criticism by not insisting that a teleological principle is at work.

third of Goux's points, collapsed in Golden Age detective fiction's metafictional tendency, are equally problematic in the epistemological shift described by Keller and Klein.

The four types of money identified by Goux—money with intrinsic worth (gold, silver), representative money (convertible paper), fiduciary money, which is only partly guaranteed, and conventional money (inconvertible paper) need not detain us. Nonetheless, the examples that I cite, from Doyle to Sayers to Hammett to Chandler, parallel the trajectory of these types, describing a passage from the first to the fourth. In *The Counterfeiters*, Goux isolates the relation between Strouvilhou and Edouard as a contest within boundaries exclusive of gold money or even representative money—literature no longer commands that faith. Instead, we have positions within partly or entirely unguaranteed fiscal systems in which currency is enforced by decree. The literary consequences for Gide take two pathways—the laying bare of a fictional, conventionalized system that deserves little respect (Strouvilhou) and the participation in that same fiction, wherein we "pretend to remain within the economic system of gold language or of representative language while at the same time evading this system by means of a clever trick" (Goux, *Coiners* 16). This trick is necessary, given the realization that an objective relation between language and the world is quite beyond our grasp—there is no subterranean fund ("The Red-Headed League") or core of value ("The Six Napoleons"), save in the fictional fantasy of its protection or dramatization by the detective's authority. Furthermore, areas of life which are assumed to escape strict institutional regulation, such as the arts, are reduced to a productive process regulated partly by the marketability of style, but lacking a one-to-one correspondence with a visible treasury (*The Five Red Herrings*). During the critical 40-year period of these texts' appearance and consumption, 1891 to 1931, at least in the UK, the gold standard was temporarily abandoned in 1915, convertibility of notes dropped in 1919, and, despite efforts to go back on gold, the standard, too, was abandoned in 1931. The problem of the circulation of unguaranteed promissory notes, a theme figuring repeatedly in *Capital*, was certainly a matter of common knowledge in the late-Victorian era. By the 1920s and the appearance of *The Counterfeiters*, Goux notes the "turning point" at which the novel appears, "straddling the nostalgic memory of a gold language or a representative language, and negative prescience that this language is no longer tenable, that it no longer corresponds to the actual conditions of the circulation of signs" (*Coiners* 19). As for my last two exemplary texts, Hammett's *The Maltese Falcon* (1930) appears at a crisis point and Chandler's *The High Window* (1942) stands in a reflective relation to fiscal change.

To generalize, the Golden Age and hard-boiled subgenres echo the choices that Goux finds in Gide. On the one hand, the system may close in on itself, becoming self-referential and logically consistent *within* the terms of its own structure. On the other, it may draw attention to the absence of transcendental forces and thereby emphasize the fact of circulation despite an inherent lack of meaning. Notably, the subgenres coexist in time; they react to the same impetus. The political undertones of both orientations can be translated into attitudes towards a shift to the increased State role in currency regulation after World War I, one in which the government resembles a manager dedicated publicly to bourgeois interests (whether or not these are served) and a bleaker vision of State capitalism in which power defines reality, where bits of paper are declared to possess value by decree. A final question concerns the ambiguity of where authority resides if the standard can no longer be seen or handled in its materiality—the question of who decides evokes the political exception whereby the event itself is capable of being defined and acted upon.

"[Y]ou have not grasped the entire meaning of this business." (Doyle, "Six" 985)

Arthur Conan Doyle's "The Red-Headed League" (1891), the third tale from *The Adventures of Sherlock Holmes,* overtly thematizes economic and class relations. Value and circulation are central, especially the problem of the fund or treasury which Holmes takes it upon himself to protect. Pawnbroker Jabez Wilson's shop is used in a bank robbery bid that involves running a tunnel from the shop's cellar to the vault of a bank which abuts the premises. Wilson's scheming assistant, Vincent Spaulding, the alias of John Clay, an aristocrat by birth and a man regarded by Holmes as high in the ranks of dangerous London criminals, engineers his entry into the slow-witted proprietor's shop by coming for half wages. The unsuspecting Wilson is got out of the way by Clay and a co-conspirator, who dupe him into believing that an organization calling itself the Red-Headed League will pay Wilson handsomely for sitting in an office for a number of hours each day to copy out the *Encyclopedia Britannica.* This ruse absents Wilson from his shop so that the criminals can finish the last stages of their tunnel unimpeded. The abrupt dissolving of the League sends Wilson to Holmes, who, after a brief investigation, recognizes Clay and reads the deeper meaning of the caper. Holmes contacts Mr. Merryweather, the bank director, then sits with him, Watson, and Inspector Jones of Scotland Yard in the dark vault, which contains a fabulous amount of French gold, the acquisition of which is intended to buoy the bank's reserves. At the conclusion, Clay and his accomplice are arrested and Wilson is advised to supervise his household more carefully.

As Knight makes clear in his discussion of this story in *Form and Ideology,* "the real threat to respectable life posed by the grim areas where the working-class and the 'dangerous classes' lived is thoroughly subdued" in favor of solutions focused upon the middle classes (94), whose follies can be subjected to the timely corrective of Holmes's rational analysis.[10] The bourgeois managers of the bank

---

[10]   As in other early stories, like "The Adventure of the Beryl Coronet" or "The Adventure of the Naval Treaty," Holmes serves as defender of an essentially unlikable or incautious bourgeoisie in cases where they are incapable of defending themselves or their interests. Atkinson, in his essay on "The Red-Headed League," takes Merryweather's

are, ironically, not that far removed from these "grim areas" inasmuch as the bank premises border the pawnshop, the poor man's emporium. The stereotyped and dubiously named Mr. Merryweather is agitated over a missed rubber of whist; the pawnbroker's business life, inseparable from his private life given the conjoining of shop and living space, depends upon the precarious finances of the poor. References in the text to the end of the month and times of day help flesh out the picture of cycles of want and need characterizing the world of Wilson's customers. And while the text inadvertently admits their predicament, it does not raise sympathy for them. At the same time, it points out the benign foolishness and fluster of the bank director, who, originally hostile to Holmes, eventually ends up fawning upon him, raising the obvious question as to why Holmes should protect this man and his interests. Likewise, we question his commitment to the police, whose representative Holmes terms "an absolute imbecile." These unflattering portraits, however, do not depict these men as stepping outside of their prescribed roles—of that they are not guilty. The real villain is the aristocrat who poses as a member of the working poor, a role evoked by the commonness of his given name and the suggestiveness of his surname, Clay. In his double betrayal, we are not asked so much to be antagonistic to the working classes but rather to reject any tinkering with class structure. Clay, in his imposture, is also a traitor to the worker in his devious usurpation of a job that might have gone to an honest man through the class treachery of accepting employment under the market rate (we recall the dozen other applicants who are turned away, implying the dearth of employment opportunities). Alternatively, if Clay had honored his social commitments, living up to his heritage and the traditions of Eton and Oxford, there would have been no social instability. Holmes rights this imbalance, again to the benefit of the parties who seem little enough to deserve it. This portrayal of the textual economy, though worth analyzing, yields only a superficial reading.

The concealed structure of the text supports an economy of meaning that is more subterranean, literally so in this text—and in fact, we must apply imagination to reading a story which competes with "The Adventure of the Speckled Band" in terms of its implausibility. Some of the more or less comic effects, such as the good-natured stupidity of the client Mr. Wilson, can be understood as parody—Diane Barsham, for instance, reads the "nominal" labor assigned by the League as a spoof on "Victorian encyclopedism" (113). Other points are more difficult to explain. For instance, how does Clay learn of the gold in the vault? Merryweather remarks that the information has leaked out, but this seems unlikely, since even the police are unaware of it. How does Clay know that the gold is still in the vault and has not been moved, as would have been prudent, given the threats Merryweather mentions? Why would the directors tolerate a doubtful situation when it could be easily rectified? But most damningly, how could anyone tunnel to the exact place where the gold is kept? Where has all the debris been taken? How

---

role to represent "the whole system of capital," remarking Holmes's intervention on the banker's behalf to have a notable ideological dimension (16).

could these bulky, heavy crates be removed from the premises without attracting notice? The whole scenario is, in fact, a fantasy,[11] a theatrical performance. It stages a confirmation of the institution's gold; our confidence is bulwarked by the protection extended by Sherlock Holmes where the efforts of the bourgeois caretakers and their labor force have failed.

The source of the anxiety over this hoard nonetheless demands attention. Goux supplies an answer, urging that gold must be seen since "as soon as the 'golden image' was no longer visible to the public eye, no longer directly worshiped and tangibly circulated but rather confined to secret bank reserves, 'gone back again into the soil,' its total disappearance was to be expected" (*Symbolic* 115)—this reading bridges the world of fiction and the readership of the *Strand*. Holmes's efforts guard value, as opposed to the business practices of Jabez Wilson, which inherently undervalues every ware that crosses the counter, and in which values are a question of negotiation if not sharp practice. Curiously, the visibility of the gold is one of the differences between the original story and its adaptation to television. In the Jeremy Brett series, we actually see the gold (referred to, incidentally, as napoleons). Unaccustomed to intrinsic value in our currency, we perhaps remain unimpressed with the solid materiality of the bulky crates and their valuable contents; we do not regard the gold as an anchor which secures the bank's solvency in a world of electronic transactions. Moreover, we are cut adrift from this static *fond*, which ensures the viability of circulation on the surface in the City, which, like the road fronting the bank, supports "the immense stream of commerce flowing in a double tide inwards and outwards" (Doyle, "Red" 306). As in "The Adventure of the Six Napoleons," the story's original readers likely needed the security of bullion resting beneath the transactions of daily life—and, we note, the anxiety around this scopic demand seems to grow as we enter the early years of the twentieth century. But for "The Red-Headed League," the standard placed in the temple is the unseen measure subtending transactions; it guarantees but does not circulate; the measure ensconced in the vault is sufficient.

The need to actually see this valuable material core becomes more pressing in "The Adventure of the Six Napoleons" (1904), a story which few critics, with the notable exception of Michael Atkinson, have given critical attention. Atkinson touches upon several of the issues present in this story: the notion of a destructive iconoclasm, the convergence of Holmes and the criminal in the repetition of their activities, and, as in the rest of his engaging *The Secret Marriage of Sherlock Holmes*, a careful inquiry into Doyle's authorial psychology. To this, we can add the sociological implications of the text in respect to the burgeoning art market amongst the professional classes (represented here by journalists and doctors), as

---

[11]   The Jeremy Brett television episode of this story attempts to bridge some of these lacunae. For instance, Merryweather explains in greater depth the secrecy around the gold, but the leak is demonstrated from the start in a receipt surreptitiously dropped in the street by a co-conspirator. The enterprise is shown to be carefully planned by Moriarty, and Clay uses the sewers as a more plausible conduit.

well as a general economic reading which encompasses questions of production, circulation, consumption, and value, culminating in the dramatization of intrinsic worth played out in front of a select audience.

"The Six Napoleons" contains in miniature most of the elements wherein the faith in gold language is still operable—though a careful reading shows that it is under strain. We have, first of all and to a striking degree for the Sherlock Holmes stories as a whole, an emphasis on economic transaction and circulation. The story commences with Lestrade's visit to Holmes and Watson and his description of what appear to be acts of criminal mania: the destruction of three plaster busts of Napoleon Bonaparte, each identical to the others (a mass-produced commodity) but each in a different location within a single district of London. Shortly thereafter, another bust is stolen and destroyed; however, this time a dead body, apparently the thief's victim, lies on the doorstep of the burgled house. Whereas Lestrade aims to identify the dead man, the murder for him being the real crime, Holmes's line of inquiry focuses on the destruction of property in the form of the busts. His search leads him to interview a merchant dealing in these *objets d'art*, to ascertain that six replicas were produced in the group and the locations of those that remain, and to visit the premises where the busts were made. The criminal is captured after Holmes correctly predicts he will attempt to steal another of the set of six—like Holmes, he knows the location of the other two, so he is checkmated by the police. In the denouement Holmes purchases the remaining bust, demolishes it, and reveals the object of these apparently irrational acts: a valuable pearl is hidden inside, adhering to the plaster. Holmes then explains that the criminal, an Italian artisan named Beppo, had received the stolen pearl from a confederate, but owing to his pursuit and apprehension by the police for a different crime, had concealed the pearl in the still-wet bust drying in the factory. Arrested and jailed for a year, Beppo had, upon release, tracked down the busts and begun his caper.

The story is the tale of two interlinked economies—money and the sign. The first foregrounds the processes of production and circulation in the manufacture, distribution, sale for profit, and purchase of art objects. We also observe certain class and labor aspects in which surplus value is extracted from exploited working class artisans (the production cost and the markup are mentioned by the factory foreman). The busts circulate like other commodities, but their identical appearance belies a value that Holmes is called upon to reveal where others see only uniformity. In his role as historian of the commodity's production and circulation, Holmes's investigation discloses the complexity of these objects beyond their merely reified end product. The investigation ends with Holmes's purchase of the remaining bust for 10 pounds—subjected to transactions, these sculptures possess a chameleon-like value which fluctuates based on market mechanisms, but whose apparent indeterminacy is concealed by the processes of circulation described in *Capital* II. Holmes's role as guarantor of bourgeois society demands the conclusive demonstration that this process is not a serpent swallowing its tail, an endless deferral of balance in the progressive accrual of value, but is based upon something tangible. In doing so, he buttresses the system's beneficiaries by revealing the intrinsic value composing the commodity's core, while the less gifted servants of these interests (Lestrade) "have not grasped the entire meaning of this business" (Doyle, "Six" 985).

In his search and desire to lay bare value, Holmes doubles the criminal, Beppo, despite their differing motives. The "disinterested" engagement in a case for which he will not be paid makes Holmes appear to be a public-minded defender of order, unlike his violent, self-serving counterpart. Beppo, never allowed to speak and associated with the criminal classes partly as a consequence of his ethnicity, is in fact described as not fully human (he is called a "simian" whose jaw resembles "the muzzle of a baboon" [Doyle, "Six" 978]),[12] and yet a more sympathetic reading of his quest reveals a metaphorical depth that indicates the real point of contrast between these characters. Obviously, Beppo fails where Holmes succeeds, but success is not so much a case of Holmes's superiority, since Beppo "[conducts] his search with considerable ingenuity and perseverance" (Doyle, "Six" 987). He outmaneuvers the police and proves almost equal to Holmes. Indeed, the description of Beppo by his former foreman as "a good workman, one of the best" (Doyle, "Six" 981) is curiously echoed at the end of the story in Lestrade's praise of Holmes's investigation as "workmanlike" (Doyle, "Six" 988). The difference lies in the juxtaposition of two parallel economies—one (Holmes) sanctioned by powerful interests, the other (Beppo) characterized as criminal despite his exploited status. As a consequence, the value Beppo searches for will never be available to him; even if he had been allowed to smash all six busts, he would have found all six empty, at least figuratively. The hidden value of the commodity's interior is the value that he literally put there himself, but it is a value which he cannot extract, namely the surplus value generated by his own labor, which has been expropriated by others. The owners of the modes of production have already pocketed this value, a process over which Beppo has no control, but one which Holmes tacitly labors to enforce. Unsurprisingly, we are manipulated to view the system through his eyes, even remaining unconcerned over the murder, since the violence is directed towards ethnic Others within the same economically depressed community.

The very form of Holmes's iconoclasm also has its sociopolitical dimension, which points towards the dramatization of meaning. The circulating token cannot be the unique—its very materiality refers to a value that is elsewhere, perhaps entirely conceptual or founded upon socially circumscribed fictions. The art object, understood as the singular product of creative genius, is treated ironically in the story, reduced to cheap, reified plaster replicas. And yet, despite their intrinsically low value, these objects bear the visage of an emperor, whose image underwrites the value of the circulating coin. In a different context, the word *napoleon* is the name of a coin (a 20-franc gold coin named for the emperor), and before reading the story we might interpret the title as referring to coins rather than to statuary.

---

[12]   Other instances of physiognomic description appear in Doyle. In *A Study in Scarlet* the dead Drebber's "low forehead, blunt nose, and prognathous jaw, gave the dead man a singularly simious and ape-like appearance" (Doyle 97). The most sustained is "The Adventure of the Creeping Man."

We should recall, too, that forgery is traditionally a capital crime which can be construed as lese-majesty in its "desecration" of the monarch's image, literalized here in an even more complete act of destruction (and subtly reinforced by Holmes's concluding remark to Watson to take out documents related to a forgery case). But the point of that destruction is to overcome a vague but persistent concern, to reveal the hidden value in the interior of a circulating piece of worthless material. The act makes value visible and offers an indisputable confirmation that the outward manifestation of the sign (and the monetary token) is indeed founded upon something tangible that transcends the shopworn exterior of the commodity form. To conclude our discussion of this story, even the dramatic means by which Holmes conjures up the pearl is carefully portrayed in that the performance takes place before an appreciative bourgeois-professional audience: "Lestrade and I sat silent for a moment, and then, with a spontaneous impulse, we both broke out clapping as at the well-wrought crisis of a play. A flush of colour sprang to Holmes's pale cheeks, and he bowed to us like the master dramatist who receives the homage of his audience" (Doyle, "Six" 986). Holmes raises his magic wand and strikes Napoleon on the head, and from the ruins a core of value is confirmed.

"Anybody could do it, given the formula." (Sayers, *Five* 8)

Dorothy L. Sayers's novel *The Five Red Herrings* (1931) ranks low in the estimation of critics.[13] Most regard the work as little more than an overly complex clue-puzzle, and in doing so seem to miss not only the novel's humor, local color, and delightful rendering of dialect, but also its sinister counterfeiting subtheme (in this instance, of art). In fact, Sayers's novel launches a serious critique of the artist as the producer of original objects of intrinsic worth in two ways: first, she contests the value of an individual style premised on non-reproducibility; and second, she demonstrates how value arises from the conjunction of powerful interests and a gullible and manipulable public. The novel's maze of timetables and suspect lists, one displacing the next, is something of a parody, which leads to an improbable solution. But the underlying critique addresses the themes of genius and the reification of artistic vision reduced to thin affectations, prone to mass duplication, and thrown onto the market, where it is subject to the whims of critics and moneyed connoisseurs. The deferral of value, delinked from the artist-producer, is paralleled by the central clue of the work, the clue that Wimsey discerns, grants value to, and employs to demonstrate to a less astute constabulary that murder was done, instead of death by misadventure. That clue, however, is an absence. It "appears" literally as a blank on the page.

The novel opens in southwest Scotland, where Wimsey is on holiday. A returning visitor over several seasons, Wimsey is well acquainted with the locals,

---

[13] Cawelti calls it "boring" and "[bogged] down in the interminable examination of clues and schedules" ("Artistic" 193; see also Cawelti, *Adventure* 120). The novel is disparaged by McGregor and Lewis (93–94), Bander (311), and Panek (*Watteau's* 94–96).

and though he doesn't paint, he does fish, and thus fulfills one of the two criteria for acceptance as an incomer. Six established and recognized painters come under scrutiny when fellow artist Sandy Campbell ends up dead. Having apparently knocked himself out from a fall, Campbell tumbled into a burn while incautiously painting *en plein air*. But we suspect that all is not as it seems. Campbell's uncontrollable temper has made him universally disliked, to the point that any of the six other painters could conceivably have murdered him in a fit of temper. Eventually, Wimsey and the police conduct an investigation in which all six men are suspects (hence the title). In addition to the clue that indicates that a crime has been committed, the killer had to pose as Campbell at the place where the body was found and to have produced the painting still drying on the easel. "Campbell" was in fact seen painting by witnesses passing at a distance; however, the state of rigor indicates that death had occurred much earlier, and the wounds are not entirely consistent with an accident. In short, whoever painted the picture was not Campbell, though necessarily the imposter was a painter and one who could reproduce Campbell's style sufficiently well to fool others familiar with his work—a demanding performance in a community brimming with painters.

Wimsey, having little to do and responsive to local gossip, hurries to the site of the "accident" upon learning of Campbell's death. After some details about the body are disclosed, Wimsey turns his attention to the unfinished and still wet canvas left, presumably, by the dead man:

> It was blocked in with a free and swift hand, and lacked the finishing touches, but it was even so a striking piece of work, bold in its masses and chiaroscuro, and strongly laid on with the knife. It showed a morning lighting—he remembered that Campbell had been seen painting a little after 10 o'clock. The grey stone bridge lay cool in the golden light, and the berries of a rowan-tree, good against witchcraft, hung yellow and red against it, casting splashes of red reflection upon the brown and white of the tumbling water beneath. Up on the left, the hills soared away in veil on veil of misty blue to meet the hazy sky. And splashed against the blue stood the great gold splendour of the bracken, flung in by spadefuls of pure reds and yellows. (Sayers, *Five* 17)

This description, represented by the omniscient narrator though ostensibly through Wimsey's eyes, employs a critical language to express admiration for the still unfinished painting: "free and swift hand," "striking piece of work," "bold in its masses," "strongly laid on," "flung in by spadefuls of pure reds and yellows." The imaginative description and sensitivity to palette discloses the masterly treatment of the subject. At the same time, it reads like an up-market enticement to a potential customer interested in adorning his sitting room with a tasteful landscape. This "critic's language," so annoying to Marxists like John Berger as a form of obscurantism which plasters over the socioeconomic relations of a represented world, is nonetheless geared to express individuality—not so much of an insight into locale or historically specific conditions, but of the artist's self-expressiveness, presumably an aspect of his particular identity and vision. Despite his apparent admiration, Wimsey nonetheless declares, "I do not believe in that painting" (Sayers, *Five* 23).

Notwithstanding language that reads like a Christie's catalog entry, Wimsey's lack of belief is not an aesthetic evaluation (though we could argue that aesthetic value is not the ultimate aim of the catalog either). Instead, and curiously in line with market concerns, Wimsey is more interested in attribution, in genuineness—is this a Campbell or isn't it?[14] Belief is connected with crime, that is, the physical impossibility of the painting. The painting becomes an abstract problem, akin to the locked room, whose challenge in this instance is to explain how the painting got onto the easel. Moreover, the crime involves passing off of one's work as another's, a substitution which retains, nominally, the value promised by someone else. The missing signature, an inscription linked to that value, is absent, not so much because the painting is unfinished (or, if it were, that it would be harder to copy convincingly) but because any number of names might be placed there. The name is inconsistent with a discrete fund of creativity having a one-to-one, cause-and-effect relation to its execution. In his investigation Wimsey ends up revealing this "original" work to be counterfeit, a work whose aura is manufactured to compel belief and, more importantly for the killer, to serve as an alibi.

Sympathy for the victim in this case, as we have come to expect from Golden Age plots, is impossible, not only because Campbell remains alive for a mere dozen pages but also because during this short span he manages to threaten or irritate everyone around him, including most of the generally likable suspects. But disdain for Sandy Campbell does not stop at his insufferable personality; it extends to his professional status in the eyes of other artists. Faulted for his excessively pecuniary outlook, and later by the suggestion of cronyism to promote his paintings (Sayers, *Five* 243), we are predisposed to look askance at his art. Near the beginning of the novel, and before Campbell's murder, painter Michael Waters describes him to Wimsey thus: "Oh, he can paint—after a fashion. He's what Gowan [another of the six painters] calls him—a commercial traveler. His stuff's damned impressive at first sight, but it's all tricks. Anybody could do it, given the formula. I could do a perfectly good Campbell in half an hour. Wait a moment, I'll show you" (Sayers, *Five* 8). Art hucksterism is subtly tainted by an oblique political allusion, namely, to being a *fellow*-traveler, one who ostensibly supports a doctrine without taking the risks of open adherence, and who, given unfavorable circumstances, may deny allegiance. Wimsey, under the dictates of fairness, responds: "Show me some other time. When I've seen his stuff. I can't tell if the imitation's good till I've seen the original, can I?" (Sayers, *Five* 8). Although this passage cleverly foreshadows later developments by which Wimsey's judgment is tested, it also displays an essential tenet of his belief system, namely that the original has a status by which the measure is taken. Much later in the novel, during an experiment conducted by Wimsey to determine how closely two of the suspected artists can replicate the faux-Campbell, Waters expands on

---

[14] Compare John Berger's *Ways of Seeing*, in which he discusses the obsessive concern over authenticity for holdings in the National Gallery collection (21–23).

his earlier remarks (in reference to the painting from the murder scene): "'That's exactly what one expects from the Campbells of this world,' said Waters. 'The trick degenerates into a mannerism, and they paint caricatures of their own style'" (Sayers, *Five* 253). Ironically, the painting in question is not Campbell's but the work of an imitator, and thus an actual caricature, though with Wimsey we are prone to suspect that a clever murderer might react to the painting in just this way. Jock Graham, the other artist present, and a more perceptive man than Waters, exclaims, "I should almost have thought I had done it myself. There's a slight flavour of pastiche about it. And there's a sort of—just look at those stones in the burn, Waters, and the shadow under the bridge. It's rather more cold and cobalty than Campbell's usual style" (Sayers, *Five* 254). Waters, for his part, maintains that the painting is "insincere"—again, ironically true in that it is a forgery—but an insincerity that is paradoxically characteristic of the painter Campbell's actual style: "that's exactly what I complain of in all Campbell's stuff. It makes its effect all right, but when you come to look into it, it doesn't stand up to inspection. I call that a thoroughly Campbellish piece of work. A poor Campbell, if you like, but full of Campbellisms" (Sayers, *Five* 254).

Even though we are predisposed to dislike Campbell for reasons already listed, none of the artists involved escape being tarred with the insincerity brush. While looking about Ferguson's studio, Wimsey assesses "an elaborate and mannered piece of decorative landscape" (Sayers, *Five* 31). This tendency to a copyable mannerism, with market-oriented decorative appeal, is immediately perceived by the careful scrutiny of other fellow commercial-travelers in the art market, such as Graham, who early in the novel claims that all the suspects have identifiable and even imitable styles (save himself, for a specific reason addressed in a moment). Thus, during a subsequent visit to Ferguson's studio, "Wimsey recognized the typical Ferguson of Graham's malicious description—the tree with twisted roots, the reflection, the lump of granite and blue distance and the general air of decorative unreality" (Sayers, *Five* 124). Graham, who serves as a kind of touchstone, though in terms of displaying the disingenuousness of the things he contacts rather than their truth, is in fact instrumental in undermining any uncontested notion of originality. This quality is displayed in a passage that deserves to be quoted at length:

> Graham pulled a piece of chalk from his pocket and set to work on the bar counter, his face screwed up into a lifelike imitation of Campbell's heavy jowl and puffed lips, and his hand roughing in outlines with Campbell's quick, tricky touch. The picture came up before their eyes with the conjuring quickness of a lightning-sketch at the cinema—the burn, the trees, the bridge and a mass of bulging white cloud, so like the actual canvas Wimsey had seen on the easel that he was thoroughly startled.
>
> [Wimsey:] "You ought to be making a living by impersonations, Jock."
>
> "That's my trouble. Too versatile. Paint in everybody's style except my own. Worries the critics. 'Mr. Graham is still fumbling for an individual style'—that kind of thing. But it's fun. Look, here's Gowan." (Sayers, *Five* 70)

And he proceeds to do Gowan, Ferguson, Farren, and Waters—four of the five people under suspicion.

Graham explains his "fault"—that is, his lack of a distinctive style—in terms that recollect Goux's monocentric vision. His complaint, though, stands in contrast to the later accusation of insincerity launched by the less perspectivally oriented Waters: "'the whole bunch of them have only got one gift between them that I lack, and that's the single eye, more's the pity. They're perfectly sincere, I'm not—that's what makes the difference. I tell you, Wimsey, half those damned portraits people pay me for are caricatures—only the fools don't know it. If they did, they'd rather die than sign the cheques'" (Sayers, *Five* 71). This self-appraisal, which is more at home in hard-boiled writing, and which figures in Marlowe's self-understanding in *The High Window*, indeed threatens to undermine authenticity, and thus sincerity or integrity, through self-consciousness. In short, Graham is guilty of not being identical with himself. Once a style is established and becomes self-conscious (the eye observing the eye, which implies more than one eye), then we are forced to judge between style and manneristic imitation. Both style and counterfeit draw attention to the constructedness of the original, and hence to the way in which value is ascribed. The critics who manage the art market, therefore, are interested in the marketability of the recognizable, which passes as currency in a money-oriented world. The counterfeit is not worth the investment, since it is only a token.

This discussion brings us back to a standard or measure by which to dispel the "threat" of mannerist imitation and reinvest the work with aura linked to distinctive and irreproducible artistic labor. Ultimately, the question is left hanging—the insincerity of the fake and its threat to value generally is defeated by bringing the crime home to its artist. To indicate that the skeptical overtones of the novel are in fact not to be taken too seriously, the culprit is implicated by the "evidence" of his painterly identity, detectable by other artists (Sayers, *Five* 309). Style, in the end, does point to unique identity after all. But what of the detective function in this dubious economy of meaning? Wimsey's first act as a detective proceeds along the lines we expect of the Golden Age investigator in one of its purer forms, namely, to be the factor which determines the exception (murder, not accident). He accomplishes this convincingly by demonstrating an impossibility, which is not explained until much later in the text: "Now, as I explained to you at the time, it is absolutely impossible for a painter in oils to make a picture without using flake white. It is the fundamental medium which he uses to mix with his other colours to produce various shades of light and shadow" (Sayers, *Five* 301–2). Of course, it is the missing tube of flake white that he and the police frantically search for at the start and cannot find. Taken in a broad and abstract sense, this absence points up the medium essential for the image to emerge, the one color described as "fundamental" for a vision, particularly an "authentic" vision distinguishable from other artists, to be committed to canvas. The absence which grounds meaning in the text, that is, the absence which brings the exception into vision, is that which binds together the pure elements (other tubes of paint or clues), both in the composition itself in a literal sense and in the larger social processes of the novel as the condition for initiating the investigation. The flake white is the *crochet* upon which the rightness of vision depends, and its identification is dependent upon its valuation by the detective-critic.

"I don't believe it or disbelieve it …. I don't know a damned thing about it." (Hammett, *Maltese* 491)

The absent core of value is thematically central to Dashiell Hammett's *The Maltese Falcon* (1930). In Doyle the fund guaranteeing circulation is literalized and placed on display in the bank vault; subsequently, the valuable core in a circulating, mass-produced token is brought to light. Not so with the falcon, a statuette whose promise of gold under its blackened exterior proves empty. The concluding episode of Hammett's novel demonstrates that the anxiety of 1904 has become reality in 1930, and the falcon's disappearance after 1912 encompasses the critical years. Demolishing the material aspect of the sign in the confidence of bringing its core to light no longer yields dividends—while it is in circulation, the falcon's value compels belief, but once it is arrested and surveyed, its golden core of value has vanished, raising the question as to whether it was ever there. Jasmine Yong Hall likens this investment in the object to commodity fetishism, in which "value is abstracted into exchange value in a capitalist economy" (85).[15] The absent core of value, once revealed, signifies epistemological destabilization, which the detective is incapable of rectifying. Narratives are generated, but the detective cannot ensure incontestable meaning. The end of the novel dramatizes the divestment of meaning in a token universe in which the advantages and disadvantages of certain narratives are weighed against others. In the process, meaning is uncoupled from a process of discovery; rather, it is minted as the need arises.

To be sure, the falcon initially issues the promise of intrinsic value. The narrative around commodity production and circulation uncovered by Holmes substantially widens in scope for Spade, to embrace a much broader sweep of history. Gutman's account provides the falcon with a pedigree that supposedly endorses its genuineness, a story that highlights circulation and ownership (Hammett, *Maltese* 499). The falcon's economic origins are feudal—a tribute linking a religious order with a suzerain. Its subsequent history develops under nascent capitalism and extends to the present of the novel. The enameling takes place around 1840; the statue, found in 1911 and then stolen around 1912, drops out of sight for 17 years, bringing us up to 1928. In the interim, gold backing for currency has been periodically suspended and is headed for collapse.

In 1930, the falcon has become a commodity whose market value is constantly in flux. As a discrete object, however, it shares little with the products of economic collectivism forming the social background to the novel (commodities as defined by Marx in *Capital* I). This point is worth noting, since it places modern

---

[15]   The notion of commodity fetishism here is developed by several critics; see also Thomas (263), McGurl (713), and especially Rzepka (193–94).

interpretations of the falcon within a specific frame of historical interpretation: the falcon is not a mass-produced object—it is unique, presumably created by self-directed artisan labor—surplus value and profit have not been generated around the object through exploited labor under capitalism. Value in this case is distant from the way value is thought of at its origins, whether or not these were violent, exploitive, or morally questionable by modern standards; rather, it is completely dematerialized, in that value is negotiated by competitive antagonists sight unseen. Feverish speculation threads the text, as the falcon's value responds to shifts in market conditions. And yet, significantly, the confidence with which Holmes penetrates exteriors in his single-minded pursuit of transcendental value is nowhere evident in Spade's groping towards meaning. Whereas Holmes appears to know full well that his purchase of the bust for £10 is a swindle (though one rendered "legitimate" by the owner's signing away of his interest in front of witnesses, as if this contractual relation obliterated ethical obligations), Spade is at the bargaining table, hoping to get his best price for something he knows nothing about. If we trace the shifting values ascribed to the "black ornament" (Hammett, *Maltese* 426), a phrase suggesting superfluity, we start with Cairo's bid at $5,000 (Hammett, *Maltese* 426), a price that is subsequently agreed to (Hammett, *Maltese* 433). Spade passes this figure on to Brigid, who replies that she can't match it. Later, she admits she was promised £500 for the bird, which was subsequently raised to £750 (Hammett, *Maltese* 465). In his first discussion with Gutman, Spade avers that he was offered $10,000 by Cairo (Hammett, *Maltese* 484). After Gutman's revelations, the falcon's price is raised to $25,000 now, the same later, or a percentage of its realization on the market (Hammett, *Maltese* 503). Near the end of the novel, after the principal players have assembled in Spade's apartment, the detective complains that what he is receiving is not what was earlier agreed upon. Gutman rejoins: "Yes, sir, ... but we were talking then. This is actual money, genuine coin of the realm, sir. With a dollar of this you can buy more than with ten dollars of talk" (Hammett, *Maltese* 545). In determining value, speculation is ungrounded, since at every junction, in Gutman's words, "the situation has changed" (Hammett, *Maltese* 545) and no original contract can be produced. Moreover, for most of the novel, the falcon is missing from the action; its material absence nonetheless does not quell speculation. In Goux's terms, the bottom line established by Gutman is the dismissal of symbolic or ideal forms, characterized by talk, the idle production of intrinsically meaningless signs subject to inflationary spirals, and the substitution of "coin of the realm."

Some of the economic ground discussed here has been sufficiently treated by Hall in the essay I've already cited, "Jameson, Genre, and Gumshoes: *The Maltese Falcon* as Inverted Romance." Although she does not use Goux's terminology, Hall understands the dematerialization of value as a loss of transcendental force. Money has displaced God, but money has lost its material groundedness (Hall 79); unlike the fixed nature of God anterior to the system, money only becomes meaningful in circulation. As the new primum mobile which impels movement, it ironically cannot serve as an ultimate measure. Thus, Hall astutely remarks Gutman's inability to determine the bird's value, "a value which he emphasizes is impossible to name" (83), not in the sense that a buyer won't make a bid, but that language is recognized as arbitrary (McGurl 708).

The arbitrariness of value is not necessarily connected to questions of genuineness or to counterfeiting. Ruehlmann's assessment of the characters in *The Maltese Falcon* as counterfeits is plausible (74); however, the bird itself cannot be termed a counterfeit since the values generated around the figurine are merely nominal; we have no anchored basis of comparison, only Gutman's story, which itself may be pure fabrication. Thomas, in an otherwise perceptive passage, also seems misled on this point, terming the last incarnation of the falcon "a counterfeit imitation of the original object" (263)—though the whole idea of original object only arises in language. Given the general untrustworthiness of the characters, we lack sufficient knowledge to erect a standard of truth that compels consensus. In fact, the stories and speculation all turn out to be worthless scrip; none can be verified by the authority of the detective's ratiocinative processes, arcane knowledge, or naked power, much less a scientifically grounded methodology. Spade's suspicions of Gutman's tale compel him to consult an expert, Effie's cousin, who teaches history at a university—he takes recourse to disciplinary knowledge, placing enough faith in the people who wield it to declare whether the story is "probable," "possible," "even barely possible," or "bunk" (Hammett, *Maltese* 507). This sort of self-conscious recourse to techniques grounded in institutional practices (discursive formations, disciplinary knowledge, legal authority, scientific methodology, legitimate police powers) does not so much supplement the detective's faulty or incomplete knowledge as draw these epistemological certainties into the maelstrom of doubt. Just as the falcon can only be counterfeited if we assume a genuine original, so does such knowledge appear to be built on sand once the ideological interests of disciplinary knowledge are laid bare. And finally, Gutman's tale is a perspective on value very much embedded in the early twentieth century, as are the responses it elicits in Spade (Rzepka 193). Although the original valuation is feudal—the tributary relation linking a religious order with a monarchal lord—the drift of the story emphasizes the economic metamorphoses traceable since the beginnings of capitalism to the present of the novel, where, in Marling's phrase, the falcon indeed serves as an "emblem of speculation" (139). This trajectory has already reached a high level of maturity by the time we turn to Chandler's engagement with the theme: the problems of genuineness, value, and circulation connected to the coin in *The High Window*.

"The story doesn't ring true." (Chandler, *High Window* 1106)

The High Window (1942) was not Chandler's favorite novel (Gardiner and Walker 211),[16] and some weaknesses, such as character development and plausibility, do

---

[16] Critics are mixed, though perhaps more favorable than unfavorable. Peter Wolfe calls it an "artistic failure" (161) and a "misfire" (236); Durham, however, dismisses Chandler's self-assessment and terms the book "one of his better novels" (43), as does Merrill ("Raymond Chandler's Plots" 5).

detract from its effect. The work bears a family resemblance to *The Big Sleep*, both in its beads-on-a-string development and its two-part structure. As in the earlier novel, Marlowe quickly brings the job for which he is hired to a close, but ends up plowing on to wrap up what he feels to be an incomplete investigation. This incompletion does not hinge upon assembling sufficient evidence within a frame already posited hypothetically by the omniscient detective; rather, the curtailment of vision disables such authoritative knowledge. Jameson also sees a link between *The High Window* and *The Big Sleep*, though in terms of Carmen's nude pictures rather than narrative development; he claims: "the Brasher Doubloon would seem to be a regression from the nude photographs of *The Big Sleep*, replacing the technological image with older forms of minted value and thereby threatening a slippage back into the more romantic formulas of the older Hammett narrative, with its falcons and curses" ("Synoptic" 38–39). Jameson consistently offers keen insights into Chandler, but this assertion is weak. The relation to *The Maltese Falcon* concerns the problems of ascribing value to the coin, which is both in and out of circulation, in and out of the economy, viewed and valued as a material object and a dematerialized aestheticism. As the novel develops, the coin's aesthetic, intrinsic, and potentially token value are jumbled, much like the confusion over character identity. Furthermore, the coin is the product of a defunct artisan labor which is counterfeited by modern scientific techniques, techniques good enough to threaten the loss of the original; finally, the coin is valuable as a unique object which ends up being mass produced for the purposes of fraud. Most of these problems function within the purview of Goux's theoretical writings.

The story, though convoluted, is not as complex as that in *The Big Sleep*, probably because unlike that work or most of the subsequent novels, *The High Window* did not involve cannibalizing existing shorter texts drawn from the pulps. Despite a greater degree of plot unity, the restricted vision and almost blind forward momentum characterizing *The Big Sleep* is maintained. Marlowe is hired by the wealthy and imposing Elizabeth Murdock to quietly recover a valuable stolen coin called the Brasher Doubloon, a prize specimen from her second husband's coin collection. Mrs. Murdock believes the coin to have been stolen by her daughter-in-law, Linda Conquest, either out of spite or in order to raise funds to desert her son, Leslie Murdock. She wants Linda located discreetly, without police involvement or social notoriety. In tracking down the coin, Marlowe meets a dangerous nightclub owner, Alex Morny, his wife, Lois Magic, and her lover, Lou Vannier, all of whom play a role in subsequent developments; Marlowe also gets tangled up with Lieutenant Breeze because he discovers two bodies, one which he doesn't report, while working on the case—both corpses are left in the wake of the missing coin. In the end, Vannier, too, ends up dead, killed by Leslie Murdock (though he is not brought to justice)—we find that Vannier had been blackmailing Mrs. Murdock for years with photographic evidence that she had killed her first husband, a crime that, puzzlingly, she had convinced her repressed young secretary, Merle Davis, that she (Merle) had committed. The coin is recovered, having turned out to be involved in a counterfeiting scam, but the criminals who survive go free and, unsurprisingly, the entire cast is criminally implicated, except Merle Davis, who, ironically, attempts to confess to a shooting she didn't commit.

Detection does not comprise the most interesting parts of this narrative: the search for the lost person, which is satisfactorily concluded a quarter of the way in, was never a major challenge, nor does the lost coin pose a significant puzzle—and although there is low-level ratiocination on Marlowe's part, we are not confronted with a perplexing clue-puzzle. None of this matters much to our study of the novel, whose most pronounced weakness is probably the lack of development around the principal villain, Vannier, with whom we have virtually no relation. Although he is clearly unsympathetic, we don't get close enough to despise Vannier with gusto— we dismiss him as an adulterer, a murderer, and a blackmailer, but his victims are not sympathetic either. The clues that finally lead to Vannier are frustratingly chance-dependent—a receipt that just happens to fall out of a pocket, a picture that just happens to fall off a wall, revealing a photograph that just happened to have been taken at the right time to prove a murder. Many of these plot "problems" are critically described by Steven Weisenburger in "Order, Error, and the Novels of Raymond Chandler" (18); he has the good sense not to dismiss them as the marks of an inferior novel but sees them as suggestive of something lying beyond a demand for verisimilitude.

For my purpose the central problem of the story is the coin and its curious, enforced noncirculation—in this respect, the coin is an object that does not correspond to its concept for more than one reason. First, the legality of the coin as tender is a barrier, not only because by 1942 gold was not circulating but also because of the nonstandard aspect of the coin; its distinctiveness is reason to remove it from the money supply. Its nonstandardness is not only a product of a variation in its form. The coin was not minted but produced by a cumbersome and obsolete artisan process which introduced discrepancies and inconsistencies, resulting in coins which were nonidentical.[17] Instead of machine-based mass production, a human element enters the equation, emphasized by the fact that the maker's name distinguishes the coin (the Brasher Doubloon). This personalization goes deeper in that the unusually perfect condition of the coin, a result of never having been in circulation, gives it a double moniker: the Murdock Brasher. Furthermore, the coin is locked up by the direction of a will, which prohibits its sale during Mrs. Murdock's lifetime—legally barring it from entering the marketplace or enabling exchange value, even if it were capable of doing so. The counterfeit scheme launched by Vannier and his accomplice, a dentist who can "mass" produce copies of the coin using dental gold-molding techniques, involves making many copies of this unique coin to sell discreetly as originals.[18] Unlike normal counterfeiting,

---

[17]   In this, it bears comparison with the philatelic content of Ellery Queen's *The Chinese Orange Mystery* and G.T. Fleming-Robert's Diamondstone story "The Crime Conductor."

[18]   This plan is reproduced in the revision of "The Final Problem" for the Jeremy Brett Sherlock Holmes television series. Moriarty engineers the theft of the *Mona Lisa*, not for the purpose of selling it, but to sell a number of clever forgeries, thus obtaining its value

this mass production of a token is not equal to its face value, its nominal value, less its value as a metal or a function of craftsmanship; rather, its uniqueness makes it worth whatever the market will bear. Thus, the value of the Doubloon is not understood by the interested parties as a material value, a point made by confronting someone not in the know with the coin. We witness this process in the scenes at the pawnshop. The pawnshop owner initially ignores the aesthetic or collector's view of the coin—instead he determines that it is gold, weighs it, and bargains over its worth, not even giving Marlowe its full value as gold (Chandler, *High Window* 1061). Neither does the cost of labor get expressed in the coin's value, since it costs more to manufacture than the market price of the metal, given that it is not produced through the cheaper modern minting process. Indeed, the ambiguity of the coin is expressed by its very appearance, related to us by the dealer Morningstar, in that the coin's reverse "showed a sun rising or setting behind a sharp peak of mountain" (Chandler, *High Window* 1056).

The value of the gold coin fluctuates as it changes hands on its illicit itinerary. Its price is subjected to haggling between Marlowe and Morningstar, between Leslie Murdock and Morny, and between Marlowe and the pawnbroker. Value is a matter of talk—the sales pitch of those hawking the counterfeits, or, more "legitimately" and, as Morningstar remarks, "[the coin] would have to have a history, of course" (Chandler, *High Window* 1031). The narrative drive suggests the convergence of the coin and the falcon, but it also shows up the complexity of both objects, especially the coin's gold content in the context of gold's function as general equivalent. Gold's self-identity is never at stake in *The Maltese Falcon*, since it turns out that all we end up with is talk—again, there is no counterfeit, since we have nothing to prove an original save Gutman's history and a string of corpses. In *The High Window* we have the reality of gold's non-self-identity as indicated by the three haggling points raised above. The coin is overvalued in that the cost of labor and materials exceeds their market price (a point recognized explicitly by Marlowe [Chandler, *High Window* 1162]); the coin is undervalued since in the real economy weak participants submit to unfavorable terms (Marlowe's interaction with the pawnbroker); finally, the coin is indeterminate: this last point, which is the most important, requires some explanation. The coin's value is problematic because it does *not* circulate; it is in enforced noncirculation which normally shouldn't be a problem, since as an ingot or piece of a treasury, gold can function to guarantee the circulation of tokens, whether they are convertible or not. The coin does not serve this function, however, and has never done so since it hasn't entered the market in use, that is, until it disappears. At this point, its value is immediately unclear. Leslie's claim that he stole the coin to satisfy a debt to Morny is weak—in response to this story Marlowe appropriately remarks: "The story doesn't ring true" (Chandler, *High Window* 1106). The coin is difficult to convert *into* money, given the restrictions on its sale; its value is market-determined.

---

several times over. The original painting's presence in the Louvre determines the value (or valuelessness) of any copy in circulation. Holmes aids the French government in recovering the original to reestablish the measure by which counterfeits are exposed.

And Morningstar's illegal possession of the coin, purchased for $1,000, allows him to profit to the tune of $200 on the promise of a quick turnaround by selling the object back to its rightful owners without scandal.

In this indeterminate mode, the coin's problematic relation to self, Chandler finds a metaphor that places the story beyond the metafictional ploys of Golden Age texts. With some frequency, the Golden Age detective compares his or her own activity to the activities of other (still fictional) confreres in contemporaneous detective novels, so that the dialogue is peppered with references, praiseful or critical, to Sherlock Holmes, Philo Vance, or, in the most extreme case, a 50-name reference list in Clayton Rawson's *Death from a Top Hat* (a passage, incredibly enough, appearing in an in-text essay claiming that the age of detective fiction is over). Occasionally, the detective is identified as a character in such fiction—this rare device appears most notably in "The Locked Room Lecture" from *The Three Coffins* and Edmund Crispin's *The Moving Toyshop*. The gesture of situating the text, however, is not an act of self-depreciation to suggest that the text is mere copy, a counterfeit of "serious" literature, of gold language reduced to an empty token. In contrast, Chandler's self-referential gesture, rare for the hard-boiled as a rule, has more serious consequences that draw attention to a general fakeness (reaching greater heights in Chandler's anti-Hollywood diatribes in *The Little Sister*). The cast of characters serves to demonstrate this principle, from the ludicrous stage names Lois Magic and Linda Conquest (both of whom unconvincingly "play" at being wives), to the pathetic and ineffectual tough-guy act of Leslie Murdock when he first encounters Marlowe, to the blundering and fatally ill-acted part of the sham detective George Philips, to the ex-actor, now nightclub owner/gambling den operator A.P. Morny. In this last case, the fake is humorously underscored by Morny's swank address in a neighborhood where he is certainly out of place, having "acquired" the property through calling in a gambling debt. Marlowe has to identify his place by a gate bearing the initials of the house's former occupant; Morny's name, more appropriately, appears on the service entrance.

At about the point where Marlowe finds Linda (his initial task) and convinces himself that she is not involved in the theft of the coin, *The High Window* loops back on itself in a way we might expect from the Golden Age, though remaining distinct through its cynical idiom. Marlowe remarks to Linda:

> "What I like about this place [Morny's club] is everything runs so true to type" .... "The cop on the gate, the shine on the door, the cigarette and check girls, the fat greasy sensual Jew with the tall stately bored showgirl, the well-dressed, drunk and horribly rude director cursing the barman, the silent guy with the gun, the night club owner with the soft gray hair and the B-picture mannerisms, and now you—the tall dark torcher with the negligent sneer, the husky voice, the hard-boiled vocabulary."

To which Linda responds:

> "And what about the wise-cracking snooper with the last year's gags and the come-hither smile?" (Chandler, *High Window* 1093)

This dialogue, in effect, closes up the first, "official" part of the investigation. It should be taken in conjunction with a second passage near the end of the book, this time in dialogue with Leslie Murdock, which essentially closes off the last murder and brings together a set of relations that allows us to explain everything, or at least to believe we can. In this interview, the uncommunicative Leslie submits to Marlowe's summing up with the remark:

> "All right .... Get on with it. I have a feeling you are going to be very brilliant. Remorseless flow of logic and intuition and all that rot. Just like in a detective book."

To which Marlowe rejoins:

> "Sure. Taking the evidence piece by piece, putting it all together in a neat pattern, sneaking in an odd bit I had on my hip here and there, analyzing the motives and characters and making them out to be quite different from what anybody—or I myself for that matter—thought them to be up to this golden moment—and finally making a sort of world-weary pounce on the least promising suspect." (Chandler, *High Window* 1160)

Like the coin, Marlowe's circulation through society (high and low) and markets (a legitimate and shadow economy of shady businessmen, gamblers, and gigolos) can no longer amount to Goux's circulation of the general equivalent. Marlowe, too, is a sham, and not just through the attempted debasing of status by detractors (Leslie Murdock) or tired cynics who have abandoned faith in a gold standard (Linda Conquest and Doctor Moss, source of the oft-cited reference to Marlowe as a "shop-soiled Galahad"). Perhaps we long for a genuineness that distinguishes him from copies of the coin manufactured by the dentist, Teager, a real value amongst the false equality of sameness, but we also remember that, in what amounts almost to a throwaway line, Teager could only distinguish the "real" coin by a tiny mark etched on its surface. Marlowe is unable to guarantee or, like Teager, inscribe the truths that he discovers in any public forum, partly because he cannot fathom them himself, despite the fact that his proximity to crime sets him up to take the rap. Midway through, he thinks to himself: "Marlowe practically knee-deep in dead men. And no reasonable, logical, friendly account of himself whatsoever" (Chandler, *High Window* 1140). Even when he is able to piece together a coherent narrative, he fails at convincing Merle Davis of her innocence and the reprehensible duplicity of her employer.

Marlowe is subject to the vicissitudes of the marketplace, first of all by Mrs. Murdock's complaints about his fee, later in being tempted by Morny with $500, which he turns down to pursue what he ends up doing for free, namely, finding the dirt on Vannier. The labor Marlowe puts into the investigation seems to exceed the going market rate, notwithstanding its volatile character, and thus, like the counterfeit coin, its very materiality falls short of the costs of production. Marlowe cannot function as the circulating equivalent in the way we expect of omniscient Golden Age types who are able to escape the bounds of a (potentially dirty) material existence for a transcendental ideality outside the restrictive social boundaries wherein transgression is managed. However, he can function to point up the absence of such equivalents and the far more compelling forces of wealth and authority that establish frames of reference in the service of interest groups. To close, we may once more cite Goux:

> What we have here is a change in the principle of *legitimation*, a change that reverberates far beyond literature—so far as to transform the sociosymbolic regime itself. It is as if we are witnessing a shift from a legitimation based *on the exchange of equivalents* and on *representation* ... to another type of legitimation, still tentative, that seeks to found itself directly on the production process itself, or, still more profoundly, on the site of Measures, which holds the meaning of this process. (*Coiners* 77)

This form of legitimation, as I will pursue it in the next two chapters, is connected to detective labor, which, like the discussion of knowledge and value so far, has distinct tendencies within the subgenres.

Chapter 5
Detective Labor

The Puzzle of Detective Labor

Few professions are tracked with the intensity of the detective story. Although other types of work are sometimes the focus of fiction, these occupations are distinguished by publicly established institutional frames and general familiarity. Virtually everyone has direct experience of military personnel, doctors, or lawyers; detectives are not a populous class of labor, neither do they have a clear institutional status, save a vague connection to police work. Likely, this inexperience with detective labor facilitates representations that would not pass muster for more common professions. The difficulty of situating the detective among the professional classes does not comfortably relegate him or her to the world of wage or salaried labor either. Time and production are not subject to calculation, since detective work is normally irreducible to measurable units (notwithstanding the hard-boiled cliché of $25 per day plus expenses). The retainer cannot be converted into a piece rate for truth, which resists expressions in quanta. Moreover, the extension of work beyond any promise of remuneration generally places the detective outside the bourgeois economic frame, in which work is commodified as a time-linked disposal of labor power. Freedman and Kendrick raise some of these ideas in the context of *Red Harvest*:

> [T]he labor of the Continental Op himself is a paradigm of the "liberated" activity that constitutes an important part of detective fiction. For detective work might almost be called a bohemian kind of labor: as work that frees the worker from the homogenized space-time of most capitalist labor and that in so doing brings the powers of the "whole man" at least potentially into play, detective work is a peculiarly nonalienated variety of labor. (13)

The satisfaction of detective labor therefore seems to lie in the convergence of one's "nature" and one's paid activity. Audrey Jaffe expresses this thought concisely in respect to Holmes, who serves as "a fantasy of professionalism as unalienated labor" and "a figure for whom slavishness cannot be an issue because his work … is the complete expression of his nature" (425). This assessment runs contrary to the suspicion that investigative work is a tedious, fact-finding grind in which trained personnel analyze minutiae, never seeing the big picture, never single-handedly solving a case, and frequently consigned to failure. Yet these suspicions are overthrown for the pleasure of the text, not merely in its denouement but in the process of tracing the devious pathways of a coveted unalienated labor. Although the curious status of detective labor is recognized by a number of critics, especially in relation to hard-boiled fiction,[1] a sustained and general inquiry into such work which incorporates Classical/Golden Age fiction is absent from the scholarship.

The level of self-determination in the labor process and the application of and control over knowledge by individuals in the production of outcomes suggest an affinity between the detective and the craftsman or artisan. Despite the similarities, the period of the detective story's ascendency corresponds to massive and unprecedented upheavals in the rhythms and scope of individual labor, both in Europe and in the United States, a period in which the artisan was definitively on the wane. Historically, the rise of detective fiction parallels the intensive development of capitalist markets and modes of labor, a fact acknowledged in studies by Thomas (3–4) and McCann (6–7), yet the status of detective work within this system is at best ambiguous inasmuch as such labor produces no durable commodities; its practitioners are subjected to neither time clock nor rationally calculable wage scale. There are no detective unions, and few detectives are subordinated to managerial hierarchies. Fictional detective work remains untouched by dilution or Taylorist analysis; in short, it represents a pocket of labor whose product (the solution) retains, if not depends upon, the unmistakable traces of the worker's identity.[2] As if to offset these advantages, the detective is often notoriously ill-compensated, yet rarely interrogates or resists the compulsion to work. The unresolved dialectic internal to detective labor, whose form in fact does *not* serve self-evidently to distinguish the subgenres, concerns the conflict between the expectation of a return (investment or debt) and unrecompensed expenditure (the rejection of rational calculation, even up to the point of death). The Golden Age gravitates towards an economic conservationism of structure in its entropy-resisting hermetic crime scenes, whereas hard-boiled writers of the Hammett variety depict a spiral of escalating, system-threatening expenditure (ideas developed in Chapters 2 and 3, respectively). In terms of labor, the subgenres overlap in the detective's willingness to work for nothing.[3] The common ground by which to measure this tendency and its social outcomes is the gift; at the same time, the social nature of this gift serves to differentiate subgenres. Simply put, the Classical/Golden Age tends to employ the apparent gift-character of much detective labor as an investment, which potentially reinscribes the gift within an economic regime; in contrast, the hard-boiled tends towards the dialectic of purposeful unrewarded labor and extravagant expenditure, which turns out to be much closer to aneconomic definitions of the gift arising in poststructuralist

---

[1]   Sample analyses are found in Freedman and Kendrick generally; Willett (6); Erin Smith (98); Hartman (224); Bargainnier (51); Hilgart (374); and Broe (182).

[2]   Critics who term detective labor *non-alienated* or *unalienated* include Freedman and Kendrick (13, 22) and Jaffe (425). Others imply it: Knight (*Crime* 113); Porter (*Pursuit* 179); Erin Smith (102); and Stephen Marcus (206).

[3]   Porter (*Pursuit* 179) and especially Žižek (41) overstate the case for remuneration. Others, such as Atkinson (15) and Knight (*Crime* 113), take a more balanced view.

thought, particularly as found in theoretical work by Jacques Derrida and Jean-Joseph Goux.

The gift-character of detective labor, in tandem with the problems of expenditure and value, is a structural principle rather than a thematic problem; it evokes Terry Eagleton's notion of ideology in *Marxism and Literary Criticism*, as well as Marc Shell's understanding of the economy of the text in *The Economy of Literature*. As a built-in principle, the transcendent mastery of a Sherlock Holmes, or other omniscient-type detective, contrives formally to venture without risk, never entertaining the real possibility of loss. The detective's regulative role, in fact, undergirds the subgenre's cherished illusion of a return to order, the idyllic sameness of a society restored through the detective's efforts.[4] In contrast, the gift as it figures in the hard-boiled canon repeatedly assumes the form of labor betrayed through the marked ingratitude of a criminal or deviant beneficiary. The volatile compound of intimacy and obligation meshes uncomfortably with the indifferent "freedom" of market relations, so that the hero's loss—for instance, Marlowe's virtuous social marginalization in Auden's "Great Wrong Place" (19)—ironically reestablishes the status quo he negates. The Classical and Golden Age structure tends to support the investment character of gift-labor. The hard-boiled tends to represent the gift as unrewarded and even socially rejected labor.

From Work to Alienation

Sociologist Kai Erikson offers three evaluative criteria to clarify our understanding of alienation vis-à-vis labor. The first entails a loss of meaning in work, either in feelings of subordination to machines or mechanical processes or to the dictates of a managerial class which controls the process, its speed, and the timeframes of the work experience, particularly to the point that intellectual content is atrophied. Secondly, alienation involves the effects of competition that undermine community. The final source of alienation, while rarely surfacing in the Classical or Golden Age subgenres, is relevant to the hard-boiled, namely, the separation of individuals from "their own nature as members of the human species" (Erikson 22). This tripartite division—relation to the product, relation to others, and relation to self—serves as a foundation for testing the levels of alienation present in the detective.

Definitions of work are typically tied to socially mediated constructions of value. Despite profound changes in the nature of work today, the inherited dominant ideology maintains work to be absolutely necessary, "the only relevant source and the only valid measure for the evaluation of human beings and their activities" (Beck

---

4   The view that the Classical and Golden Age detective enables a return to order is endorsed with reservations by Aydelotte (70), Hilfer (xiii), and Margolies (5) and generally supported by Erin Smith (86), Klein (5), Bargainnier (10), and Mahan (2). McCann (91) and Rabinowitz (120) are among the few scholars who assess this claim critically.

10).[5] At the beginning of the twentieth century, the gigantic investment in fixed capital expenditure tremendously increased the productive capacity of industry so that overproduction and, increasingly, underconsumption led to widening cycles of disemployment between booms in which relative unemployment, euphemistically understood as "normal unemployment," rose markedly. David Montgomery, in his survey of nineteenth- and early twentieth-century labor, *Workers' Control in America*, indicates conflict areas that throw light on detective work. Montgomery's research into the status of US labor and the history of labor relations between workers and a burgeoning managerial class suggests that laborers had significant independence in the second half of the nineteenth century, due primarily to their generally skilled status. Increases in scale and, significantly, the introduction of methods derived from time-motion studies had deleterious effects on levels of worker control and produced antagonism between plant owners and labor unions. The precarious position of the worker arose from "dilution," which itself was partly an outcome of scientific management—the shift of knowledge and the power it entails into managerial hands, where it was further atomized. Though Frederick Taylor's *Shop Management* was not published until 1913 and was only implemented piecemeal at first (Montgomery 113), the scientific management of the workplace in terms of increasing efficiency had been practiced in England for some time. Taylorist applications "had found favor in almost every industry by the mid-1920s" (Montgomery 113), which places its widespread growth concurrent not only with the explosion of hard-boiled American detective stories, but also the precursors to the Golden Age, as well as the Golden Age itself. Although the three focal points identified by Montgomery—"management's standardization of tasks, the conversion of laborers into machine tenders, and the controversy over incentive pay schemes and job classifications" (114)—had particular relevance for readers of the American pulps, the large-scale consolidations of monopoly capitalism in fact touched a much broader readership, including the more white-collar, middle-class audiences of Golden Age fiction.

Although it seems evident that Dupin could only emerge in a relatively developed capitalist society (given the story's police methods and modes of media reporting), Dupin's and Holmes's societies in fact reflect different moments in the development of capitalism. Poe is certainly a visionary, but in terms of labor, Dupin is disengaged from the realities of either American or French society—Holmes, on the other hand, reflects the beginnings of a newly emerging class

---

[5]   The mismatch between this ideological position and the realities of modern productive capacity are documented in many sources. A concise historical overview appears in Stanley Aronowitz and William DiFazio's *The Jobless Future* under the subheading "From Craft Era to Fordism" (26–30). Other general treatments include André Gorz's *Reclaiming Work: Beyond the Wage-Based Society* and *Paths to Paradise: On the Liberation from Work* and Maurice Godelier's essay "Some Things You Give, Some Things You Sell, but Some Things You Must Keep for Yourselves." For a discussion of the modern sociopolitical effects of this ideology in an American context, see Joel Handler and Yeheskel Hasenfeld's *We the Poor People: Work, Poverty, and Welfare.*

structure at the beginning of monopoly capitalism. Poe's era was the zenith of a chaotic competitive capitalism, which favored confrontation in the marketplace between small-scale producers. By the last decades of the nineteenth century, capital had become concentrated in combinatory forms (trusts) which increased the scale of production and began to manage the entire productive process, from the extraction of raw materials to the marketing of finished products. To offset a tendency towards declining rates of profit, cartels crushed small competitors and eventually reached agreements, secret or tacit, to stabilize or manipulate prices to insure constant rates of return. With the increased role of banking institutions and the general internationalization of operations, enormous concerns developed that had little in common with the myth of the self-made man in the fledgling United States or the rugged individualist bent on the conquest of the American West. This latest stage of capitalism was already perceived by bourgeois economists and summed up in 1916 by Lenin in his widely read treatise *Imperialism, the Highest Stage of Capitalism*. Despite attempts to impose controls on monopolistic practices, governments themselves eventually succumbed, since State policy could hardly resist the powerful interests embodied in their gigantic economic operations.[6] A relevant question concerns the status of detective labor and the class interests or complicity of the detective-worker with these dominant social and institutional power formations.

In the early stages of capitalist development, the social division of labor, though implying a measure of specialization, was still linked to completeness in terms of knowledge and a direct relation to the total work process. This earlier configuration differed from the detailed division of labor which reached much more radical forms under Taylorism. As a result of scientific management, the partitioning of tasks, the integration of machine and human labor, and intensified levels of scrutiny were applied to all labor processes in a complex social milieu. The transformation of nineteenth-century competitive capitalism during the Progressive Era into monopoly capitalism was, for those in the middle and bottom levels of society, a shift (often a loss) in skills as artisan labor was transformed into semiskilled wage work. From the end of the nineteenth century, the decline in self-employment or entrepreneurialism was marked, despite the widely believed myth of unlimited opportunity in the United States (Braverman 53). The demands of efficiency occasioned "the separation of hand and brain" (Braverman 126), first in heavy industry and subsequently in management and office work (Braverman 307–8; Mills, *White* 196).

---

[6] Useful historical and contemporary sources on this transformation include Lewis Corey's *The Decline of American Capitalism* and *The Crisis of the Middle Class*, Paul Baran and Paul Sweezy's *Monopoly Capital: An Essay on the American Economic and Social Order*, Harry Braverman's *Labor and Monopoly Capitalism: The Degradation of Work in the Twentieth Century*, and Jeremy Rifkin's *The End of Work: The Decline of the Global Labor Force and the Dawn of the Post-Market Era*.

The exploitive potential of scientific management is obscured by its compelling argument for efficiency (Doray 131), which potentially gives rise to ambivalence in those whose stated aim is the welfare of the worker. Lenin, for instance, though deploring Taylor's ideological commitments, was enthusiastic about his system.[7] Despite gains in output, for the worker, Taylorism results in atomization to meet the "higher goal" of economic collectivism, or in Taylor's own words, "under scientific management absolutely every element in the work of every man in your establishment, sooner or later, becomes the subject of exact, precise, scientific investigation and knowledge" (52). The nature of this knowledge, however, is unavailable to those engaged in the process itself, which has fundamentally lost meaning. Given this depressing experience of work, it seems unsurprising that wage earners of all sorts would feel compelled to "escape" into detective fiction of any type, into representations of work which offer a completeness unavailable to the great majority of its readers in real life.

The detective's all-encompassing relation to action is the means to achieve completeness of knowledge. Detective labor is non-alienated labor inasmuch as the worker is linked, at virtually every step, to both process and solution. Whether the truth is restricted to private consumption or publicly circulated, some degree of closure is conferred upon the work process. This public/private divide has little structural importance to labor and its relation to production, production that after all relies largely, if not exclusively, upon the detective's ratiocinative and/ or physical efforts. Despite some duplicity amongst the Classical and Golden Age detectives, we typically are rewarded with public, institutionally sanctioned disclosures. Hard-boiled outcomes of the Chandleresque sort are more likely to be divided between a narrative for general consumption and a private reserve of truth hidden away under institutional lock and key. Although the impulse to arrive at a solution may dominate many readers' interest in the genre, much of the focus is on the labor behind the process of disclosure: the ways it is initiated and conducted, boundaries drawn, and the endorsement of interests that subtend it. The valorization of socially useful labor, which in fact defines an activity as labor, threatens to deprive the detective of control over the public outcomes of his or her efforts. An example of this problem is the double-bluff played on Marlowe by the police in *The Long Goodbye*: in that novel the fantasy of detective labor which escapes the alienating effects brought about by a loss of control is effectively laid to rest.

Even before Marlowe is subjected to this ruse, the price of non-alienated labor in Chandler's world is "heroic" poverty, which confers upon him Erikson's second criterion of alienation (self to other). Marlowe's lonely closing remarks in *The Big Sleep, Farewell My Lovely*, and *The Long Goodbye* say as much. Throughout the novels, his decision to remain aloof from community, whether or not this is

---

[7]   Lenin's notes on Taylor's *Shop Management* appear in his unpublished *Notebooks on Imperialism* from 1916 (152–56) and in an even more striking and developed form in the unpublished version of "The Immediate Tasks of the Soviet Government" (79–80).

actually a choice, is also a decision to remain connected to self and to a modicum of control over the process by which his labor is conducted. Formulated this way, we question whether his detachment differs substantially from the outsider status (transcendence) suggested by the Classical and Golden Age figures (indeed, Porter places Spade and Marlowe "outside the system" [*Pursuit* 179]). In both cases, though, we observe how the problematic relation to community is the condition by which community is sustained—the gift of labor which buttresses such enclosures, but which ideologically includes or excludes, lauds or denigrates that labor.

The gift is the continuation of the labor process in the face of institutional- or client-mediated closure or in the open-ended expenditure of labor outside the promise or guarantee of any return. This is the true basis of Bataillian expenditure for the hard-boiled hero—it is symbolic and differs sharply from the practice of real expenditure, which is merely narrowly symptomatic (for instance, alcoholic excess or violence). The former type of expenditure is labor irreducible to the norms of capitalist economics. This important distinction illustrates the divide between mere content-based evidence pointing towards excess to a structural principle, connected also to the first-person narrative as an act of writing. The determination to circumvent or exceed the economy in terms of use or exchange value is characterized by the inability to call a stop to the investigation, a structural point recognized by Knight, though understood partly as a commitment to "justice" (*Crime* 113), and, we might add, as the detective's means of escaping Erikson's first and third forms of alienation. Thus, Knight concludes that "though the private eye is a professional—a paid worker like most people—he is not, in the crucial part of the story, an employee: his time, his courage, above all his values, are controlled by himself" (*Crime* 113).

Labor in the Classical Analytic Story

If we regard Poe's Dupin stories as the definitive origin of detective fiction, we cannot ignore the fact that the representation of labor and its motives are inconsistent and problematic from the onset—inconsistent even given the brevity of the series. Dupin is the great nonworker, a fact underscored by his pretense to an aristocratic heritage that holds labor in disdain. His personality, predilection for nocturnal ramblings, and dilettantish nature also interfere with the regular rhythms of employment. Dupin's willingness to perform investigative work sends mixed signals: he enters the fray when a friend is threatened by a false accusation in "The Murders in the Rue Morgue"; in contrast, his involvement in "The Purloined Letter" seems motivated by the promise of a large reward, laced, of course, with scorn for the Prefect's ineffectuality. Dupin, unlike Holmes, makes no claim that work is its own reward. To be sure, William Crisman locates in the trajectory of the Dupin trilogy a tendency towards "an increasing professionalism" (215), which indicates a fissure at the beginning of the genre between the disinterested search for truth and the desire to profit. This dialectic dimly foreshadows the New Class professional appearing later in the nineteenth century, but it is only tangentially important to

Dupin himself. Unlike Holmes, who as far we know has no claims to old money or an aristocratic pedigree, Dupin regards himself, notwithstanding his poverty, as heir to aristocratic sensibilities, bowing only grudgingly to circumstances. We note, however, that the labors of both Dupin and Holmes have at best a shaky relation to utility. Alvin Gouldner reminds us that the nineteenth century gave birth to a concept of usefulness which gauged itself against the nobility: "the useful were those whose lives manifestly did not turn on a round of leisure and entertainment, but who worked at routine economic roles in which they produced marketable goods and services" (*Coming Crisis* 64). The nineteenth-century middle-class view, which became a social standard in western Europe generally, would likely have had trouble fully digesting Dupin (the aristocrat) or Holmes (the intermittent worker), or indeed Watson (the loafing invalid), were they to appear outside of fiction. In the end, Holmes's work is marginalized because true labor is "energy expended in conformity to some cultural requirement or standard, a norm" (Gouldner, *Future* 27).[8] As I have demonstrated, this marginality should be read as buttressing the homogeneous field of productive relations.

Whether or not there is a reward, we easily forget that the detective is working for someone and that "*all* working ... remains always in principle a working for, which is entirely other than a being-with" (Shershow 76)—this working-for and being-with is commonly conflated inasmuch as ideologically mandated interests are served. At the same time, the detective, who by haughtiness, bohemianism, or intellectual tour-de-force camouflages the working-for in the Classical/Golden Age formula, is by virtue of eccentricity someone with whom being-with proves difficult. Save for some ultimate social goal, his or her outsider status problematizes the ontological relation on the personal level, a situation that holds for both Classical and Golden Age labor. Looking to the Golden Age, Robin Goodman recognizes this point structurally when she singles out Lord Peter Wimsey, Miss Marple, and Sherlock Holmes as "protected from the law," "marginal to the economy," and "outside the wage system," respectively (33)—in short, on the fringes of what passes for work. If, as she continues, they end up endorsing the State's "rule of law," they do so as a function of not being fully integrated into that State. Their forms of labor, in fact, place them outside: Lord Peter as the flush aristocrat, Miss Marple in her complete absorption into the private sphere (narrowed further by her age and absence of family responsibilities), and Holmes in his (public) renunciation of both wage labor and membership in any established profession—the first, and presumably only, consulting detective, as he is wont to tell us in *A Study in Scarlet*. Holmes. As with Holmes, the same distinction applies to Craig Kennedy in the Arthur B. Reeve series, who is idealized in his submission to a system of self-negating work, and whose arcane knowledge is just an esoteric version of submitting himself body and soul to the demands of the workplace. Kennedy, like Holmes, represses anything that obscures that devotion.

---

    [8]   James Werner's characterization is apt in terms of "[Holmes's] indolence as regards 'productive' and 'socially valuable' labor" (10; see also Rzepka 76).

The position is summed up by Futrelle's Professor Van Dusen in "The Problem of the Crystal Gazer" in his remark to a client: "I never accept fees .... I interest myself in affairs like these because I like them. They are good mental exercise" (274).[9] Another early detective figure, Dr. Thorndyke, likewise judges the value of cases on their intrinsic merits—his attraction to what he believes will become textbook cases. Thus, he instructs Dr. Berkeley in *The Eye of Osiris* (1911) to "make it clear to him [an impoverished client] that I am doing this entirely for the enlargement of my own knowledge" (Freeman 74).[10]

In a text like "The Adventure of the Speckled Band" Holmes downplays money while espousing a work-for-work's-sake philosophy, evident in his remarks to his client: "As to reward, my profession is its own reward; but you are at liberty to defray whatever expenses I may be put to, at the time which suits you best" (Doyle 370). We should be cautious, however, in unreservedly attributing this attitude to Holmes. Atkinson's subtle analysis reminds us that our access to Holmes is mediated by Watson's pen—as well as his hero-worship. Hence, the same story contains passages like this: "working as he did rather for the love of his art than for the acquirement of wealth, [Holmes] refused to associate himself with any investigation which did not tend towards the unusual, and even the fantastic" (Doyle 368). These are, in fact, Watson's perceptions and representations of Holmes, which conform to the lines of Holmes's public persona, namely, "that his own untainted rationality is as free from economic concerns as from social mores" (Atkinson 15). In a number of cases we note the tendency to interpret the whole body of the detective's actions as subordinated to some work goal.[11]

The problematic status of Holmes's labor is most striking in "The Man with the Twisted Lip" (1892), brilliantly analyzed by Audrey Jaffe in her essay "Detecting

---

[9] For similar dismissals see Futrelle's Thinking Machine stories "The Mystery of the Man Who Was Lost" (97) and "The Leak" (519).

[10] This attitude characterizes Thorndyke's approach generally and throughout the Freeman corpus—for instance in *A Silent Witness* (1914) in his explanation of a specialist's duties (90–91), in *The D'Arblay Mystery* (1926) where Thorndyke jokingly remarks that he should pay the client for "indulging" him in his "pet hobby" (70), and a late and sustained example in the 1938 novel *The Stoneware Monkey* (38, 105).

[11] Journalist-assistant Walter Jameson expresses these attitudes in several Craig Kennedy stories from *The Treasure Train*: "I could see no sense in the proceeding, yet knew Kennedy too well to suppose, for an instant, that he had not some purpose" (Reeve, "Truth-Detector" 36); or: "Impatient though I [Jameson] was at this seeming neglect of the principal figures in the case, I knew, nevertheless, that Kennedy had already schemed out his campaign and that whatever it was he had in mind was of first importance" (Reeve, "Vital" 203); or: "I could see the old restless fever for work which came into his eyes whenever he had a case which interested him more than usual. I knew there would be no rest for Kennedy until he had finished it" (Reeve, "The Sand-Hog" 162). The same idea surfaces in Futrelle's Thinking Machine stories: "Beneath the irritated voice, behind the inscrutable face, in the disjointed questioning, they all knew intuitively there was some definite purpose" ("Haunted" 481).

the Beggar." Jaffe, correctly understanding labor to be "only what a culture recognizes as labor," goes on to demonstrate how begging is consigned, as a matter of course, to non-labor (415). But a positive definition of labor entails many tacit assumptions. The social forces at play in recognizing productive activity are rarely defined, though negative examples in the form of deviant individuals are easily held to be representatives of threatening social groups. The self-evident character of productive labor draws attention away from what deserves investigation, namely, how a society generating immense wealth can tolerate comparably extreme levels of destitution. In Doyle's story the problem is inadvertently brought into vision, since our beggar is not a "genuine" non-worker, but an imposter who "works" at begging because it is lucrative. Within a larger social context, this labor of non-labor serves as a reminder of the illicit gains (illicit by its own definition in earning without labor) generated by speculation and the "magical" transformations of price in the market, which obscure the exploitation that generates surplus value. Nonetheless, the outrage of a fake beggar who refuses to offer an honest day's toil becomes the invisible frame that negatively defines the conditions of genuine male labor.

Jaffe's investigation of "The Man with the Twisted Lip" raises the paradox of readers' inconsistent understanding of and ideological position towards labor. She suggests this incongruity in remarking how Holmes frequently reduces strangers to professions based upon outward signs so that identity becomes a function of the work one does (405), a point also noted in Doyle's "A Case of Identity" by Thomas (81). This practice invites us to reflect upon Holmes himself. What in fact does Holmes do, and what traces of that labor are borne upon his person? Watson's well-known list of Holmes's abilities (or lack thereof) in *A Study in Scarlet* (1887) resists integration into normal work schemes as Watson, the staid late Victorian, figures it. He enumerates his companion's strengths and qualifications, puzzles over them, and eventually casts them into the fire, unable to plug this skill base into any capitalist work regimen. As an index of what professional work is and what it is not, Holmes's labor is perplexing: he remains outside the normal economy of work in terms of a regimented schedule or well-defined periods of labor, and the service he renders rarely involves any physical rearrangement of matter and thus is generally free of measurable qualities. It is precisely these qualities that link him to the criminal of the piece.

In this well-known text, Neville St. Clair, formerly a journalist, discovered in the process of writing up a story on begging in London that with a little cosmetic artistry and repartee, large sums could be made by sitting with one's cap on the ground. Eventually, St. Clair, under the name Hugh Boone, took up this "profession" full-time, profiting to the point that he could marry and integrate himself, under his proper name, into respectable society. His chance sighting by his wife, who knew nothing of this ruse (highlighting the gulf between domestic and public spheres of work), in a disreputable part of London leads to his "disappearance"—ironically, he is arrested by the police in his beggar's guise as the murderer of himself, that is, of Neville St. Clair. Holmes, who believes St. Clair to be the victim of some plot, must establish a link between the men to solve the case. To do so, he hangs about in opium dens with the scum of the city, takes long drives into the country in his client's trap, sleeps in a well-appointed bedroom in his client's house, and smokes large quantities of tobacco—not an investigative procedure we would condone in a professional police force, if we recognize such behaviors as work at all. Jaffe, well aware of this, concludes that the text "displays anxiety about labor that appears not to be labor, often mentioning the fact that, when working, Holmes appears to be doing nothing." She continues with this poignant remark: "Both Holmes and Boone live by their wits; neither is perceived to be working when he is actually hardest at work" (421).

This labor which is not labor has an oblique relation to knowledge—since Holmes is, reputedly, a complete idiot when it comes to facts expected of any educated person (the heliocentric worldview) and a polymath in respect to obscure minutiae (tobacco ash). His lecture to Watson on the "brain-attic" in *A Study in Scarlet* (Doyle 89), whereby he remarks that only that knowledge useful to his enterprise should be retained, is baffling, given the fact that any given crime may demand any specific form of knowledge. The encyclopedic learning associated with Classical or Golden Age detective omnipotence is thoroughly confused by such statements. Both Dennis Porter and Tim Roth rightfully point out that Holmes is not represented consistently this way, since clearly in practice no one could adhere to the brain-attic concept of knowledge.

I cited Jaffe's comment about Holmes's establishing of identity through the traits inscribed by labor on the body, which in the context of "The Man with the Twisted Lip" comes back to confuse us, since St. Clair cannot be classified positively within the capitalist frame—neither in some managerial capacity, as capitalist (despite his claim of "interest in several companies in the City"), nor as wage laborer. St. Clair/Boone is not at the margins; he seems to be outside the system itself, an Other to the system, since his removal of money from circulation cannot be justified within a capitalist ideology—and yet, he only seems to be, since in fact he betrays precisely the sleight of hand that a Marxist critique lays bare, namely, the unearned income removed from the system as revenue and reemployed as capital. This confusion is played out in the relation between the detective and the criminal, who in terms of labor are, in fact, more akin to each other than different, since "Holmes's profession ... depends upon exactly the kind of indeterminacy he finds inappropriate for St. Clair" (Jaffe 422). Naturally, we understand this parallelism as merely formal, and that functionally they stand at polar extremes: as Other to a system of capital, circulation, and the exploitation of labor to extract surplus value, Boone helps define "proper" society by the negation of its norms. That he would form an alter ego to "contain" this negation within a disreputable exterior is no surprise. But Holmes likewise exceeds the system, uncovers this negation so that the dialectic works properly. He occupies a position on the outside that conceptualizes totality and guarantees the management of waste. As such, Holmes is a guarantor rather than a productive element within the frame itself; he endorses the frame by which meaning means (discussed in Chapter 2).

The discomfort of the story is the eye turning upon itself, not only in the suspicion that things are not as they appear (the false beggar), but that signs themselves have no absolute basis. In line with our discussion of a fund of meaning, the bank's gold reserve (Chapter 4), Jaffe observes how "the 'false beggar' makes visible the system of exchange wherein sympathy, coin, and identity can circulate endlessly, never drawing upon any fund of truth" (411). The overlap between Holmes and Boone risks placing Holmes's labor in a similar position, thus threatening the boundaries of meaning that he works to uphold.

Golden Age Labor

The idea of routine work, usually shunned by the Golden Age omniscient type, is not rejected simply out of boredom, absence of official status, or lack of technical expertise. Chief Inspector Parker privately grouses over Wimsey's freedom to avoid the grind, but we are nonetheless reminded of Bunter's first-rate photography setup and Lord Peter's knowledge of toxicology. Other pairings—District Attorney John Markham and Philo Vance, Chief Inspector Masters and H.M., Inspector Japp and Poirot, Sir Richard Freeman and Fen—or, among the professionals, Sergeant Fox and Inspector Alleyn and the laboratories of the Sûreté and Bencolin—function to segregate aspects of the investigation. The former painstakingly accumulate and methodically analyze the material evidence necessary for a conviction; the latter engage in flights of analytic abstraction. Though readers are aware of such divides, most of the time we are manipulated in our sympathies to favor the abstract. In Nicholas Blake's *There's Trouble Brewing* (1937), for example, Inspector Tyler investigates the murder of the town's leading industrialist. The Inspector is unappreciative of Nigel Strangeways, whom he figures to be a lazy interloper unable to withstand the burdens of a proper investigation. He remarks: "Plenty o' routine work to be done before [making an arrest]. But you amateurs aren't interested in that, are you? Too much like hard work, eh?" (144). Such throwaway lines, emulative of Scotland Yard pigheadedness from Holmes to Poirot, foreshadow the amateur's victory

Superficially, the mental exercise of analysis both contrasts with and underscores the dullness of routine, but more to the point, the detective's analytic strength is almost always a solo affair, lauding bourgeois individualism in the face of a forensic collectivism which parallels the economic collectivism that had been attained by the turn of the century (with the obvious exception of the Thorndyke stories). The official detective is analogous to a manager who directs labor, receives orders from above, and is subject to public scrutiny. The private detective resembles the artisan, out of place in a collectivist world, who maintains the myth of control and an essentially complementary parallelism with major social institutions. More than one scheme might be used to categorize major types of Golden Age labor; here, I suggest a taxonomy which covers a swath of texts: the scholar-professional, the dilettante, and the institutionally linked worker-professional. To this we might add a maverick class whose members only partly correspond to any type.

The first category encompasses the professions, sometimes those requiring an extended technical training such as in medicine or law, but all demanding a high level of educational attainment. Within this group we include Gladys Mitchell's Dame Beatrice Lestrange Bradley (psychoanalyst and MD), John Dickson Carr/ Carter Dickson's Sir Henry Merrivale (lawyer) and Dr. Gideon Fell (humanities scholar), and Edmund Crispin's Professor Gervase Fell (Oxford professor of English). We could add an early version of Arthur B. Reeve's Professor Craig Kennedy (research chemist at an unnamed New York university) as well as Jacques Futrelle's Professor S.F.X. Van Dusen and R. Austin Freeman's eclectic and long-lived John Thorndyke. Though ostensibly closer to the hard-boiled type, Perry Mason is on the margins of this group, given the frequent clue-puzzle focus of Gardner's novels. Robert Van Gulik's Judge Dee also fits into this category due to the examinations he must pass to qualify for his post. The second group, the dilettante, occasionally includes professionals. They tend to write if they need income and to have no clear occupation if they do not. Anthony Berkeley's Roger Sheringham, Nicholas Blake's Nigel Strangeways, Dorothy L. Sayers's Peter Wimsey, S.S. Van Dine's Philo Vance, and Ellery Queen fall into this category. We might also include Ngaio Marsh's Inspector Roderick Alleyn—though a police officer, we cannot discount his Oxford training or his aristocratic background, which erases the dire necessity of labor. He is also an authority on police investigative methods, as indicated by his standard textbook on the subject, *Principles and Practice of Criminal Investigation*. A third, relatively small group consists of professionals whose labor generates income. The ranks of Golden Age private detectives in this group are limited, or, as often, they represent hybrid forms—narratives with clue-puzzle foci that straddle subgenres. Anthony Boucher's Fergus O'Breen, not really a hard-boiled type, and Clayton Rawson's Great Merlini are in this group, the latter distinguished by being an amateur whose real working life is described convincingly in parallel with his interest in criminal investigation. Poirot, though an ex-police officer dedicated to private investigation, tells us from the first that he is in (unsuccessful) retirement and that he is a wealthy man. The point of convergence, though, for this list of detectives is that they typically make little or nothing for their efforts, at least not in terms of money.

A maverick class contains figures who cannot be situated clearly into this three-part schema. As a rule, these characters are semi-comic and function sometimes as parody. Thus, Father Brown falls into the professional class while Miss Marple and Ambrose Chitterwick parody, somewhat critically, the dilettante and the man of leisure. These three detectives in particular are further linked by their inoffensive, and thus deceptive, exteriors, belying their ratiocinative and psychological acumen.

Evidence of uncompensated labor is easy to find in the sources. Mrs. Bradley "works" some of the time—for instance, she takes on the position of Warden at Cartaret Training College in *Laurels Are Poison* (1942)—but this expenditure of time and energy is a screen for her investigation. The question of payment is comfortably forgotten, given her immense personal wealth. Her professional commitments, referred to in *When Last I Died* (1941) and *Death and the Maiden* (1947), are sandwiched between other, unpaid pursuits. Professor Gervase Fen, another professional, though one with more obvious institutionally mediated responsibilities, also seems curiously free from encroachments on his investigative pursuits. Although Fen makes occasional reference to marking assignments and university duties, he seems unencumbered by his professorship when his fancy is captured. Even granting that work schedules at Oxford in the 1930s differed substantially from most professorial work today, Fen, and his earlier American counterpart, chemistry professor Craig Kennedy, seem to have time on their hands. The fact that Fen is never paid for this labor raises questions about his motives, which the narrator has a hard time explaining; he satisfies himself by reference to something "at the basis of Fen's personality," described as "a kind of passionless sense of justice and of proportion, a deeply rooted objection to waste" (Crispin 199). And yet in terms of waste, his own expenditure of labor is altruistic to an extreme. Kennedy is an even more perplexing figure in that he barely finishes one case to be engaged on another. The pattern of Reeve's stories in *The War Terror* (1915) consists of one story segueing into the next. The apparent lack of job pressure, which also characterizes Kennedy's journalist roommate, Walter Jameson, allows the pair to dash off at a moment's notice without the bother of a lecture schedule or office commitments. Though paid by the university for his professorial work, Kennedy is not above discreetly making a buck on the side; in any case, his clients, almost without exception members of the New York elite or insurance companies, can well afford to pay for his services.

The dilettante class of Golden Age detectives also seems strangely free from the pressures exerted upon rank and file individuals, especially given the lean years in which these stories and novels appeared. Though his father, Richard Queen, clearly has official work commitments within a well-defined structure of authority, Ellery seems indifferent to payment. In *The Chinese Orange Mystery* (1934), for instance, Ellery goes to elaborate lengths to demonstrate the modus operandi of the crime, though no reward or even reimbursement is forthcoming. We find similar devotion to the cause without payment in other early novels: in *The Roman Hat Mystery* (1929), *The Dutch Shoe Mystery* (1931), and especially *The Egyptian Cross Mystery* (1932). Nigel Strangeways, another overeducated dilettante, also moves among society's upper reaches, which form the source of his clientele. From the start, however, in a novel like *Thou Shell of Death* (1936), the detective receives nothing (save an introduction to his future wife) in that he is hired by the victim who, once dead, also turns out to be the culprit. More unpaid labor appears in *There's Trouble Brewing*, when Eustace Bunnett tries to hire Nigel to identify the person who threw his dog into a vat at his brewery. Nigel requests a substantial fee of £25 and £5 pounds per day, presumably to put him off; in effect, his money demands function to erect barriers to work. Bunnett apparently ends up dead the next day, so the fee is out, but Nigel stays on to help his hosts, the Cammisons; no money is forthcoming, nor does his original reason for the visit—to lecture on his new book—profit him. Dilettante expenditure is taken to fanciful extremes in Sayers in the early story "The Adventurous Exploit of the Cave of Ali Baba" (1928), in which Lord Peter fakes his own death in order to assume a disguise by which he infiltrates a well-organized criminal syndicate—he spends two years living in poverty, separated from his friends and family, all of whom believe him dead!

Even the professionals of the Golden Age and its affiliated clue-puzzle element end up working for free. In John Dickson Carr's *Castle Skull* (1931), Bencolin, *juge d'instruction* at the Sûreté, is called in with his German counterpart von Arnheim—this special request, we learn early on, will net him nothing in terms of a pecuniary reward (a similar, though more twisted situation arises in Carr's *The Lost Gallows* [1931]). His "client" D'Aunay remarks to Bencolin at the beginning:

> "For my purpose, I want the best in the business. With you, then, I will not insult a man who has followed your course by saying that you may name your own fee. At the present time, you are on a vacation. Good. I want you to take my case. I will not pay you one sou. But, when I have outlined it, I think you will work for me, because it will be the strangest affair you have ever handled." (Carr, *Castle* 6)

On the other side of the Atlantic, and somewhat closer to the limit of the Golden Age's generally agreed-upon timeframe, Anthony Boucher's Fergus O'Breen is unmistakably working within the shadow of a more dominant hard-boiled context. Because his livelihood depends upon retaining his license, he contemplates turning down the chance of a fee from Lucas Quincy, since his business possibly requires breaking the law:

> He could not make up his mind on [Quincy's] proposition. It was all very well to go dashing off quixotically to save lives ..., but a fee would help. And yet Quincy's stipulation, that all evidence should be turned over to him exclusively and kept secret from the D.A., made the job not only unethical but goddamned risky. It would take a fine fee to make up for being booted out of your profession. (27)

The word *quixotically*, which appears again later in reference to O'Breen's labor, is self-consciously mocking—an inner need compels the detective, though one that is out of step with social norms of reimbursement for labor. In this novel, the ability to work outside of these norms is a fantasy of liberation that concedes the relative powerlessness of the private individual within the boundaries established by legitimate labor (Boucher 53, 83).

Hard-Boiled Labor

Classical and Golden Age detectives working within the clue-puzzle form generally have access to a social totality (albeit a constructed one); they establish patterns based upon a totalizing vision. Their labor functions to determine meaning within set parameters by fixing events and determining clue values, culminating in the authoritative narrative comprising the denouement. By entering the crime scene and engaging the criminal, such detectives offer a circulating general equivalent, at the same time transcending the system to act as a guarantor. Such distance is denied to hard-boiled detectives, who cannot frame and determine events with the certainty or authority of their Golden Age counterparts. Most of these detectives nonetheless exhibit a curiously broad circulation. Their movements appear to forge links between wealthy clients and a marginalized underclass, but careful scrutiny, Jameson reminds us, reveals the detective's investigative voyage to confirm "the fragmentary, atomistic nature of the society he moves through" ("Raymond Chandler" 131). In contrast to Golden Age anteriority, the "privileged experience in which the whole social structure can be grasped no longer exists" (Jameson, "Raymond Chandler" 127), either in fantasy or in reality. To be sure, the "social structure" that Jameson writes about is not much more convincing than what we find in the so-called microcosms of the Golden Age. The inclusion of racial and sexual minorities, women, the mentally ill, or the poor and petty bourgeoisie is not intrinsically positive, given the consistently hostile depictions of these groups. If the range of voices exceeds Golden Age limits, the tone of the narrative voice rarely does. Ralph Willett only mildly exaggerates when he remarks that "the hard-boiled novel reproduces the bourgeois individualistic diegesis of capitalist society, discovering crime but mystifying and concealing class, race and gender relations" (7).

For its target audience, though, hard-boiled labor offers an escape from the monotonous grind of common work experience—it remains irreducible to time or motion studies governing the repetitive, usually non-thinking tasks to which most workers are condemned. For Erin Smith, the pulps were, in part, a coming to terms with Taylorist developments in industry and a nostalgic fantasy of artisan independence. The worker, faced with greater speeds, deskilled labor, and a volatile job market, sought relief from these anxieties. Smith warns that the experience of reading these texts was not unalloyed in that the medium in which they appeared introduced conflictive messages, largely a product of the advertising that accompanied the stories. Competing value systems are evident, and the "texts negotiate an uneasy rapprochement between residual artisan culture centered on skilled production work and an emergent consumer culture that valued men for the commodities they could (or couldn't) buy" (11). Nonetheless, she maintains that the texts consumed by the pulp audiences employed crime as a medium for storytelling, but that the real focus was the "private eye's struggles for autonomy at work" (17). More speculatively, we might view the attractiveness of such texts to lie in the investigator's rejection of collective effort, though this renunciation of collectivism does not serve to glorify bourgeois individualism; rather, it conserves the value of labor. In any case, Smith is correct in observing that "the hard-boiled detective seems an unlikely proletarian hero," especially since "the private detective is usually hired to protect the interests of those with significant property" (79). The hard-boiled detective's working conditions are but one of several distinctions related to labor, and in fact the differences from most workers' reality cuts deeper. Not only does the detective escape the time clock and the enclosed place of work, but he (or, rarely, she) is free of obligations to spouse and family and professional affiliations or membership in ethnic community, church, and neighborhood. The excision of these background features common to most of the readers aids us in viewing the detectives as "individuals completely defined by their work" (Erin Smith 80). However, the special status of this work has little to do with work in the Marxian sense of productive labor in the late nineteenth or early twentieth centuries.

The fantasy of detective labor is just that—a labor that escapes the forces of institutional gravity, though this escape manifests itself in different ways. Margolies claims that the private eye's popularity derived in part from evading bureaucratic control (86; see also Broe 168). Porter finds retrogressive or anachronistic value systems to govern the hard-boiled detective's regimen (whether a chivalrous knight, self-determined and autonomous worker, or ascetic workaholic) ("Private" 96). Yet Marlowe's anti-social qualities and his unusual work practices (coupled with his intermittent income) are tolerated, for his poverty is ostensibly self-determined and his work ethic is never questioned. The detective's calling, with its oblique allusion to what mystery writer Robert Parker conjoins with America's Protestant roots, could be read as a latter-day manifestation of the driving force associated with American frontier history: "Here surely is the ultimate expression of the Protestant ethic, a total commitment to the job which neither money nor sex can seduce" (28). But the motivation for this "total commitment" remains vague, if not dubious, particularly in the romanticized version given us by Cawelti, who holds that "the hard-boiled detective has chosen this way of life because honor and integrity mean more to him than fame or fortune" (*Adventure* 157). Even unsympathetic reader-critics are stirred by this question, such as in Geoffrey Hartman's query: "What is there in it for him? The money is only expense money …. Their motives are virtually the only things in these stories that are not visible" (224; see also Roth 78–79). If we posit more abstract forms of satisfaction—as unlikely as this may sound, given the precarious lower middle-class position occupied by most PIs—we come up against other obstacles. The willingness not only to work without the promise of recompense, but also to undertake particularly dangerous work, is hard to accept; Roth enumerates other unlikely motives—"the need to maintain an orderly society, the satisfaction of being a professional"— which he sensibly dismisses as "too much at variance with the overt semantics of the texts to be creditable" (114).

Erin Smith's work on the pulps again gives us the best insight into how to understand the representation of work in these stories; for Smith the private eye of this period "had everything to do with changes in the structure of work in the early decades of the twentieth century" (80). These changes, however, do not include radical labor agitation or the struggle for a fair wage. For instance, in several of Nebel's Cardigan stories the protagonist is cognizant of the social situation but offers few criticisms of social inequalities. The first installment of the

Cardigan series, "Death Alley" (1931), promises to address labor issues, since part of the conflict arises from the assumed retaliation against a boss for his attitudes towards striking workers. Cardigan dismisses this accusation and even appears sympathetic to the strikers, but the theme is quickly dropped. In a much bleaker story, "A Truck-Load of Diamonds" (1932), a thief is abetted after the fact by an impoverished jewelry store employee who is about to face dismissal. The wealthy patrician partner in the jewelry firm announces to Cardigan that the employee, Micah, will be let go—not, however, due to the theft or any dereliction of duty in 10 years of service: "He received notice the first of the month. Times are hard. We've had to cut down. I have utmost faith in Micah. This was indeed unfortunate. There has never been an irregularity in the house of Traum and Fleer. We could, you understand, hardly afford it" (Nebel, "Truck-Load" 356). The irony of the expressions "Times are hard" and "This was indeed unfortunate"—referring to the theft and not the dire straits of the employee—coming from a man dealing in $60,000 diamond necklaces is brutal. Micah's complicity with the crime is not prompted by revenge against his unfeeling boss, but by the crushing medical bills accrued by a sick sister, who has bled him of all his savings. Micah intended to shake down the thief for a cut of the take to help cover these expenses. After the caper crashes down around them, he commits suicide. Cardigan reflects at the close: "It was this sort of thing that often cropped up in his business—men down to bedrock, men who turned criminals over night for a reason that no law would recognize. Cardigan had read the letters [from the sister] in Micah's room. He knew" (Nebel, "Truck-Load" 376). Though effective in their understatement, no real social protest arises from these observations. Despite Cardigan's own impoverished origins, his priorities are aligned with the interests of the patrician owners.

Narratives highlighting the autonomy of the detective exude ambivalence: though seeming to reproduce the world familiar to workers, they comprise a backward glance towards dead forms of independent labor and anticonsumerism and glorify a type of individualism out of step with reality. In *White Collar*, C. Wright Mills points out how the myth of American individualism, threadbare by the turn of the century, was nonetheless perpetuated in school and "reinforced and even created, especially in white-collar times, by the editorial machinery of popular amusement and mass communications" (xiii). In the same text Mills offers us a definition of the craftsman, who seems uncannily close to many hard-boiled detectives, particularly Hammett's Op, Chandler's Marlowe, and Macdonald's Archer. A number of popular though lesser lights reflect shades of these figures: Coxe's Flash Casey and Kent Murdoch, Nebel's Captain MacBride, Whitfield's Ben Jardinn, and, paradoxically, Spillane's Mike Hammer. What unites these figures in particular is their willingness to place work before remuneration, and in this we note their difference from other hard-boiled amateurs and private detectives, such as we find in Carroll John Daly, Nebel's Donahue, much of Norbert Davis, Jonathan Latimer, Hammett's Sam Spade, and, to a lesser degree, in semi-hard-boiled figures like Gardner's Perry Mason.

Among the features Mills isolates in his definition of the craftsman, termed an "idealized model of work gratification," we note especially the focus on production for its own sake, the intimate relation between mind and hand, control over the labor process, the beneficial professional consequences of experience, and the collapse of distance between work and nonwork activities (*White* 220). Mills goes on, however, to state that these job qualities are practically nonexistent at the time he was writing (early 1950s) and had been anachronistic for some time (*White* 224). To the idea of control, we should add the experience of totality, of which modern workers, almost without exception, are deprived. The Golden Age detective's grasp on totality does not stem from the craftsman ethos, which is a subjective relation; rather, the totality for Classical and Golden Age fiction is measured from the outside. To return for a moment to the Golden Age typology, the outsider in this case is not the alienated individual increasingly evident as the hard-boiled genre develops through the 1940s; instead, the outside is a function of professional status, the upper echelons of the new middle class: the medicolegal profession, represented early on by Dr. Thorndyke and later by Mrs. Bradley; the professor, its Classical form in Craig Kennedy and its Golden Age version in Gervase Fen; the lawyer-politician in Gideon Fell and H.M. (also a qualified medical doctor); remnants of the aristocracy in Lord Peter; or simply the privileged, such as we find in Philo Vance. We might extend this a bit further by including the supernatural—the outside of nature or its suggestion—in Father Brown, and by a stretch of the imagination, the Great Merlini.

Marlowe and Archer, both college-educated, come of age in a period in which great confusion begins to appear in the white-collar labor market. The obvious advantages of education in the first decades of the century, which allowed the children of wage earners to climb into the white-collar ranks and then to seek promotion within that system, began, by the 1940s and 1950s, to confront the overproduction of educated individuals. Graduates competed for fewer positions due to technological advances and the application of scientific management to the office; at the same time the scope for imagination, intelligence, or application necessary to perform the job declined. In this light, Geherin's remark is apt: the detective's "compensation comes in the sense of satisfaction he gets in demonstrating once again his superior intellectual skills rather than in any form of monetary reward" (2). The frustration of the automated workplace, once associated with labor in factories, invaded the office to the degree that employers preferred to hire individuals of humbler academic attainments, claiming that more education interfered with performance, given the grinding monotony of the job (Mills, *White* 247). Mills makes much throughout *White Collar* of the fantasy, still maintained in his day, of the opportunities offered by white-collar work. Both Marlowe and Archer worked within the bureaucracies of law enforcement; both left these institutions to do what Mills maintains is nearly suicidal without substantial capital. This movement is more evidence of the fanciful quality of detective fiction, even if we ignore the unlikely types of cases they are involved in. To cite Mills:

> In their daydreams about the kind of work they would really like, workers are
> concerned about the variety of work, the using of skills, and contact with other
> people; as many want white-collar jobs as want skilled labor; less than a fifth
> have in mind small businesses. We have already seen what is likely to happen
> to the 0.2 per cent of the adult population who try to start small businesses and
> be their own bosses, and we know that farming is not an economically over-
> crowded business. (*White* 277)

And even within the ranks of the detectives, the economic whittling away suggests
stages in this struggle. Between the 1920s representations of the collective
efforts of the Continental Detective Agency and the solo efforts of the 1940s and
beyond, we observe a dramatic drop in the number of personnel. Although we are
stretching a point by referring to an agency, the tendency to throw operatives at
a job is pervasive in the Op stories (allusions to an army of investigators all over
the nation with contacts worldwide). Spade has a secretary, as do Ben Jardinn and
even Norbert Davis's Ben Shaley. By the time we get to Marlowe in *The Big Sleep*,
the secretary is gone and Marlowe has to endure insults from Vivian Regan about
his lack of front.

Keeping within the hard-boiled subgenre, we again take our range of
representative positions as bounded by Coxe and Chandler (Spillane stands
beyond Chandler and forms a special case). The hard-boiled interest in work is
documentable from its supposed origins in Daly's "The False Burton Combs,"
though it usually gets discussed in the much-cited passage from "The Gutting of
Couffignal" (1925) in which the Op waxes rhapsodically about work for work's
sake (later in the story demonstrating this through his rejection of bribes, material
or sexual). The Op's self-identification with work, so much that we know him
under no other guise save the occasional mention of a poker game, is completely in
line with Mills's craftsman, someone "who does not flee from work into a separate
sphere of leisure," someone who "brings to his non-working hours the values
and qualities developed and employed in his working time" (*White* 223). The
Op, a functional element in a larger corporate body, cannot maintain the illusion
of convergence between ownership, management, and labor to the degree that
Marlowe might, but in the end, the question becomes how complicit this enjoyable
labor is in the affirmation of an order that is both exploitive and committed to
creative input and the grasp of totality. For all his apparent freedom in pursuing
a case, the Op nonetheless is ultimately confined by the system's demands. This
point, best described by Freedman and Kendrick, is most obvious at the end of *Red
Harvest* in the reestablishment of "bourgeois legality":

> this alliance [between the Op and "bourgeois legality"] points to a crucial
> ambiguity in the very identity of the private detective. Though he is on one level
> independent of the police—and hence free of certain statist constraints on the
> individualist or "whole man"—his entire position as a respectable entrepreneur
> ... ties him to the state and makes him function, in the last analysis, as an adjunct
> to the official forces of law and order. (Freedman and Kendrick 18)

At the same time, the Op's cynical rejoinder at the end suggests, again in Freedman and Kendrick's view, his "awareness that his own labor has inevitably been reified into an instrument wielded for the benefit of the despicable capitalist boss Elihu" (27). These boundaries are illustrated in the unselfconscious commitments to a world of individualistic professionalism, represented well in Coxe, and the impossibility of functioning within corrupt institutional frameworks, best characterized by Chandler. The spectrum of hard-boiled labor will be taken up in Chapter 6, initially in the institutionally linked detectives in Coxe, through degrees of ambivalence or cautious respect in Whitfield, Hammett, and Chandler, to the extreme position presented by Spillane.

Detective Work and the Gift

Understanding detective labor as gift-labor clears up some of the bafflement expressed by critics like David Bazelon, who see the Op as "primarily a job-holder"—an employee for whom "*competence* replaces moral stature as the criterion of an individual's worth" (469). Bazelon does not understand the Op's instrumentalization to be an attack by the left-leaning Hammett on America's labor woes. Rather, the critic bemoans the detective's lack of a private life and his intense job commitment: "One might think he was in it for the money—but his salary is never made known, is apparently not large, and he isn't even *tempted* to steal" (470). The gift-character of hard-boiled detective labor, whose ground is prepared by Hammett (and others, such as Nebel and Whitfield) and which flowers with Chandler and Ross Macdonald and attains overripeness in Spillane, remains invisible to Bazelon. Perhaps it is the irrationality of this gesture which blocks its obvious application to detective fiction, a genre that ostensibly celebrates the triumph of rationality.

The next move in this dialectic compels us to turn to theology. Theology tests the limits of such rationality in terms of self-sacrifice and altruism, and so perhaps the theological dimensions of the gift shed light on the detective's paradoxical selflessness. And indeed, such contractions are evident in John Caputo's discussions of sin and forgiveness. On the one hand, Caputo asserts the gift to be an absolute offering; on the other, gifts are frequently understood to be conditioned, interested, or even interest-bearing. In the latter case, they imply the attachment of debt and obligation that inscribe the gift within economic circuits of value and exchange. Caputo analyzes the tortuous logic of the gift of forgiveness, likening it to a wage-mentality in its conditional mode. Forgiveness is offered, granted that the sinner stops sinning and makes restitution, if in no other way but by demonstrating contrition. Yet such demands conflict with the necessary conditions for forgiveness in that it is the sinning sinner who is the proper recipient, not one who has stopped (and by definition is no longer a sinner): "But what is a sin? It is a sinner sinning, a concrete, factical deed, datable in time, locatable in space" (Caputo 120). Yet such forgiveness, if offered, possesses another side, namely that it is offered for nothing, a gift that is undeserved in that it receives nothing (the sacrifice of sin itself, since it has already been renounced) in return. Summarizing ideas in Derrida's *Given Time I: Counterfeit Money* and other texts, Robert Bernasconi understands Derrida's notion of the gift as equally paradoxical. The problematic first principle is non-participation in exchange, a principle which prohibits reciprocity. This prohibition echoes Caputo's concept of forgiveness, which presumably is a one-way act, but which also is not given for anything else. If it is—for instance, in deference or thanks, a mere gesture of acknowledgment—then the gift character of the act is threatened. We arrive at a conundrum and a series of questions, expressed concisely by Bernasconi: "Even to refuse it, is to acknowledge it and so, in a sense, give a return. The problem is still more acute in the case of the giver: how can the giver not be aware of giving? Insofar as the giver is conscious of doing something good in giving, is not its gratuitous character compromised? This leads Derrida to ask if the conditions of the gift are not the conditions of its impossibility" (256).

Such abstruse problems seem distant from everyday notions of giving, conditioned by several centuries of capitalist development. Nonetheless, few of capitalism's advocates are as blunt as George Gilder in *Wealth and Poverty* in inscribing the gift within an economy of calculation and unblushing greed: "The gifts of advanced capitalism in a monetary economy are called investments. One does not make gifts without some sense, possibly unconscious, that one will be rewarded, whether in this world or the next" (24). Instead of representing a vestige of nonmarket selflessness, Gilder's psychology of the gift questions whether the ego is ever displaced, or even could be. And we cannot overlook the conundrum raised by the gift once understood from this perspective. It wavers between expenditure in its free sense (Bataille's summit experience and summit morality) and the expectation of return (its discursive formulation in decline). This conundrum forms the foundational problem for several critics, conveniently listed by Scott Shershow (86). Shershow also describes the tension of the gift, which "presents itself as a radical Other of the commodity," to nonetheless "constantly to be drawn back under the horizon of rational exchange," which establishes or reestablishes a relation to labor, wage, profit, and a host of other terms that seems to betray the word's everyday sense (5). Derrida indicates the ambiguity of the gift to stem from the subjective processes of the giver caught in a net of social relations. The problem confronting us in detective fiction and the gift-character of detective labor or, more accurately, its representation, is posed in Shershow's question, namely: "Can a gift truly be given freely, with no thought of reciprocation, which would necessarily reinscribe the gift in an economy of exchange—and thus reveal the gift to be itself a form of work?" (87). This tension is preserved in my use of the term *gift-labor*, which maintains the idea of a mutual conditioning.

A shift or transformation in our own historically grounded understanding of the gift is not simply a disruption traceable to the capitalist revolution, with its consequent alienation and reification of life.[12] In its Classical/Golden Age formulation, labor is pursued outside of obvious money relations because social stability suffices (represented as the victory of reason over forces threatening to production). For hard-boiled texts the escape allows freedom from the fragmentation of work experience in the modern workplace, the separation of hand and mind and the fracturing of processes of production that obscure any sense of totality, but also the severing of labor, management, and ultimate control and interest. The gift seems to exist in defiance of these conditions. A couple of difficulties arise in this reading, however, the first of which concerns the larger timeline of the gift, encompassing periods and cultures that exceed the scope of modern capitalist or bourgeois relations or even the notion of the West. Here, we confront the Maussian and Bataillian concern of registering the gift beyond a narrow frame to encompass a history that extends to the precapitalist past and to the surviving practices and mentalities in so-called primitive economic forms. This concern deserves comment in that the specific manifestation of the gift, within the form of literature, leads us to suspect complicity with the forces that precipitate escape in the first place. That the detective hero is complicit with bourgeois norms of legality, justice, and social good is obvious enough in the Classic/Golden Age formula, even in cases where the detective's own class interests are at odds with this ideology. But we suspect that the hard-boiled hero, despite marginalization, is not that different,[13] though for more subtle reasons.

Mauss's treatment of the gift in terms of linear "development" (46) and the vocabulary of modern economic transaction is the point of departure for recent philosophical inquiries, namely those of Rodolphe Gasché, Derrida, and Goux, among others. The suspicion that the gift is more akin to Gilder's crude formulation than we might first admit is sufficiently demonstrated in the questions initiating Mauss's influential study *The Gift* (1924): "*What rule of legality and self-interest, in societies of a backward or archaic type, compels the gift that has been received to be obligatorily reciprocated? What power resides in the object given that causes its recipient to pay it back?*" (3). Mauss's remarks on the *hau*, the spirit informing the gift, brings us back to the contemporaneous socioeconomic concerns troubling him in the Interwar period. This period includes Bataille's (partly Mauss-inspired) venture into economics as well as much of the detective fiction under scrutiny in Chapter 6. Given the Classical and Golden Age's propensity for conservation and the regulation of value within a bounded, homogeneous milieu, labor for nothing

---

[12] James Carrier attempts to trace the ambiguities around modern notions of gift, and its survival in the face of insistent commodification, to the transformations of labor and the impersonality of modern economic transactions (11), that is, as a reaction against these phenomena.

[13] Margolies opines that Hammett's inability to write reflected his distaste for his own heroes' support of exploitive social mechanisms—their own labor was dedicated to serving a system which they could not in fact condone since it operated to maintain the hegemony of the privileged few. The conflict, he suggests, was exacerbated by the Depression as well as Hammett's own political allegiances (17–18).

seems destabilizing. The uncertain relation to wage or reimbursement that appears time and again in the very nature of much detective labor is therefore confusing. The practitioners of the Classical and Golden Age subgenres are avid to balance accounts, going so far as to generate highly artificial hermetic, anti-entropic worlds in order to do so. Enmeshed in a milieu dominated by the logic of a capitalist praxis, such relations are extended to every sphere of life, though to be sure they do not escape ironic self-consciousness. We note this in Gladys Mitchell's first novel, *Speedy Death* (1929), in which her heroine, Mrs. Bradley, is on trial for a murder that she did in fact commit. Although she brings about the death of an insane killer who she fears will commit additional crimes in the future, her defense avoids such sidelights; rather, it proceeds along the lines of technicalities over evidence, since actions outside the norms of calculation are regarded with suspicion. The Chief Constable, explaining his take on the case to an inspector, expresses it concisely: "The British public doesn't believe in disinterested actions, and it is just as well it should be so. An absolutely disinterested action with an altruistic motive is a very unusual thing" (Mitchell, *Speedy* 151).

A more tortuous and typically less humorous approach to the problem arises in hard-boiled fiction, reaching its apogee in Chandler. Although hard-boiled detective labor is bought on the market, the economic transaction is superseded by a different set of connections to the client than we find in most Golden Age texts, or at least this relation remains in tension. The fact that betrayal is a recurring theme does not in any way lessen the sense of gift—rather, after Derrida, we are strengthened in our conviction that return is more effectively blocked through ingratitude. Ingratitude, however, is not quite enough, since by reversing gratitude, it still works within the same universe of acknowledgment. The volatile compound of intimacy and obligation exceeds the indifferent "freedom" of the market relation alone. The deep irony pervading tales in which this relation cannot be sorted (the most insistent example being *The Long Goodbye*) is the injury suffered by detectives in the mismatch between the economy of their actions and the self-interest dominating market relations, an injury of which they and we are uncomfortably aware. The conjunction of these modes of experience is only partially expressed in Carrier's juxtaposition of "economic transactions as impersonal and rational" with "social transactions as personal and affective" (10), since these existential modes are generally indistinguishable in figures for whom these barriers are ill-defined; moreover, following Gasché, we would be wise to avoid recourse to "the radical otherness of archaic societies" as a recuperative strategy whereby universal reification of relations could be dissipated (103). The experience of capitalism tends in one way only, and that is towards the liquidation of all such "otherness" and its reappearance in suitably marketable forms—the figure of the circle which closes off and accounts for all exchanges, avoiding the threat of Hegelian absolute negativity or of Bataillian heterogeneity as Others of discursive homogeneity. But how do we preserve this knowledge without its reintegration into the boundaries of a framing device? Gasché offers an answer in his critique of Mauss:

any exchange becomes possible for Mauss only through the project of a recuperation of an alienated self by an ego who conceives himself, however, as out of the circle and, by that very conceit, as an irreducible plenitude, as much an imposture as the object thrust into the circuit, which is merely the substitute for his self [*propre*]. This primary exchange of what would have been lost opens and limits the exchange. The alienation of self is fictive, since the ego that enters into the exchange believes himself to be outside with respect to the exchange, believes himself to be an irreducible plenitude by virtue of the occultation of the originary alienation, which causes him to be always already caught up in the exchange and which is added to the alienation as a repetition of the originary loss, a repetition that procures the illusion of a recuperable, conditional loss. (112)

The "plenitude" is the fullness of the equivalent in its role of establishing value (which is also the reader's position), its function as measure, which like gold is identical to self. The circulation of that value-measure, despite the trials of the marketplace, is not thereby diminished by the experience: the "alienation" remarked by Gasché is not existential but rather the rendering visible of a transcendental principle to help reestablish boundedness within an erstwhile homogeneous space, its guarantor. The detective appears "out of the circle" but also circulating (as a "substitute," though one which is convertible)—this engagement is limiting ("limits the exchange") since it conceives of all relationships within the vision of that outside accessible at once to the omniscient detective. If the self is gambled in this engagement, it is a "loss" which is calculated to yield a return, the promise of that self's restoration. We do not have much trouble in reconciling the experience of the Golden Age detective with this formal pattern; however, the hard-boiled detective presents some challenges. Does the apparent risk of the self in the hard-boiled text, coupled with the loss of transcendental status, reopen the possibility of uncalculated expenditure? Or does the transmission of the text reclose a circle whose opening was merely illusionary? And is this closure a function of discourse itself, which suggests a fundamentally economic nature of language?

The labor of the hard-boiled detective places him or her within the purview of death, as we have seen most explicitly in examples from Hammett and Chandler. As all are threatened and many die, we are reminded of that risk and danger which dog the detective's steps, even though this path is engaged by choice. The freedom to choose is present; this labor is not imposed by dire necessity, as it is for the laborer who works to eat, must work, and even must "choose" dangerous work to reproduce labor power. Rather, such detectives determine to put themselves in harm's way; they are complicit with self-sacrifice. But this risk is deceptive. The story, by virtue of its existence, is a testimony to survival. This sacrifice is an engagement with and a displacement of death. Why this illusion? And what are the consequences for gift and labor? These questions take center stage in the next chapter.

Chapter 6
Hard-Boiled Gift-Labor
and the Aneconomic Gift

The Gift of Labor

In Marxian terms, the concept of gift-labor is oxymoronic. The end of labor, though perhaps not leading to marketable commodities, nonetheless does produce use-values. If we argue that the unpaid detective plods on to a solution to satisfy a private need, we cannot *necessarily* speak of this product or service as possessing commodity status or exchange value, at least not according to Marx's definition in the first chapter of *Capital* I: "He who satisfies his own need with the product of his own labour admittedly creates use-values, but not commodities. In order to produce the latter, he must not only produce use-values, but use-values for others, social use-values" (131). The detective's efforts might be read as an activity which extends the normal boundaries of how services are understood by its relation to the individuality of the detective worker. Marx, in the "Productive and Unproductive Labour" section of "Results of the Immediate Process of Production," does state that such services (those inseparable from the worker) "are yet capable of being directly exploited in *capitalist* terms," though he goes on to remark that they "are of microscopic significance when compared with the mass of capitalist production" (*Capital* I: 1044–45). Here, Marx understands such work as a form of wage-labor which "has scarcely reached the stage of being subsumed even formally under capital, and belongs essentially to a transitional stage" (*Capital* I: 1044). This form of labor has arrived in the public consciousness as fantasy labor in the form of the detective, whose largely unclassifiable labor (service? wage? altruism?) nonetheless makes claim to a social use-value, though one coopted to serve certain interests.

The notion of a social use-value in the truth-bearing narrative might be useful if it enjoyed circulation. Whether or not the audience buys the solution does not discount the labor necessary to its production; indeed, "a use-value ... has value only because abstract human labour is objectified or materialized in it" (*Capital* I: 129). Here we run up against notable differences between representative writers from the Classical/Golden Age and hard-boiled genres. The labor that generates solutions for Holmes, Poirot, or Lord Peter may or may not be paid—likely it isn't, or if it is we hear nothing about it (Watson 177)—but in any case, it is useful labor in that its products are endorsed by members of the dominant culture in the public sphere. It matters little whether or not the solutions are true. The shielding of criminals in narratives like "The Adventure of the Abbey Grange," "The Adventure of 'The Western Star,'" and "The Unsolved Puzzle of the Man with No Face," to cite examples from the detectives just enumerated, does not offer any obstacle to an official solution to which the detective himself acquiesces, perhaps even suggests. Detective labor here is validated, understood as productive. In a number of hard-boiled detective narratives, especially those that depart from the strict clue-puzzle omniscience model, the diffuse nature of responsibility erodes the capacity to offer a packaged product, or at least one that passes official inspection. Delaguerra, at the end of "Spanish Blood," remarks: "Downtown they like it the way it is. It's swell politics" (Chandler 233). This statement refers to a string of murders pinned on the wrong people, but admissible because the killers themselves are dead. Political expediency masks, if not obliterates, Delaguerra's dangerous labor, whose complicity is not the buttressing of a society in which he is invested, the shielding of a client whose interests he shares, or personal profit.[1] We might argue that the detective's labor is essential to a solution which does pass muster—that labor possesses value because, again in Marx's terms, it is "an object of utility"—but this is merely exploitation, the cooptation of that labor and squeezing of value from it for the benefit of those who control it (that is, Downtown). To continue with an earlier citation from Marx: "If the thing is useless, so is the labour contained in it; the labour does not count as labour, and therefore creates no value" (*Capital* I: 131). The conundrum is whether the usefulness of truth to the detective outweighs the recognition of that truth outside the confines of his or her world-consciousness. This form of hair-splitting is most applicable to existential readings of hard-boiled alienation and departs from the social meaning of that labor to focus upon individual psychology. The social character of this labor is, in fact, akin to the gift.

To conflate labor with gift-giving smacks of a euphemism—the theft of surplus value generated through the exploitation of the worker, who makes a "gift" of what goes beyond the capacity to reproduce labor power. Furthermore, a confusing juxtaposition arises from attaching gifts to any form of economic activity, a point pursued by Derrida in the first parts of *Given Time*. Taking a somewhat reductive approach to Derrida's oblique style in the beginning of his text, we come to question whether any gift can be conceived outside of an economy, understood as a bounded and regularized system of exchange based upon the recognition of value and use, since its noneconomic status depends upon the preexistence of the economy as a reference point—or, to put it differently, the regularized, homogeneous space of "normal" social life is framed by such relations to the degree that any deviation from exchange is viewed suspiciously. The concern is not so much that we step outside the historical reality of highly

---

[1]   Chandler admired Nebel, whose Captain MacBride resists the opportunities for illegal gain surrounding him, of which he is well aware. As a consequence, "MacBride had never been affluent; he was always in debt, there were bills always to be met; graft lay around him within easy reach but he scowled at it, went on driving a shabby car, went on being in debt" (Nebel, "Rough Reform" 14). For similar sentiments, see Nebel's "Ten Men from Chicago" (105).

developed market relations, but that we question whether the gift is "that which interrupts the economy" by its ability to "[suspend] economic calculation" and to shut down exchange (Derrida, *Given* 7). The "circle" of exchange is broken and the relations of one to another (and to self) are rendered unstable, different, perhaps irrecoverable. Importantly, Derrida makes this distinction: the gift has a relation to the circle but this relation is "a relation of foreignness" (*Given* 7). That the relation slips back into memory testifies either to the strength of the economic frame, or, as Bataille might have it, the slippage into a something (or nothing) not the self. The inconceivability of this disintegration is either the ideological block demanding a class-based understanding of stability or the Bataillian *crochet* whose discursive potency obscures its own point of reference.

The recognition (validation) of gift-labor and the capitalization of its service in the marketplace is a form of reciprocity that is not merely economic but connected to the establishment of the ego, the secret desire for power that results from the impotence of the donee and the hoped-for, and impossible and thus rhetorical question: "How can I ever repay you?" For Derrida, this recognition leads to the establishment of identity as property (*Given* 11). If this labor escapes notice, or if it is crushed under institutional obstructions to circulation, does the detective become the anonymous figure whose labor is valueless? And would this valuelessness be within the scope of the gift? What becomes of the detective's identity, which hangs precariously unrecognized because it is unreciprocated? These questions, derived in part from Derrida and Goux, point towards a gift that remains a gift only insofar as it cannot be returned or reduced to a cycle of return in the counter-gift connoting debt (Derrida, *Given* 12–13).

In his "Seneca against Derrida: Gift and Alterity" Goux demonstrates that this concern over the economics of the gift goes much deeper in Western thought than the nineteenth-century rise of anthropological interest in the nature of exchange. Goux summarizes the conception of the gift in Seneca and in the broader sense in Stoicism as thinking the gift without return, but also without the anxiety of debt. To achieve this, the gift must not only be lifted from situations in which material objects are bought and sold and loaned for interest, the exchange of tangible objects, but must be placed into the context of the intention and the soul. Thereby, sacrificial and cultic practices are eclipsed by the good will, and later to a Christian principle (which understands the Divine gift—the sun as symbolic of God—as irreducible to calculation). Ingratitude then vanishes in the face of a return that is never made and could not be made, only a chain of gifts which have not "properly" established notions of reciprocity. Gifts attain a sort of positive or even idealized form when their return is impossible, since it obliterates expectation, investment, and debt:

> Nothing puts more light on the essence of generosity, nothing gives a better demonstration that it cannot lean on interest (*utilitas*) and on a vile calculation ... than the kind deed given to the poor, to the dying person, to the traveler, to the stranger, to the unknown person. In all, these cases show the goal of the kind deed as precisely what it should be: "Not the profit ... nor the pleasure ... or the

fame ... of the one who gives" (IV, 11, 1), but the advantage (*utilitas*) of the one who receives. (Goux, "Seneca" 150)

We note here that the quotations in Goux are from Seneca.

Taken to an extreme formulation, as in the case of Spillane, the corpse is logically the best recipient, since the dead are unable to make any return; furthermore, knowledge itself is eclipsed since it is irrelevant. And if possible, to go even further, to place one's very ego at risk to "benefit" the dead seems the height of expenditure, an act "against the interest ... of the one who gives it" (Goux, "Seneca" 150). This blind or aggressive giving is in line with the impossibility registered by Derrida, "the double bind of the gift," since it is the dead recipient for whom "the gift [does] not even appear" and for whom it is neither "perceived [nor] received as gift" (*Given* 16). By not acknowledging this gesture, by denying the reciprocity which will establish the detective's identity, and not allowing a "reappropriation" of that identity, the measure of value disappears. The use-value of the gift-gesture likewise is incalculable. The measure or the equivalent, important to establishing the boundary of the outside whereby the homogeneity of the inside is guaranteed, is thus not the gift, but gift-labor, whose existence at the margins of the economy are boundary-establishing.

Readings of texts by Coxe, Whitfield, Chandler, and Spillane allow us to explore a range of positions related to these theoretical considerations of the gift. Though my series does not follow strict chronological order (Chandler's *The Long Goodbye* postdates the first six Spillane novels), the sequence does mark a trajectory. Coxe's heroes work comfortably within benign institutional frameworks in which rewards do not depend upon money values. These men's labor is unproblematic in that it is directed towards an abstract principle which never gets much attention. From Whitfield to Chandler, we come up against more complex forms of labor—self-sacrifice for principles that are increasingly under scrutiny. Chandler represents the highest point of this self-reflective development. Spillane goes one step further, shutting down reflection, but by doing so, twisting out of the consciousness of debt-relations in terms of his pathological gift-labor.

"There's nothing the matter with the job; it's just that every job seems lousy some of the time." (Coxe, "Murder Mix-Up" 223)

Coxe's heroes, despite their fierce individualism, are complicit with a hierarchy of labor relations premised upon the fantasy of benevolent interdependence. The Flash Casey short story "Murder Mix-Up" (1936) depicts an institutional framework in which accessible authority figures acknowledge and reward the worker. Casey is the most proficient, most successful, and therefore best-paid photographer in Boston. His professionalism makes his position unassailable, so much so that he can manipulate authorities like the police and his immediate boss, Blaine. He demonstrates loyalty to the job, the paper, and his colleagues. His behavior, though violent, drunken, and insubordinate, invites no censure. Although not entirely in control of his assignments, he is in charge of how the production process unfolds; he not only finds and cases the situations, but takes the pictures and develops them—from start to finish he is there, and he partakes of the intellectual as well as the manual labor. No chasm looms between mind and hand despite the context of institutional control and managerial hierarchies.

At the end of "Murder Mix-Up," after a tumultuous night of violence, Casey enters the office of the Managing Editor, MacGrath, to vent some grievances about his job. A warmer and more accessible incarnation of the Old Man, MacGrath hears Casey's complaints about his disillusionment with his work. MacGrath tries to convince Casey that his labors are worthwhile, and that Casey would be bored and even more disillusioned with some other line of work, notwithstanding its comparative safety: "He was a keen judge of men, MacGrath. He knew human values and his gaze was both searching and understanding" (Coxe, "Murder Mix-Up" 222). When Casey declares his intention to find some other outlet for his talents, MacGrath counters:

> "You wouldn't like it" .... "If you couldn't get a front row seat to fires and accidents and shooting—if you didn't have some excitement and get slapped around a bit you'd go nuts. You're the best camera in the city, you get the most money, and you lie if you say you don't like it. There's nothing the matter with the job; it's just that every job seems lousy some of the time." (Coxe, "Murder Mix-Up" 223)

This is a point of view to which Casey acquiesces. MacGrath then receives the photos Casey got beaten up for, promises him a bonus, and remarks that if he weren't already too sober, he'd join Casey on the resumption of his bender. In this work fantasy, money is downplayed in favor of competence, a value shared and exemplified by authority figures: the hard-working editor deserves his position by remaining in his office long after hours and demonstrating complete dedication to the job. Managers are able to recognize talent and to reward it, but they also realize that money has its limits.

In a later Casey vehicle, *Murder for Two* (1943), the relations between loyalty, commitment, and work again come to the fore, and again work is characterized by a high level of variety, independence, and interest for the worker. The creative dimension of Casey's vocation, as well as his professional commitment, is underlined in a scene in which criminals have ransacked his desk, destroying part of a photographic collection he considered representative of his best efforts:

> Casey recovered what he could. There were not more than thirty or forty [photographs], but to him they represented something that could not be replaced. Of the thousands of pictures he had taken over the years, these were the ones he had thought worth saving, spot-news shots mostly, that told a documented story, a history story really, of his profession. He had collected them as a connoisseur of paintings collects old masters, though with Casey there was a stronger attachment, since these were his own creations and the result of luck, enthusiasm, and hard work. (Coxe, *Murder for Two* 74)

This paean to unalienated labor emphasizes worker control over the labor process. Casey evades the compromise between creative labor and the demands of institutions, partly by blurring the parameters of how work is defined—not by a system which constrains but through the cultivation of a personal standard and definition that escapes the time-space parameters of exploitation. The emphasis on uniqueness ("could not be replaced," "own creations"), expert status ("a history ... of his profession"), and, most surprisingly, a reference to developed taste or connoisseurship evoke thoroughly New Class values.

Institutions, when their power is felt, are nonetheless depicted as under the control of accessible and humane individuals with distinct personalities. MacGrath is approachable and altruistic. Blaine, though acerbic, is reliable, professional, and ultimately fair. The higher levels of the organization do not consist of dim, anonymous figures; their visibility allows Coxe to circumvent, with sentimentality to be sure, the bleaker vision of Latimer's world. In Latimer's Bill Crane series, Colonel Black remains a distant figure who communicates by telephone and who lacks the benign, paternalistic qualities in his tendency to figure everything by time versus cost. Coxe's MacGrath and Wyman dispel the pessimism arising from the journalist's up-close exposure to the sordidness of the urban landscape. In contrast, Crane's distressing portrait of 1930s work insecurity is worlds away from the closing remark in *Murder for Two* in which Casey declares, "Taking pictures for a big city newspaper might be a headache, but for him it was the only job in the world and there was no other that could compare with it" (Coxe 240).

"I hadn't seen any stones, but I believed they existed." (Whitfield, *Green Ice* 125)

The fantasy of uncoopted hard-boiled labor, whether institutionally linked or freelance, reaches a high point in the early 1930s. The first type is well represented by a series of Frederick Nebel vehicles, including his MacBride-Kennedy pairing and his private detectives Donny Donahue and Jack Cardigan. Donahue is willing to work under grim conditions and for rewards that seem outweighed by risks. Although Donahue, like Cardigan, is money-driven, both men's professional commitments transcend dollar values. In "Spare the Rod" (1931) Donahue delivers this speech on work:

> I'm just a plain everyday guy trying to make a living—as honestly as possible. There's not a hell of a lot of romance attached to my business. I'm no drawing-room cop. One day I'm here—the next day, somewhere else. That's not romance. It's damned monotonous. When I take on a client, I expect a break. I expect the truth. If it is the truth, I'm just as liable to risk my neck for the guy as not. (Nebel 190)

In another story, when urged to halt the investigation by a client who cites the dangers of further probing, Donahue replies: "Hell, I might as well stick." When the client asks, "What's the use of inviting a bullet?" he responds, "I'd hate my guts if I gave it the go-by now" (Nebel, "Save Your Tears" 416).[2] Similar ambiguity arises in Whitfield's Jo Gar stories. Although references are made to retainers and the financial status of the client, at other times Gar is unconcerned with fees. "I do not work always for money" (Whitfield 80), Gar remarks in "Enough Rope" (1930). Or, in his ongoing battle of wits with the official police force, represented by Lt. Ratan, he says, "I am retaining *myself* .... My reward will be obtained in a way familiar to you, Lieutenant. I shall be amused at you" (Whitfield, "Siamese Cat" 385). In "China Man" (1932) he reflects that "his fees were not big; he accepted almost any case that was interesting, and many of his clients were not rich. If he were to move into better quarters he would perhaps not be able to accept cases that interested him, and his contacts would be different. He had decided that he would lose more than he would gain" (Whitfield 357).

Returning to Nebel's Donahue, we note the complex combination of dangerous action, commitment, and indeterminacy exemplified in stories like "The Red-Hots" (1931). In line with the chaotic conditions described in Hammett's "Bodies Piled Up" (Chapter 3)—violence, confusion over identity and character relations, lack of motive or at least an indistinct motive—we start off with almost nothing but a client, who happens to be dead. Donahue is called upon to visit Robert Crosby at his apartment, where Crosby will specify his business. After waiting for some time in Crosby's apartment, to which he has been admitted by a "roommate," Donahue finds Crosby's body in a ransacked room. The object prompting the search remains unnamed until the end, and only after a number of deaths have occurred. The detective, though working for a client through the Interstate Detective Agency and the promise of a bonus from Crosby's wealthy family, is willing to put himself in harm's way, negotiate, and commit crimes without any positive knowledge of what he is doing. He crosses paths with several dangerous criminals: Alfred Poore, Irene Saffarrans, and Babe Delaney, violent thieves who in turn compete with each other as much as they work together. There is no clear center of gravity or cooperation, so that halfway through the story Donahue, having tracked down Irene, is still uncertain what is going on.

"He Could Take It" (1932) begins abruptly with Donahue returning home to nurse his battered body, the result of abuse meted out in the previous installment of the series. Working discreetly for District Attorney Frank Castleman, Donahue is instrumental in acquiring documentary evidence of criminal activity that points to corruption in the New York City police force. The story makes no pretense to investigative practices or deduction; rather, Donahue stays one step ahead of

---

[2]   Donahue makes similar remarks elsewhere: "I don't know why I'm in—but I'm in it. It keeps me in butts and I see the country and I don't have to slave over a desk. I get places. It's not a pretty game, and no guy ever wrote a poem about it. But it's the only hole I fit in" (Nebel, "Rough Justice" 18). Cardigan, too, shares this sentiment: "Sister, I like my job. The head office sent me out here because 'Boss' Hammerhorn thinks I'm a swell, elegant guy. He wired me to hang onto this job till my guts hurt. I liked the way he put it. And I'm in it—this job. Up to my neck" (Nebel, "Six" 92).

violent criminals intent upon recovering the papers while being badgered by the official police, especially Detective Kelly McPard, who is unaware of Donahue's true assignment. The criminals relentlessly pursue Donahue, first attempting to pay him off through a corrupt lawyer, then subjecting him and McPard, who is captured along with Donahue, to gruesome torture. Donahue and McPard are eventually rescued and the documents apparently reach their destination—Donahue has submitted to torture and almost certain death to prevent the criminals from obtaining the papers. As McPard must admit, the police believed that Donahue's only purpose in holding out was the chance of profit (a view also shared by the crooks). The title refers to the abuse that Donahue must accept for a principle— ironically, one that threatens him professionally, given his unwelcome efforts to expose graft in the police force. At one point in the story, McPard asks Donahue, "Now what did you get out of that fight?" Donahue appropriately responds: "Welts and abrasions" (Nebel, "He Could Take It" 309). Whatever financial reward or official recognition he receives never gets mentioned.

Raoul Whitfield's *Green Ice* (1930) serves as a novel-length example which complexly gathers together all these labor-related elements, especially the impetus to place oneself at risk for minimal or unknown rewards. In terms of plotting, character psychology, and work ethic, Whitfield is ultimately unable or unwilling to offer a plausible explanation for the actions and motives of his hero, Mal Ourney. *Green Ice* abandons the institutional complicity of Coxe's Casey and Murdock characters, but we must wait until Chandler to delve into the complex psychology of gift-labor, even though Whitfield's first-person narrative offers some direct insights into his protagonist. The novel begins *in medias res*: Ourney, just released from Sing Sing after serving a two-year sentence for manslaughter, is only minutes out of jail when things start happening. From the beginning, two interconnected themes—the disproportionate relationship between punishment (or suffering) and justice and the sacrificial gift—are fused in Ourney's labor. Complex forms of gift-giving are constantly linked to Ourney, who, we learn early on, is innocent of wrongdoing in the manslaughter charge. In order to protect Dot Ellis, whose drunk driving caused the deaths for which he takes the rap, Ourney pretends to have been at the wheel, an act that appears all the more selfless in that he was planning to end his relationship with her that very evening. Reference to Ourney's "good deed" of keeping Ellis out of jail consistently crops up; this action is revisited at intervals, becoming the principal leitmotiv of the book.

Moments after Ourney is released, Ellis calls to him from a cab, trying to convince him to join her; he refuses, and a short while later she is gunned down. Later, we learn that far from offering a welcome or proposing a reconciliation, Ellis met Ourney in an attempt to frame him. She hopes to plant on his person some hot emeralds, the "ice" of the title, though her reasons for setting up Ourney remain incomprehensible until we are halfway through the novel. Upon the heels of her murder, we gather several apparently disparate threads, obscure connections, and deceptions whose confusion is heightened by Ourney's (and our) limited perspective on and knowledge of events. Looking back from the end of the novel, in which some semblance of official narrative form is given to the chain connecting a dozen murders, we understand the violence to have begun with the killing of a South American gem dealer in New York and the theft of emeralds believed to be worth around $300,000. A quarter of a million of this money is concentrated in five very large stones; 15 smaller stones account for the balance. The first murder is orchestrated by a midlevel crook who tries to put one over on some mob bosses. Although two of the big players are killed at the end, most of the deaths are concentrated at the small-time end of the criminal ladder, individuals who are in fact used as fodder by the big crooks—whom Ourney repeatedly refers to as "crime-breeders"—to take the blame for their own crimes or to commit crimes for which they are not "compensated." Ourney is constantly on the scene of the various killings, though he is never seriously suspected by the police, with whom he enters into a sort of uneasy partnership, especially a New York police detective named Donelly. Ourney's involvement, however, is not accidental—his presence is typically connected to his search for information that will lead him to the big operators, the "breeders" whom he wishes to bring to justice. Convinced that these individuals are the real source of social decay, he conceives the idea of using his sizable inheritance to pursue reforms and personal vigilante campaigns, much to the chagrin of the police, who view his interference as harmful at best. Ironically, his successes cost many lives, mostly from the lower tier of criminal miscreants he ostensibly wants to help. Ourney acts upon an overblown and generally unselfconscious code of chivalry (lacking Marlowe's capacity for self-irony in *The Big Sleep*) whose vision of the world is divided chiefly into victims and victimizers; how he arrives at this ideology is as mysterious as the antecedents of the emerald caper, and therefore, the risks he takes to rid the world of evil as he understands it collapses into sentimental do-gooder speechmaking, delivered up with street patois and hard-boiled violence. Three aspects of this novel related to the gift deserve examination, allowing us to situate it between Coxe and Chandler—a look into Ourney's self-described motives and their problematic foundation, the nature of Ourney's labor, and finally the mismatch of social reality and Ourney's fantasy objectives, which threatens to draw attention to the flimsy premise initiating the action.

Ourney is upfront about his plans, however incompletely thought out, poorly organized, or damaging they eventually turn out to be. Upon release, he intends to enlist the help of other like-minded souls—ex-cons—to attack the sources of the problem: "I got the idea that just a few humans were using a lot of other humans as they wanted, then framing them, smashing them—rubbing them out. It looked pretty rotten to me. I'm not sentimental—I'm curious. I'd like to smash some of the ones who use the others up" (Whitfield, *Green* 78). Later, when talking to two women about the murder of his friend Wirt Donner (unaware of their own complicity in this killing), he embroiders on the theme: "Wirt Donner and I were going after the big guns in the mob that was using up a lot of underdog crooks. We were going to use my coin and go after 'em hard" (Whitfield, *Green* 100). Aside from the intimation that his prison stay had opened his eyes to the manipulation of little people by a few evil higher-ups, we remain in the dark about the obsessive nature of Ourney's altruism. We are not much better informed of the parallel case with Dot Ellis, whose ingratitude only amplifies the confusion—Mal's rationale for throwing away two years of his life is reduced to the fact that Dot was drinking his liquor and that he didn't want to make his bad news of breaking off with her worse by saddling her with jail time over her own criminal negligence! Although everyone seems aware of Ellis's guilt, virtually no one sees his act as reasonable or particularly noble. Ourney's baffling attitude isolates him ideologically, a fact that is underscored when his would-be helpmeet, Wirt Donner, is gunned down in front of him in Chapter 2 and a second possible helper, who turns out to be Ellis's killer and gunning for Mal himself, is shot with Ourney's help in Chapter 3. Ourney is self-contradictory when it comes to tallying up scores. The dominant institutionally entrenched view in *Green Ice* is that a lot of deaths simply don't count. Chief of Detectives Lenz, speaking to Ourney in his office, says of four murders happening within hours of each other: "That's a lot of killing—but it's all right. None of it was important" (Whitfield, *Green* 55). He concludes: "They come in batches—but they don't mean anything" (Whitfield, *Green* 56). Dobe, a newspaper editor, has similar attitudes towards violence in the poor districts of Duquesne: "there was a double murder. But then, there was a triple murder in Duquesne last week. And a single one the week before. There's so many up there that they don't count" (Whitfield, *Green* 93). Virgie Beers, who turns out to be one of the principal crooks, says of this Duquesne double murder: "It doesn't count. … Some mill worker did it" (Whitfield, *Green* 82), which is even echoed later in Ourney's reflections: "The Widow's death didn't count" (Whitfield, *Green* 89).

Ourney's vague philosophy and inconsistent value system parallels the difficulties in the bizarre work fantasy that he embodies. Ourney's labor does not correspond to an everyday sense of the term in that it is enabled by his independent means, disconnected from institutions, patrons, or clients, and non-remunerative. If anything, it consists of an unrelenting placing of the self at risk, though this endangerment must be looked upon with suspicion, given the recurring sense of unrecognized egoism in Ourney. Unlike the argument forwarded in Chapter 3, that the hard-boiled detective's first-person confrontation with death takes us beyond that (strictly speaking) uncrossable line, the sequentialization of Ourney's deaths in being battered into unconsciousness three times in as many days undermines the effectiveness of this trope. Ourney's strong sense of self and his "calling" place him relatively close to the criminals he combats—also strong, self-assured types who likewise do not work for wages. The principal characters who do have jobs are also curiously free of the restrictions and responsibilities we might expect of them. Donelly is "working" but not in his jurisdiction, and we are never told why a Manhattan detective has the authority to be in a different state on the job. Dobe, Ourney's newspaper editor friend in Pittsburg, seems to have plenty of time to support Ourney's interests. These men are juxtaposed with taxi-drivers, police officers, hotel and hospital staff, and steel workers who by necessity are engaged in making a regular living.

Ultimately, the relations between the crime-breeders and the small-time criminals who are "victimized" by them parallel the larger operations of capitalism. The monopoly on violence in the upper echelons of crime duplicate the State's prerogatives, whereby big capital is protected and the lower-middle-class, small-time operator is manipulated and ruined. The word *breeder* itself is clearly linked to production, though in truth it involves a harnessing of productive forces (albeit criminal ones) through exploitation. The contradictions in Ourney's philosophy reveal that it does no more than reproduce the support of hegemonic interests obvious among the small-time hoods. The emeralds of the title themselves serve as a metaphor for this confusing ideological system (Ourney: "I hadn't seen any stones, but I believed they existed" [Whitfield, *Green Ice* 125]). We learn midway through the novel that the emeralds are counterfeited, or at least there are both fake and real ones in circulation. Because it is difficult to tell the difference, we and the principal players are uncertain whether what is being fought for and killed for is real or not. This uncertainty parallels the motivating factors premising Ourney's actions as well as several other characters' actions in the novel. Indeed, the final story "works" because the major players are all dead.

Marlowe and Work

Professional ethics and commitments figure prominently in *The Big Sleep*, where Marlowe rejects or resists sexual temptations, personal safety, and ill-gotten gains in the service of abstractions like honor, loyalty, and fairness. Marlowe's rebuff of Carmen's unwanted advances is linked explicitly to his job: "It's a question of professional pride. You know—professional pride. I'm working for your father. He's a sick man, very frail, very helpless. He sort of trusts me not to pull any stunts" (Chandler, *Big Sleep* 707). He responds to District Attorney Taggart Wilde's incredulity that Marlowe would take the risks he does for $50 a day: "I don't like it …. But what the hell am I to do? I'm on a case. I'm selling what I have to sell to make a living. What little guts and intelligence the Lord gave me and a willingness to get pushed around in order to protect a client" (Chandler, *Big Sleep* 674). Finally, Marlowe stands up to the client himself, General Sternwood, by offering to return his fee when disputes over methods arise:

> "When you hire a boy in my line of work it isn't like hiring a window-washer and showing him eight windows and saying: 'Wash those and you're through.' *You* don't know what I have to go through or over or under to do your job for you. I do it my way. I do my best to protect you and I may break a few rules, but I break them in your favor. The client comes first, unless he's crooked. Even then all I do is hand the job back to him and keep my mouth shut." (Chandler, *Big Sleep* 750)

Over the trajectory of the novels, however, Marlowe's characterization of work shifts; his views culminate in *The Long Goodbye*, the most complex statement on the self-divided nature of Marlowe's attitudes.

Marlowe's disdain for the idle rich, a constant in the novels, stems from their not living up to his expectations of whatever constitutes a fair day's work. Thus, in *Farewell, My Lovely* (1940), when he says of Lindsay Marriott's living room that "it was a room where anything could happen except work" (Chandler 801), sympathy is unequivocally withdrawn from Marriott, not only for his effeminacy, but for his unwillingness to labor. Marlowe's jibe at Marriott is nonetheless perplexing, given the stretches of time Marlowe seems to kill sitting in the office, another room where work rarely happens and whose chief difference from Marriott's place is its lack of elegance. His dismissal of "a salaried job" (Chandler, *Farewell* 907), echoed in other works (*Long* 625), and his rejection of petty bourgeois enslavement to the treadmill are ironic, given his own self-induced idleness, a state which is alternately praised and berated. In *Farewell, My Lovely*, Marlowe discourses on his occupation to Mrs. Grayle: "There's not much money in it. There's a lot of grief. But there's a lot of fun too" (Chandler 859). In *The Long Goodbye* we get Marlowe's synopsis of "a day in the life of a P.I.," which registers a shift in his assessment of the profession:

> You don't get rich, you don't often have much fun. Sometimes you get beaten up or shot at or tossed into the jailhouse. Once in a long while you get dead. Every other month you decide to give it up and find some sensible occupation while you can still walk without shaking your head. Then the door buzzer rings and you open the inner door to the waiting room and there stands a new face with a new problem, a new load of grief, and a small piece of money. (Chandler 549)

What remains constant and what changes is of interest—obviously, the poor pay and headaches remain, the fun does not. What also persists is the question of what a fair day's labor is and what it is worth, ironically enacted in *The Little Sister* (1949). The passage back and forth of the $20 fee—half the day rate, as we learn later (Chandler 312)—paid by Orfamay Quest eventually ends up where it began: in her undeserving pocket. Marlowe's willingness to labor for half-wages is embroiled in self-contradiction: he takes on the job because, as he puts it, "I didn't have the heart to tell her I was just plain bored with doing nothing" (Chandler, *Little Sister* 214). Ironically, his "cheap" labor is dismissed by Orfamay a few chapters later: "'I paid you twenty dollars, Mr. Marlowe,' she said coldly. 'I understood that was in payment of a day's work. It doesn't seem to me that you've done a day's work'" (Chandler, *Little Sister* 231).

The critical assessment of Marlowe's labor occupies a range of positions. David Geherin attributes Marlowe's work ethic to "curiosity" and to empathy with others, rather than excitement, much less a financial motive (74); he remarks how Marlowe appears "[willing] to suffer on behalf of others, including some who aren't even his clients" (75), a quality he shares with Ourney. This view meshes with Marlowe's own remarks in *Farewell, My Lovely*, where he mentions curiosity as a motivating force in the case, as well as his inclination for work over non-work, or, as he puts it: "Even a no-charge job was a change" (Chandler 780). Mahan takes this idea somewhat farther by giving Marlowe's self-sacrifice a theological orientation, a trait that Mahan understands Marlowe to share with Ross Macdonald's Lew Archer (15). This concern for the Other does not encompass the full range of Marlowe's work consciousness, however. For instance, John Irwin views Marlowe's chosen occupation, one which insures poverty, as an effort "to achieve the maximum independence of his life-as-being" (231) as opposed to "life-as-having," though this also entails "a personal life sacrificed to a professional one" (231). In the end, though, Marlowe's marginal economic position turns out to be an indicator of "the independence and disinterestedness of his actions" (Irwin 234): we might read this as a source of ambiguity rather than selflessness—in fact, we are confronted with a dialectical movement between the independent self (the self-aware and focused ego) and the forgetting of that ego through the gift of time, energy, resources, and possibly life itself.

Chip Rhodes's more negative assessment of Marlowe's work regimen, in his analysis of *The Little Sister*, contrasts sharply with those of the critics in the preceding paragraph: "Much of [Marlowe's] work through the first half of *Little Sister* is simply to get somebody, Mavis Weld or her studio head, Ballou, to hire him so that he can justify his ethical mission and fantasy of saving them, of working with them against the hostile, outside world" (8). Rhodes's critical psychological portrait points up McCann's insightful assessment of a shift in Chandler's vision from the 1930s towards the critique of post-War consumerism (173). But to say that Marlowe's philosophy is merely anachronistic would also be wrong, since we must question whether he ever genuinely takes the Other over his own narrow vision of service. In a perceptive passage, Sharp criticizes Marlowe (in contrast to the more empathetic Lew Archer), who "never cares to know why Carmen Sternwood was emotionally disturbed, why she couldn't tolerate rejection from men, why she killed Rusty Regan. He is bound to protect her by his sense of duty to his client, General Sternwood, but he feels little more than contempt for her, and the fact of her guilt in the case is simply another detail to manage" (9).

Although Chandler is credited with introducing psychological depth into the hard-boiled tale, it would be more apt to term him an intensification of an existing tendency, one which we see in Frederick Nebel (a writer admired by Chandler) in well-developed form in the early 1930s. Nebel's Donahue story "Red Pavement" (1931) bears comparison with Chandler in respect to my analysis of *The Long Goodbye* in that the detective-hero foreshadows Marlowe's willingness to act on the behalf of strangers, even to the point of risking his own safety and freedom. As the story commences, Donahue picks up a drunken stranger, Charlie Stromsen, literally out of the gutter and helps him on his way uptown. They end up in a taxi, and Donahue agrees to take on an apparently easy job: picking up Stromsen's fiancée at Penn Station and getting her to a hotel while he cleans himself up. One hundred dollars change hands. On the way to Penn Station the taxi is shot up, killing Stromsen and leaving Donahue in possession of his wallet and a promise to pick up the fiancée, Laura. After meeting Laura and claiming a bag checked by Stromsen at the station, Donahue conducts her to his apartment, where he breaks the news. This shock is followed by another: the checked bag contains over $14,000. On the heels of this discovery, Detective McPard arrives, ostensibly to check up on Donahue's involvement in the shooting, but also to inform him that Stromsen was a former convict who had done time for a robbery in which the money was never recovered. Like Marlowe and Spillane's Mike Hammer, Donahue seems unconcerned about the antecedents of the stranger he has promised to help, and his unwillingness to cooperate with the police intensifies the discomfort of his position.

One distinction between this story and Chandler's, however, is its much more transparent dialectical bent. Donahue weighs his actions, oscillating between selflessness and self-interest in an internal dialogue: "No mock heroics. The guy with the death gurgle in his throat asked you to do something, and like a sap you did it. The girl turned out to be a pop-eyed little thing from the sticks. You broke the news to her as gently as you could. You didn't have to be gentle about it, but you were, anyhow. Then you felt relieved: it was simple" (Nebel, "Red Pavement" 393). Laura's departure, apparently a timely response to overhearing McPard's remarks about her fiancé while she was locked in Donahue's bedroom, seems to absolve Donahue of further responsibility, except that she cannot be found at the station where she said she would be. Her absence leads Donahue to assume that she is threatened by the same killers who pursued Stromsen. This situation prompts reflections that allow no place for chivalric fantasy:

> He was not being gallant—not now. He was intent on saving his skin, his license to operate, his sense of superiority born of his always having been on the right side of the fence when the cops got gay. When you got right down to it, the girl as a personality meant nothing to him; she was significant only for the fact that her death would bring the cops down on him. (Nebel, "Red Pavement" 394)

Ambivalence persists, however: Donahue successfully tracks her down, but he refuses to take possession of the money, even though he learns it was stolen from an illegal gambling enterprise in the first place. Donahue's oscillation between a commitment to a fair day's work and the pragmatic demands of self-preservation strike a balance that Chandler upsets—Marlowe becomes his vehicle to illustrate the tipping of that balance towards a self-defeating gift-labor.

"The stranger can keep going and pretend not to hear." (Chandler, *Long* 433)

The Long Goodbye (1953), Chandler's longest novel, is flabby—its length results from a combination of Marlowe's disgruntled sermonizing, tangential digressions, and uneconomically handled and overly complex character relations.[3] This

---

[3]   That said, Robert Merrill contests critics of *The Long Goodbye*'s uneconomically handled plot in an important essay, "Raymond Chandler's Plots and the Concept of Plot." He argues that establishing the guilt of Eileen Wade—which occurs 50 pages before the end of the novel—is not the novel's true focus. To put it succinctly: "the plot really focuses on Marlowe and not the murders he investigates" (11).

departure from genre expectations is complicated by an almost metafictional quality in Chandler's curious treatment of time, in which the temporal frame of reference is fast-forwarded or occasionally led off into indefinite or even inconsequential channels, at least for what purports to pass as a first-person narrative. To take these claims in order, Marlowe's frequent grandstanding is obvious to any reader of the novel—the work is peppered with bitter invective on the state of postwar American society and culture. As for other digressions, we are subjected to a number of passages whose function in the overall economy of the standard detective plot is perplexing. Connections that might be handled more efficiently, such as Eileen Wade's introduction to Marlowe, are diverted through tortuous channels in the form of Roger Wade's publisher, Howard Spencer. In respect to the time element, we are given information that problematizes the locus of narration—for instance, the paragraph detailing the fate of Terry's abandoned car (Chandler, *Long* 453) is a bizarre departure from what we would expect Marlowe to know or the general reader to care about.[4]

A series of implausible or chance happenings are required to splice together the disparate narrative threads. But for all that, the novel offers a complex vision of labor and of the psychology of the gift in a society dominated by market relations, money, and reification. Instead of the firmly established but basically unobserved self of Whitfield's Mal Ourney, Marlowe constantly oscillates between the selfless act and (self)-consciousness of that selflessness. He participates in the reformulation of the self, which momentarily escapes vision. This struggle is not entirely his own, but seems to pervade a gamut of essentially unhappy characters caught up in the irrationality of the gift, the sensitivity to gratitude, debt, counter-gift, and the stirrings of an impulse to begin the gift sequence anew.

Though there is little to call plot in terms of the traditional, ratiocinative clue-puzzle story, there is a sequence of events. Central to the story, though physically absent from most it, is Terry Lennox. Lennox, whom we find out later to have been Paul Marston, is married to Sylvia Potter, daughter of wealthy media magnate Harlan Potter. Marlowe finds the drunken and incapacitated Lennox outside a club and takes charge of him. After a subsequent meeting, Marlowe develops an offbeat relationship with Lennox, who divorces and later remarries Sylvia. One morning, Terry shows up at Marlowe's home and demands to be taken to Tijuana, and Marlowe helps him to get there. As it turns out, Sylvia has been killed, which leads to a police visit, interrogation, and jail for Marlowe through his refusal to be of material assistance. The official story out of Mexico is that Terry has committed suicide, so the police must grudgingly release Marlowe, though he is immediately warned off investigating the circumstances of Terry's death by Potter's lawyers,

---

[4] Other examples pertaining to time can be cited: the missing wife investigation (Chandler, *Long* 546–49) is solved within an ambiguous timeframe—a paragraph separates the problem and the result for a process that must have taken at least several days. Marlowe's fast-forwarding of events to describe Captain Gregorius's dismissal and death also unexpectedly breaks the narrative.

Terry's gangland friends, and the police. Some time passes and, in what appears to be an unrelated set of events, Marlowe is "employed" to help a writer, Roger Wade, and his wife, Eileen Wade. After some involvement with the drunken and unstable Wade, Wade is killed in an apparent suicide, though it turns out that his wife, formerly attached to Terry when he was Paul Marston, had killed both Terry and Sylvia. Eileen commits suicide, leaving a note to explain her actions. Marlowe obtains a copy of this note and allows it to be published by a newspaper to clear Terry's name. Subsequently, he is threatened by Terry's friend Menendez, who might have killed Marlowe if undercover police officers had not intervened. Menendez's purpose in threatening Marlowe is to maintain a cover-up. Whether or not they think Terry is innocent, Menendez and another friend, Randy Starr, help him set up a ruse by which Potter's lawyer is fooled into believing Terry is dead. In fact, Terry is still alive and has undergone plastic surgery to make him look Latino. He returns to see Marlowe, first to try, in character, to convince him that Lennox is dead, and then, when this doesn't work, to explain himself. But Marlowe rejects his overture.

Marlowe's initial motivation to help the drunken Lennox in the opening scene of the novel is unclear. His Good Samaritan attitude contrasts with Sylvia's coldness and the club doorman's cynical lack of sympathy: "Okay, sucker. If it was me, I'd just drop him in the gutter and keep going. Them booze hounds just make a man a lot of trouble for no fun. I got a philosophy about them things. The way the competition is nowadays a guy has to save his strength to protect hisself in the clinches" (Chandler, *Long* 421). Pure altruism is never possible, though, in this novel; in Marlowe's thought rejoinder to the doorman he conflates his actions with labor: "He was partly right of course. Terry Lennox made me plenty of trouble. But after all that's my line of work" (Chandler, *Long* 421). Social attitudes, however, are equally mixed. In their next meeting, again one in which Marlowe intervenes to keep Lennox out of stir on a vag charge, a helpful taxi-driver approves of Marlowe's selfless actions (Chandler, *Long* 425).

As with Marlowe, we more than once question Lennox's motives—the precariousness of his life and false poverty are unnecessary, given his wife's wealth and his connections. Instead, he refuses to seek help, relying on people like Marlowe. When Marlowe questions why he doesn't enlist the aid of his wealthy relations, Lennox responds, "My kind of pride is different. It's the pride of a man who has nothing else" (Chandler, *Long* 427). We might regard this suspiciously, however, in that this pride is a reserve, a fund which, remaining unexpended in relation to Marlowe, eventually loses him that friendship. The carte blanche Lennox wields with wealthy friends like Menendez and Starr goes unused— Starr's help, for instance, is rejected "because he couldn't refuse." When Marlowe raises the idea that Starr might welcome a chance to repay Lennox a debt (which, as it turns out, Starr does owe), Lennox counters that he wants neither "favors" nor "handouts"—"But you'll take them from a stranger," replies Marlowe. "He looked me straight in the eye. 'The stranger can keep going and pretend not to hear'" (Chandler, *Long* 433). The fact is, no relation can escape the intrusion of money, of calculations of repayment, even when that debt—life itself in the case of war heroism—is incalculable. In this context, we are left wondering whether the events of the previous 20 years for these characters, including the Depression and World War II, are not indicted by Chandler as shaping, beyond their own will, a fundamental obsession with such questions. Even after Terry absconds with Marlowe's help—aid which Marlowe offers with the demand that Terry not explain any of the circumstances around his request—the questions of gratitude, debt, repayment, and interest arise. Indeed, as Terry prepares to board the plane in Mexico, money intrudes: "And remember, if things get tough, you have a blank check. You don't owe me a thing. We had a few drinks together and got to be friendly and I talked too much about me. I left five C notes in your coffee can. Don't be sore at me" (Chandler, *Long* 446).

Marlowe's complex psychological response to Terry's death, whether by his own hand or at the instigation of the Mexican authorities, is in part motivated by the problem of unbalanced accounts—his own "investment" in his friend has been destabilized by Terry's posthumous remittance of $5,000, delivered in a letter sent from Mexico shortly before Terry's "death." This problematic gift cannot be repaid, much less returned, since the donor is dead—a sort of ideal potlatch that leaves Marlowe holding the bag.[5] This feeling, however, is already evident before the letter arrives:

> Maybe it was like that with Terry Lennox and me [the relationship was just incidental and not intrinsically meaningful]. No, not quite. I owned a piece of him. I had invested time and money in him, and three days in the icehouse, not to mention a slug on the jaw and a punch in the neck that I felt every time I swallowed. Now he was dead and I couldn't even give him back his five hundred bucks. (Chandler, *Long* 476–77)

Terry, it turns out, is a disruptive gift-giver who spreads anxiety amongst the recipients of his thoughtless munificence, exemplified by his unwillingness to accept help from his friends, two wealthy men whose lives he saved at great personal risk during the war. The circumstances around his heroics demand some attention, since it is the "unthinking" character of Terry's actions that raise concerns over the gift's motivation. The thoughtless gift appears to be outside the economy, that is, an economy understood through market relations of exchange and value. Menendez details Terry's actions in conversation with Marlowe:

> "We were three guys in a foxhole eating," he said. "It was cold as hell, snow all around. We eat out of cans. Cold food. A little shelling, more mortar fire. We are blue with the cold, and I mean blue, Randy Starr and me and this Terry Lennox. A mortar shell plops right in the middle of us and for some reason it don't go off. Those jerries have a lot of tricks. They got a twisted sense of humor. Sometimes

---

5   The potlatch relation is noted explicitly by Joanna Smith: "Terry's money becomes for Marlowe a kind of potlatch, a gift whose goal is 'humiliating, defying, and obligating a rival'" (194).

you think it's a dud and three seconds later it ain't a dud. Terry grabs it and he's out of the foxhole before Randy and me can even start to get unstuck. But I mean quick, brother. Like a good ball handler. He throws himself facedown and throws the thing away from him and it goes off in the air. Most of it goes over his head but a hunk gets the side of his face. Right then the krauts mount an attack and the next thing we know we ain't there any more." (Chandler, *Long* 480)

Terry's almost instinctual response undermines notions of calculation, but nonetheless starts off a chain of debt that is felt more deeply due to his subsequent disappearance and suffering. The unthought gives rise to the thought, bringing actions into an exchange mode that, once recognized, precludes thoughtlessness or in which thoughtlessness pains. Marlowe wants his gift of friendship to Terry to escape the bounds of this calculation, but the precluding of further relations brings to the surface the thought, cited above, that "I had invested time and money in him."

When Lennox returns as Maioranos, he recounts how he has taken up others on this debt, acknowledging that they owed it to him but that the initial impulse that started these cycles was merely a reflex—"And when I needed them, they delivered. And for free. You're not the only guy in the world that has no price tag, Marlowe" (Chandler, *Long* 733). This complex end to the novel, on the penultimate page, shows us the crisis for Marlowe clearly, if we keep Derrida in mind. That gift of life—the dying for the other which displayed no trace of forethought, instinctual giving—is converted into a debt, and the debt is made good "for free." That debt needs to be borne, as it was earlier when Lennox took without return the boon of Marlowe's expenditure. He suggested that he was incapable of maintaining this relation with the hidden money and the $5,000 bill, a note that is permanently removed from circulation (and which, as far as Marlowe knows, originates from a dead man's pocket). He looks to continue this with his false confession, which substitutes his life for the undeserving life of his former wife, Eileen Wade. But in fact it is calculation that covertly employs Marlowe (against his will in terms of the compensation) and calls in favors from those who owe him. This breaking of trust, of reduction to economic transaction, is what Marlowe cannot condone.

The collapsing structure of *The Long Goodbye*—collapsing since the time manipulations evident throughout the text would preclude the "surprise" of Lennox's survival and the problematic anxiety over the gift—plays up the notion of the detective novel consuming itself by confronting the constraints of its own structural limits. Routledge recognizes in this text Chandler's "undermining the assumptions of the 'clue-puzzler' type, the format of which implies an ability to determine truths from a fixed and therefore assimilable structure of objects and events" (102). And Weisenburger correctly diagnoses *The Long Goodbye* as a "self-reflexive" novel which uses a curious economic metaphor, one in which "Raymond Chandler was writing checks against an account of orderly, deterministic aesthetic conventions for detective fiction that his own narrative practices (or *any* writing) would drive into bankruptcy" (24). This passage suggests that Chandler inhabited a form whose structural conventions guaranteed sufficient meaning to serve unquestioned as a crucible for strikingly new material, a work in which the detective element becomes incidental. To close this section, we might also cite McCann's assessment of *The Long Goodbye* as a sort of complementary case to Hammett's *Red Harvest*—both novels serving as examples of a limit. The Op's unsuccessful search for a scapegoat condemns the community to disunity, if we can speak of community at all. Chandler's novel, McCann writes, "is similarly unable to create a substantial sense of solidarity, but for a contrary reason. Chandler finds, in effect, too many scapegoats, banishing every feature of the postwar world and leaving Marlowe no one to feel communal with" (197). What McCann might have added, though, is that we are unable to decide whether or not Marlowe prefers it this way. In a competitive society in which money values and exchange are dominant, Marlowe requires the moral high ground of impossible payment and return. His ambivalence is like an ague whose periodic return reminds us of an infection whose subsequent and perhaps unending cycles we are unable to escape.

"A private dick. And I'm not hired by anybody either." (Spillane, *Gun* 195)

The endlessly cited chivalry theme among Chandler critics is undermined from his first novel by irony and defeatism. Nonetheless, Chandler heavy-handedly litters his texts with allusions which encourage readers to view Marlowe as his knight-errant. Marlowe is not a Don Quixote, breaking through his mad misappraisal to acquire a pragmatic understanding of nascent capitalism's disenchantment of the world; rather, Marlowe's demystification process is the existential query into his own battered subjectivity, and the suspicion that he is little more than a determined quantity in a matrix of relations defined by power and money. This self-assessment climaxes in *The Long Goodbye*, where his resistance takes the form of a quest for pockets of private experience still untainted by such determinations—however, these become purely formal exercises, ironically structured around playing over championship chess games from manuals whose predetermined outcomes mock his efforts. Mike Hammer suffers no such moments of self-reflective anguish; he is a man who has scant trouble expressing his limited range of emotions. It requires an uncomfortable stretch of the imagination to call Hammer's behavior chivalrous. He views the parade of hoods, pushers, pimps, racketeers, gamblers, Communists, and, most importantly, duplicitous women to be the dragons of the modern world—they deserve to be slain, and we should not be too concerned over how it is done. Chandler reminds us of chivalrous conundrums, recognizable in Tristan or Lancelot, in which the individual comes up against social codes and practices that seriously undermine his or her ability to act. No such obstacles for Hammer: "the very thought of anyone touching his virginal secretary Velda," Cawelti notes, "reduces Mike Hammer to a gibbering homicidal mania" (*Adventure* 151).

Spillane's novels therefore cannot be comfortably fit into the existential chivalry of Chandler's oeuvre, even as hyperbolic chivalry; rather, the notion of chivalry itself collapses under the extremity of the textual situations. Spillane is one step beyond *all* verisimilitude and one step away from comic book–type suspension of disbelief.[6] Hammer is the comic book character who erupts onto the scene because institutions fail—governmental and police authority, science, and the press are impotent onlookers in the face of villains who are little more than evil caricatures. It is easy to dismiss the Hammer series because we are offended by the immaturity of Spillane's vitriolic outbursts. Instead of berating this body of work for lacking any socially redeemable qualities, we would be better advised to pursue interpretations which probe their thematic obsessions with the aim of explaining both why they achieved such stunning popularity and, more academically, how they relate to a broader trajectory of development within the genre. One means of achieving this link is through understanding Hammer's gift-labor, to which I will shortly return.

From a formal view, the pervasive unreality of the first six novels in the Hammer series does not depend solely upon his being unkillable or his inexplicable attractiveness to women. The very procedures he employs and his relations to institutional forces mark the stories as having self-consciously crossed a threshold. This point resonates with Mandel's historical understanding of crime-solving methods and the complexity of cooperative investigative procedures, increasing division of labor, and specialization in modern police and forensic methods. Ruehlmann demonstrates the implausibility of virtually any private detective novel against the legal limits placed upon real-life investigators. He cites extracts from New York state law which destroy any shred of believability in Spillane's work (3–4), concluding that "the private eye of fiction is, then, an invention; only a literary heraldry can account for him" (4).

In the foreword to Ruehlmann's book, Aaron Marc Stein hints that the psychological investment in violent narrative is not a particularly American trait, in answer to the charge that Hammer is nurtured specifically by American soil. He points to sales of Hammer novels in translation outside the US to substantiate this claim. Indeed, for Spillane and his pulp and paperback colleagues, "these American Private-Eye stories are an export commodity. Their great sales are not limited to the home market. Their foreign market sales are also massive" (Ruehlmann xi). The explanation offered by Stein is that the revenge model of "justice," barred by law, is hungered for by the masses. He further suggests that modern life stimulates "a universal itch to take justice into our own hands" and "to let us good guys have a share in the intoxicating joys of sadism" (xii).[7] Later, Ruehlmann supplies a twist to this reading by suggesting that Hammer never acts out of some public concern, nor is he interested in forms of labor that entail responsibility to others.

---

[6]   Perhaps unsurprisingly, Hammer started life as a comic book figure. Van Dover remarks the comic book quality of the Hammer novels (93-4), as do Margolies (13), Collins and Traylor (38), and Geherin (127).

[7]   Margolies views Hammer's violence to be in line with traditional American popular heroes. The primary difference lies in the absent idealism that tempers, explains, or justifies this violence (14). Curiously, it is the "radical failure to establish positive values in his fiction" that Van Dover views as paramount to Spillane's success (151).

Rather, "he operates out of personal interest alone" (Ruehlmann 98)—and by doing so, he removes the mediating obstacles of institutions (Coxe's Flash Casey and Kent Murdock), loyalty to the company and its protocols and professional ethics (Hammett's Continental Op), and the interests of his client (Chandler's Marlowe)—and, we might add, the class interests to some degree bound up with all of these figures. Ruehlmann continues: "Hammer, middle class and anti-intellectual, embodying the middle-class man's suspicion of government and faith in the will of 'the people,' is easy for an American to identify with; his vendettas are his readers" (98). These vendettas take on the form of a calling. This link is already suggested by Cawelti, who sees in Spillane an intensification of distinctly American patterns expressed more subtly by more talented writers, by which Spillane taps into a "popular evangelical tradition"—hence the "central themes of hostility toward the sinful city with its corrupt men of wealth, its degenerate foreigners, and its Scarlet Women" (*Adventure* 190).

Given these characterizations, Spillane criticism is generally and unsurprisingly superficial, concerned with either a gloating defense of Spillane against the liberal intelligentsia[8] or denunciation which rarely goes beyond surprise and dismay at the popularity of the novels.[9] Understanding Hammer's obsessive violence in the context of labor and gift has not been examined. The first six Mike Hammer novels, written between 1947 and 1952, demonstrate a changing relation to the gift, which subtly moves from the more or less straightforward debt relations of *I, the Jury* (1947) to the gift as inexplicable expenditure in *Kiss Me Deadly* (1952). Stein's and Ruehlmann's arguments about identifying with Hammer in order to achieve justice through vengeance is understated—this argument is more in line with milder forms of the genre, hidden in that the execution rounding out the Golden Age story appears in an unwritten but nonetheless real chapter beyond the novel's end. The Golden Age is the attempted settling of debts by which calculated retribution represents the ideal—the association of pleasure with such reckoning is present in a muted form (with the possible exception of the vengeance-minded Thorndyke novels), but transferred to the beaming couple that typically finds the obstacles to their happiness removed. The uncalculated violence exuded by Hammer is, if we are to believe some of the critics I have cited, the very source of satisfaction—innocence, if it exists, is mowed down along with guilt. Justice as revenge is not an equation but a praxis that dispenses with careful calculation. At the same time, this violence is consistently framed by the gift in the early novels, one which at first is bounded by an economy of debt and of settling accounts, subsequently by friendships, however brief or lapsed, and which eventually occurs in the wake of anonymous, chance encounters. Indeed, the impossibility of the gift is heightened by the fact that Hammer's beneficiaries are, without exception, dead.

---

[8]   See the introductions by Max Collins and Lawrence Block to the New American Library compilations published in 2001, as well as the entirety of Collins and Traylor's *One Lonely Knight*.

[9]   The most concise source for antagonistic reactions is Geherin (120–21).

Spillane's first Mike Hammer installment, *I, the Jury*, opens with the brutal murder of Hammer's close friend, former police officer Jack Williams. Mike's longstanding relation to the victim is deeply influenced by Jack's wartime self-sacrifice, in which he saved Mike's life by taking a bayonet in the arm. Jack's action led to an amputation that spelled the end of his career in the police force. The vengeance killing is therefore tangibly motivated by the demands of repaying an otherwise unpayable debt, though a debt that some reflection reveals to be problematic, given Hammer's sexualization of his war experiences with Jack ("Jack Williams, the guy that shared the same mud bed with me through two years of warfare in the stinking slime of the jungle" [Spillane, *Jury* 5]).[10] The mindless hostility expressed later in remarks to Hal Kines and George Kalecki, in which Hammer suggests that Kines and Kalecki are lovers (Spillane, *Jury* 20), is gloatingly confirmed in a subsequent inspection of their apartment (Spillane, *Jury* 34)—his virulent homophobia opens up questions about how excessive violence compensates for Hammer's debt of gratitude. Nonetheless, on the level of plot, relatively conventional notions of debt function to justify Hammer's understanding of his responsibilities. The problem of the gift thus remains embryonic in this text. Jack, who is treated sympathetically, is in fact the center of an extensive gift network, a fount of self-sacrifice which leaves other characters in impossible circumstances. As a police officer before the war, Jack rescues Myrna Devlin from an attempted suicide brought about by heroin addiction. On his own initiative, he helps her through rehabilitation, and, after his return from military service, plans to marry her. Later, Jack is revealed to have several other irons in the fire, associating with the lowest ranks of society out of compassion—Eileen Vickers, a prostitute, reveres him as the one who offered her encouragement instead of judgment; Hal Kines, one of the villains of the novel, is given the opportunity to avoid jail time through Jack's intervention. Ironically, Jack's kindness leads to his murder.

The next Hammer novel, *My Gun Is Quick* (1950), addresses the gift in more complex terms, first of all by blurring Mike's obligation to its recipient and by introducing the figure of the false-giver. The book is still preliminary to the spectacular giving of *Kiss Me Deadly* a few years later, partly because the story is framed by Mike's address to the reader, in which he circumscribes his violence within the boundaries of a perverse labor, thus placing himself within a fantasy space for his audience: "I'm not you," he asserts, "and looking for those things [violent action] is my job" (Spillane, *Gun* 153). The inciting moment occurs in a cheap Manhattan diner, where Nancy—a prostitute whose name we only learn much later—strikes up a fast friendship with Mike. Mike's chivalrous defense of Nancy against her vicious pimp and his subsequent gift of money to encourage her to get off the street evokes Jack's role from the first novel. The suspicious circumstances around Nancy's death the next day prod Mike to investigate, first to give her a name, subsequently to figure the death as murder, provide a proper

---

[10]   Jack is not the only man he has "shared a bed" with—in the opening segments of *Vengeance Is Mine!* (1950) Mike wakes up in the same bed as another old army buddy.

funeral, and finally to exact revenge. In establishing the name, Mike counters the villain, Arthur Berin-Grotin, who, unbeknownst to the reader until the end of the text, turns out to be Nancy's grandfather.

A distinguishing feature of the Hammer series, recognized by Geherin (123) and to a lesser extent by Collins and Traylor (34), is Mike's proclivity to work for free. Hammer is, as he flatly asserts at one point in the novel, "A private dick. And I'm not hired by anybody either" (Spillane, *Gun* 195). He works out of emotional attachments that have no basis in a shared history, as in *The Big Kill* (1951): when someone asks Hammer who is paying for his investigative services, Mike answers, "Nobody .... I'm on my own time and my own capital" (Spillane 197). What briefly appears exceptional in *My Gun Is Quick* in fact only confirms the rule, not only in that Hammer would have acted in the same way had no client appeared, but in that the client himself turns out to be the evil mastermind behind the nefarious scheme. Berin, an exceptionally wealthy man, pays Mike handsomely to look into Nancy's murder; his selflessness masks a vested interest: to keep abreast of developments and influence their outcome. Before this double-cross comes to light, though, Mike must first grapple with Nancy's own questionable activities— not the exploited prostitute, the fallen woman who can be forgiven and "raised up" to normal life again through the intervention of Jack Williams or Mike Hammer, but a blackmailer who photographs johns and who crossed the wrong people. In this novel of reversals, however, Hammer sorts out the threads.

The novel eventually contrasts two forms of giving—the calculated giving of the publicly lauded philanthropist Berin with the authentic giving of the public menace Hammer. We are set up from the start: "Arthur Berin-Grotin is a sucker for hard-luck stories ... besides being one of the city's biggest philanthropists" (Spillane, *Gun* 168). Given our expectations of Spillane, we are suspicious of Berin's motives right away; his obsession with death or, more accurately, his obsession with remembrance, contrasts with the efforts of Lola, a second prostitute, with whom Mike falls in love. Lola helps Mike break into Berin's call girl racket, despite her protests of fear: "I don't want to die for something like that" (Spillane, *Gun* 211). Of course, Lola is "brought around" to view sacrifice as service, and, naturally enough, she dies for her commitment. Her decision is echoed on a personal level in that more than once Lola expresses her love for Mike with the demand that he not return it (Spillane, *Gun* 269).

The next four novels, *Vengeance Is Mine!*, *One Lonely Knight* (1951), *The Big Kill*, and *Kiss Me Deadly*, run along Spillane's familiar thematic lines of violent revenge; however, the beneficiary is marginalized to ever greater degrees. A lapsed army friendship is all that connects Hammer with the victim, Chester Wheeler, in *Vengeance Is Mine!* Wheeler, with his prosperous Midwestern business, his warm family life, and his community standing, contrasts sharply with Hammer, who is held in contempt by all the official institutional organs of society despite his efforts to solve the crime. In the last three novels, Hammer crosses the victim-recipients' paths by chance; they are all strangers, and, more interestingly, all are in fact deviant from Hammer's narrow sense of normalcy: a Communist who is driven to suicide, a recidivist thief who abandons his infant son, and a gangster's mistress and former prostitute who attempts to enrich herself through the sale of narcotics stolen from the Mafia. In short, the impulse to give, the gift cycle, and the promise of return are undercut in acts of senseless expenditure in that they are irrational, excessive, and completely unreciprocated.

The most extreme formulation of the gift is found in *Kiss Me Deadly*. At the same time, we reach a sort of furthest limit in what Hammer can hope to accomplish as an individual, the last stand of bourgeois individualism erupting in a demented orgy of violence before it succumbs to social forces greater than itself. The specter of organized crime, in the form of the Mafia, is characterized as an impenetrable organization whose leading figures are far beyond the reach of the law. If, by luck and bloodshed, a kingpin is brought to heel, he is simply replaced, Hydra-like, by another. In this respect, the novel is essentially hopeless in its inability to offer the closure found at the end of the other books (even *One Lonely Knight*); instead, we are impressed by the futile resistance to well protected, global conspiracies. Individual acts of violence do not end, at least temporarily, in the destruction of some evil, which in effect eradicates root and branch the particular threat central to the novel. This situation is in line with Mandel's analysis in that the private detective must necessarily yield to the police procedural—institutional collectivity meeting criminal collectivity.

A more striking feature, though, is that the recipient of the revenge-gift, once again dead, is rendered less deserving than previous donees. In novels like *I, the Jury* and *My Gun Is Quick*, the friend is avenged or the victim turns out to have given her own life to attack injustice. Retribution is largely unproblematic with such sympathetic victims. In *Vengeance Is Mine!* and the novels which follow, the friend is pushed to the sidelines: Hammer's dedication to finding the killer takes place without our emotional involvement with the victims or even our approval. We confront the perverse enactment of a gift which, in light of Goux's discussion of the gift-concept in Seneca and Stoicism, radically excludes the material object and the interest-bearing loan. Proffered to corpses who as living persons were essentially unlikable, Hammer's gift abolishes reciprocity from the horizon of the possible. But that is not all: Hammer's uncalculated expenditure is that very offering which receives in return the universal condemnation of calculating society, and one which inversely parallels the uncomfortable patriarchal authoritarianism of investment.

Conclusion:
The Theatrical Economy

Detective fiction, in its various modes, stages social concerns; this dramatic representation or enactment is both polyvocal and dynamic. The representation of social reality is refracted through ideology and fantasy, sensitive to the idiosyncrasies of writerly production and the market limitations complexly imposed by distribution and readerly consumption. These representations are suspended within a social medium responsive to centers of gravity and power, events, and paradigmatic limits. These generalizations, adequate in terms of the grand tableau, do not offer insight into specific works. If such generalizations are applied now to this genre, close readings invariably show that texts resist being pigeonholed or convincingly polarized. Thus, I have argued that generically defined detective stories exhibit *tendencies* with economic structures that in fact hold good for the trajectory of generic development, especially from the late nineteenth to the mid-twentieth centuries. To be sure, even within this structural configuration, multiple interpretations are the norm. It follows that the implicit totalitarian "solutions" of the Golden Age could be more benignly characterized outside of an overtly political context as a fantasy of correspondence between sign and world. That it potentially takes on the appearance of political totalitarianism, particularly during the 1920s and 1930s, is not a grim indictment of human nature or Western European culture, but one tendency within an unstable, generally exploitative, and frightening sociopolitical framework. That it expresses anxiety towards the establishment of definitive meaning has equal historical relevance, given the breakdown of such correspondences in linguistics and avant-garde art—detective fiction is a popular expression of such crises. As for the hard-boiled side of the coin—again, the same coin within the same generalized economy—we repeatedly and increasingly find the dramatization of failure or partial failure, which complements the Golden Age's anxious theater of success. In the stories we have focused on, that concrete historical framework is the historical transformation of capitalism from the chaotic marketplace of competing small producers, to the consolidation of capital into powerful blocks of interest in the late nineteenth and early twentieth centuries, and, finally, the arrival of massive trusts, monopoly, and finance capitalism in the first quarter of the twentieth century. Within this generalized frame, we note the tendency to define individuals as elements within economic relations: their position within the marketplace has cosmological significance, and this cosmology has totalizing ideological consequences. In their role as economic abstractions, detectives take on the function of the general equivalent, which, in this case, and even in respect to murder, most often involves mediation between property owners. As I have consistently emphasized, such relations reflect a convergence of genre formation and historical substrate, conditions that have their economic correlates. In *Capital*

Marx himself uses curiously theatrical language to describe this phase of social development in regard to what qualifies as a viable person: "Here the persons exist for one another merely as representatives and hence owners, of commodities. ... the characters who appear on the economic stage are merely personifications of economic relations; it is as the bearers of these economic relations that they come into contact with each other" (I: 179).[1]

For my purposes, and unlike the claims of the later Marx and his popularization in Engels, this economy cannot be analyzed in strictly scientific terms; neither does it hold a utopian promise. Trotsky recognizes this limit in an article from 1931, "What Is a Revolutionary Situation?" where he notes several of the disruptions that have occupied us, namely, the decline of empire, the cooperation between capital and government forces (whether totalitarian or liberal) to combat falling rates of profit and defuse the threat of socialism, disemployment and the victory of economic collectivism without a change in the ownership of the modes of production—these historical factors, Trotsky maintains, constitute the economic and social conditions favorable for revolutionary action (353). In a sense, the production and consumption of detective fiction within the subgenres examined in this study serve as evidence that the psychological response is ambivalent, and that for better or worse, what we find dramatized is the victory of property relations and the subordination of individuals to the economy, either as facilitators or as individuals who draw their status or roles based on an economic scrip(t). This return to order, actually a return to a certain kind of imbalance, is paraded as a confirmation of social rank, to overcome the criminal disruption which "threatens the community's ability to distinguish what hierarchical combination is appropriate" (Pyrhönen 202).[2]

Detective fiction nonetheless constitutes a range of popularized discourses refracting *and* manipulating the socioeconomic and political discourses concurrent with its appearance. In sympathy with Mandel, I began this project by referring to the ideological shifts subtending the rise and transformation of detective fiction from its nineteenth-century origins in Poe. Structural parallels were examined in terms of Bataille's theories of homogeneous social relations and nonproductive expenditure, Goux's claims about the economic dimensions of abstract art and the breakdown of correspondence theories of signification and reality vis-à-vis the gold standard, and the transformations of work under scientific management and the loss of worker autonomy. In this conclusion, we can appeal to one more transformative approach, namely Peter Szondi's characterization of the Drama. Szondi's ideas in *Theory of the Modern Drama* (1965) are relevant, given the commitment to explicating the historical groundedness of genre, though in philosophical terms that are at once aesthetically oriented and general. Referencing

---

[1]   See also Goux on this point (*Coiners* 56–57).

[2]   See Loïc Wacquant's "Crafting the Neoliberal State: Workfare, Prisonfare, and Social Insecurity" for a contemporary discussion of how crime and punishment are theatricalized in terms of popular television shows to benefit a political elite (206).

Hegel, Lukács, Benjamin, and Adorno, Szondi explains how form becomes conceptualized historically; though applied initially to the basic Aristotelian genres, the self-consciousness of this historicization persists in any genre-based study. Szondi's basic presentation of the problem and the rationale for his book need not be confined to theater; it suggests the very form-content confusion expressed in much detective fiction—perhaps because its formal constraints are so vividly impressed upon the general reader's mind:

> The possibility arises ... that the statement made by the content may contradict the form. If, when there is an equivalence between form and content, the thematic operates within the framework of the formal statement as a problem contained, so to speak, within something unproblematic, a contradiction arises, because the indisputable fixed statement of the form is called into question by the content. It is this inner antinomy that causes a given literary form to become historically problematic. (Szondi 4–5)

Szondi notes how manuals on technique, such as the Freytagian model of the well wrought play, appear, owl-of-Minerva-like, at the eclipse of an era, at a point where the form starts to disintegrate due to internal contradictions. For the Drama, that self-contained, parallel universe in which we voyeuristically peep through the invisible fourth wall, the crisis deepens through the formal innovations of avant-garde playwrights. Szondi documents the "crisis of the Drama," which begins with Ibsen and proceeds through Strindberg, Chekhov, Maeterlinck, and Hauptmann, before moving on to what he terms rescue attempts.

The overlap between the notions of theatrical enclosure and boundaries (both in space and content) and detective fiction are striking, even more so given the further relation between these boundaries and an economic structure. This connection, though usually only receiving passing comment, is alluded to by Roth, who notes that "most detective fiction does take place in strictly confined space" (30). Aydelotte refers specifically to the country house tale, whose settings "are more like theatrical sets than real estates. The characters who inhabit them are known to each other only by virtue of the roles they play, roles that they resolutely pretend are real, though most of them have 'offstage' activities, carefully concealed from the other players" (124). This space corresponds (though self-consciously and sometimes anxiously) to the Drama, and in many respects to the criteria established by Freytag in *The Technique of the Drama*—a space that differentiates an outside from an inside, a formalized understanding of time and space relations and limits, a commitment to rational motives and analyzable human actions, and, perhaps most questionably, the rejection of the *deus ex machina*. Although these formal limits are in place, the Classical/Golden Age drama develops, curiously enough, along lines of crisis that threaten the substance of its very formal designation, specifically in the reassurance of its meaning-generating function. In Malmgren's adept phrase, "detective fiction often stages for its readers a crisis in signification, the fall of the sign. As it discloses the arbitrariness of various signifying systems, it inevitably draws attention to itself as signifying practice" (*Anatomy* 113). As we have seen, this crisis eventually becomes insurmountable (the problem of universal guilt in Chapter 1; the problem of enclosure traceable in Christie in Chapter 2; the misalignment of detective and institutional interests in Chapter 3; the attribution of value in Chapter 4).

The persistence of this framing problem is widespread. The increasingly elaborate frames of reference in Christie and Carr have been mentioned (Chapter 2), but in fact the obsessive attempts to establish viable frames and the submission to the *deus ex machina* in the form of the outsider-detective reaches a limit in *Ask a Policeman*—parody, in this case, is less an homage than an indication of the form's collapse (which nonetheless enjoys an afterlife as Golden Age nostalgia to the present day). From Futrelle's "The Problem of Cell 13" (1905), with its surveillance space that is undercut by the detective who moves across boundaries and thereby violates the sanctity of the theater space, to Carr's *The Problem of the Green Capsule* (1939), in which the dramatization of crime and its real execution are indistinguishable and subject to mechanical reproduction and manipulation, the belief in the formal theatrical space is both preestablished and subjected to probing questions. Like Hamlet's scheme to indict the guilty Claudius, the play-within-a-play is standard detective fare, the culminating reconstruction of the crime, a recurring ploy in Reeve, Queen, and a host of others. This performance space, which Panek notes is perhaps most pronounced in Ngaio Marsh's predilection for literally staging murder (*Watteau's* 195)—such as in *Vintage Murder* (1937) and *Overture to Death* (1939) or more figuratively in *Artists in Crime* (1938) and *Death at the Bar* (1940)—is in fact the basic logic of the Golden Age's anxiety-compelling and anxiety-reducing therapy.[3] The complex dramatic questions raised by the staging of crime are partly the outcome of the metafictional tendency, well illustrated in the problem of spectatorship. The audience does not consist simply of a reader; the narrative is mediated by forms of staged spectatorship, with multiple levels of surveillance, that approximate reader positions. We can explore this situation in two brief analyses.

Returning to Carr's *The Problem of the Green Capsule*, analyzed in terms of enclosure in Chapter 2, we find a narrative mediated by Inspector Elliot's official point of view. Initially, in the opening segment in Italy, this takes on the form of a drama: we share his perspective on the Pompeiian "performance" (though we are still unaware of who he is) within the larger frame of an omniscient narration. These competing frames of understanding, relevant to much detective fiction, are brought to notice, if not destabilized, by the skepticism of Marcus Chesney, who maintains with some heat, "Over and over again I've proved my contention …

---

[3]   The tremendous number of Classical and Golden Age murder mysteries relying upon actors and theatrical settings cannot be accidental. Just to list a few in addition to the ones already mentioned: Freeman's *The Mystery of 31 New Inn* (1912), Queen's *The Roman Hat Mystery* (1929), Christie's *Lord Edgeware Dies* (1933), Mitchell's *Death at the Opera* (1934), Boucher's *The Case of the Seven of Calvary* (1937), and Crispin's *Swan Song* (1947).

that the average person … is absolutely incapable of reporting accurately what he sees or hears. You don't observe. You can't observe" (Carr, *Green Capsule* 4). In addition to foreshadowing later events, in which the demonstration of the limits of observational powers is entwined with the dispatch of a crime, the challenge to our own observational powers as readers of detective fiction is also raised, as is the way in which a situation is taken in by the official mind represented by Elliot.

Elliot, having been called in by Scotland Yard to investigate the poisoning case since the eruption of hate against the Chesney family escalates upon their return, arrives just in time for Marcus's murder. The theatrical overtones are reinforced by the description of the setting: the light from the house "gave the smooth grass a theatrical green; it illuminated every yellow leaf on the chestnut trees, throwing theatrical shadows under them" (Carr, *Green Capsule* 19). This impression is strengthened by the crime scene: "Here was the dead man sitting behind a table that faced the double-doors across the room, with a strong light set to shine on him. It was like a stage—with illuminations. If those folding doors were open, and people were sitting beyond them to look in here, this room would be like a stage" (Carr, *Green Capsule* 21). The audience, too, is carefully constructed: Marjorie, George Harding (research chemist), Ingram (professor of psychology), and Joe Chesney (MD), though Joe is absent because of professional duties. If Marjorie, to employ stereotypes that are not foreign to Carr, represents the emotional response, the others suggest aspects of trained scientific minds: methods derived from the physical sciences, psychology, and physiology, respectively. As it turns out, at least by Marjorie's description, the murder was the unexpected culmination of a performance designed to test the observational powers of the audience (in which we must eventually include the institutional representatives who investigate it as well as ourselves). Death itself is dramatized, that is, by Marcus, who "dies" in performance—his collapse at the end is feigned, or as Marjorie remarks: "That was only pretense: that was only a part of the show: it signified the end of the performance" (Carr, *Green Capsule* 31).

Of course, the performance ends with an actual death. In the play Marcus was forced to swallow a capsule containing poison, which, instead of simply being mimed, actually occurs. This variation is accomplished through the substitution of one actor for another, the original actor having been struck unconscious before the performance began. These complications point to a double performance which threatens to spill out of the boundaries of the book. The staging of the crime, in a quite deliberate way, is framed by a "real" crime investigation which duplicates the first performance; this relation potentially leads to a tertiary level of investigation. Many of the efforts of the police, then, seem aimed at finding a means to stop the expansion of the crime—and, to generalize, such efforts have the aim of localizing crime within known parameters and eventually to attribute disruptions of normalcy to the aberrations of individuals. This much is indicated by the relief of the officers in the case. Major Crow: "'But look here Inspector—even so—to do that—my God, are we dealing with a lunatic?' 'Looks like it, sir.' 'Let's face it,' said Major Crow. 'A lunatic, or whatever fancy name we want to call it, from this house'" (Carr, *Green Capsule* 36)—that is, an aberrant individual within a defined and bounded space. Later, Dr. Fell, too, makes a similar suggestion: "They are not natural crimes; they are calculated abnormalities, and the person who perpetrated them is about as safe to have about the house as a king cobra" (Carr, *Green Capsule* 78). Much of the investigative process that follows is an attempt to close this site and keep it closed.

As I have pursued in Chapter 3, the framing capacity of the detective, a problem that extends to the attribution of value (Chapter 4), comes under scrutiny in much hard-boiled work. Establishing a viable cast of characters becomes more difficult once the nature of the enclosure loses definition. The problem is thematized in an important metafictional text, Berkeley's *The Poisoned Chocolates Case* (1929), by Mr. Bradley, who in Chapter 11 of that novel ironically qualifies the situations in fiction and in real life. The "closed" and the "open" refer to murders which occur within parameters that isolate a site from the chaos of everyday social intercourse (138). This distinction applies to the hard-boiled narrative of the haptic type—open refers not so much to specific spaces, but to the limited vision of the detective, whose position moves from director to spectator, and often remains there until the end.

To illustrate, Dashiell Hammett's "The House in Turk Street" (1924) is a tale whose initial uncertainties escalate, through the misapprehension of spaces, to life-threatening proportions. The Op seeks a man who cannot, with precision, be assigned spatial coordinates, who has in fact run away from home. This nameless individual only functions to spur action; his identity remains exceptionally vague: "I had been told that the man for whom I was hunting lived in a certain Turk Street block, but my informant hadn't been able to give me his house number. Thus it came about that late one rainy afternoon I was canvassing this certain block, ringing each bell, and reciting a myth that went like this: ..." (Hammett 93). Invited by an elderly couple into their home, the Op is absorbed into the quiet, stereotyped domesticity oozing from his hosts, that is, until he is threatened at gunpoint by members of a gang, including the erstwhile benevolent couple. The irony of his situation—having misapprehended the couple but having been equally misread by the criminals, having been in search of a man with possible criminal antecedents, and having, in spite of himself, found just that—is increased by a hint of satire that involves the complex theatricalization of authorship. Two gang members debate the Op's fate off stage—a "cultured British" voice which contrasts with the ugly punk, Hook, who speaks an ungrammatical, slang-encrusted American patois—the British voice offering a series of reasoned premises to dissuade Hook from killing his prisoner, the American gangster advocating shooting first and not asking questions later (Hammett, "Turk Street" 99). The argument, of course, puts us in mind of two types of detective story associated with these respective modes of speech, a sort of altercation between authors of very different mindsets. The Op, tied to a chair and thus curtailed in his movements like a theater spectator, is party to a theatrical experience that culminates in the physical confrontation of the two male antagonists, that is, the genres personified. This impression is strengthened by the Op himself: "According to the best dramatic rules, these folks should have made sarcastic speeches to me before they left, but they didn't. They passed me without even a farewell look, and then went out of sight into the darkness of the hall" (Hammett, "Turk Street" 107).

The theatrical aspect is heightened by other features—the Gladys Mitchell–type stage management exhibited by Tai, the Chinese criminal with the cultured voice, who manipulates the Op so that he will kill the untrustworthy Hook. Tai's finagling with bullets allows the Op to eliminate Hook without retaining a dangerous weapon. But the acting is not all on their side, as the Op himself confirms when waiting to confront Tai after concealing the stolen bonds at the root of the caper: "Then I turned on all the lights in the room, lighted a cigarette (we all like to pose a little now and then), and sat down on the bed to await my capture" (Hammett, "Turk Street" 111). Humorous overtones invade the story as the British-accented antagonist prepares to "traffic" with the Op for the Bonds: "As a basis for our bargaining, we will stipulate that you have hidden the bonds where they cannot be found by anyone else; and that I have you completely in my power, as the shilling shockers used to have it" (Hammett, "Turk Street" 113). This establishment of rules (and the subsequent metadiscursive description by Tai of how the narrative might turn out) is, naturally, the laying out of a boundary in whose enclosed space we can confidently expect the rule of law, and in fact which both detective and criminal are supposed to enter willingly for the dramatization of their struggle. The resurgence of the American version commences with the reappearance of the elderly couple, now suitably transformed into gun-toting, insult-slinging mobsters. As they did at the start, they reintegrate the Op into their frame of reference by suggesting he has been Tai's ally all along. Tai, for his part, insists on enforcing the dramatic metaphor by attempting to convert the room back into a manageable theatrical space with properly scripted roles; he remarks: "I was about to extract the information [about the hiding place of the bonds] from him when you so—ah—dramatically arrived" (Hammett, "Turk Street" 115–16). The upshot is the disbelief expressed by Tai that the Op has no knowledge of what any of this is about, which, naturally, he does not.

What the theater implies, then, is escape from the confines of a boundedness over which we have no control—over the threatening aspects of real expenditure (the collapse of law or discourse), the ascription of value founded upon ordained standards, or the alienation of modern working conditions. The apparent dissolving of reference points in exemplary hard-boiled situations, particularly those found in Hammett and Chandler, is brought back under scrutiny through the resurrection of the hard-boiled operative, most dramatically after the (frequent) near-death experience. The eventual breakdown of this recuperation is evident in the postmodern tale, for instance in *The New York City Trilogy*. Alford's analysis demonstrates Auster's textual economy to lack an abstract reference point or measure by which to establish value or truth (to which he could have added productive labor). Alford cites Georges Van Den Abbeele, who "notes that the *oikos* is not a geographical location but 'a transcendental point of reference that organizes and domesticates a given area by defining all other points in relation to itself'" (623). The rug is pulled out from under us at the end of *City of Glass* in that Auster wants to have it both ways—the discursive recuperation of the survivor's tale (the hard-boiled first-person past tense) and the invisible locus from which that discourse is generated. The transcendental selfhood of the Golden Age omniscient type and the limited but stable selfhood of the hard-boiled detective give way to indeterminacy.

Although I have discussed open and closed sites as a problem of definition and ideology, the physical qualities in both cases suggest a dramatic backdrop. Crime fiction of all types stages the crisis of community or more generally of law under the aegis of aesthetics, offering solutions to this essentially dramatized (aestheticized) problem. Cawelti makes a reasonable argument when he states that a profound change in the representation of crime constitutes "a shift from an essentially religious or moral feeling about crime to what might best be called an aesthetic approach to the subject" (*Adventure* 54–55). The sociological response might view this aesthetic turn more aptly as a hegemonic practice, one which not only converts murder into a fine art, but also rereads police violence as aesthetically engaging, and therefore not in conflict with the so-called egalitarian promises of western democracy.[4] In any case, the fact that detective fiction resorts to the dramatization of the event prompts an equally "dramaturgical criticism," a form of inquiry which "does not prod a viewer to do something or change something, but simply to 'appreciate' something in its givenness" (Gouldner, *Dialectic* 169). The theater defuses the problem of hierarchy, either its exploitive potential or its crisis of legitimacy and potency, in aesthetic obfuscation. Thus, in this critical mode, detective fiction is at once a site of expenditure and a resolution and return to productivity, a recuperation of self which is lost temporarily in the suspension of knowledge. Whether this tension is alleviated by deference to the omniscient possessor of arcane knowledge or whether it works out through the surrogate of the tough guy may lead to similar outcomes, but, we hope, its persistent self-referentiality does not necessarily return it comfortably to the Same.

---

[4]   See Alvin Gouldner's chapter "Ideology and the Bourgeois Order" in *The Dialectic of Ideology and Technology* for a discussion of how such societies "blur the existence of hierarchy and ... conceal domination" (205).

Works Cited

Ackershoek, Mary Anne. "'The Daughters of His Manhood': Christie and the Golden Age of Detective Fiction." *Theory and Practice of Classic Detective Fiction*. Eds Jerome H. Delamater and Ruth Prigozy. Westport: Greenwood P, 1997. 119–28. Print.

Alewyn, Richard. "The Origin of the Detective Novel." *The Poetics of Murder: Detective Fiction and Literary Theory*. Trans. Glenn W. Most. Eds Glenn W. Most and William W. Stowe. New York: Harcourt Brace Jovanovich, 1983. 62–78. Print.

Alford, Steven E. "Spaced-Out: Signification and Space in Paul Auster's *The New York Trilogy*." *Contemporary Literature* 36.4 (1995): 613–32. Print.

Aronowitz, Stanley, and William DiFazio. *The Jobless Future: Sci-Tech and the Dogma of Work*. Minneapolis: U of Minnesota P, 1994. Print.

Atkin, Nicholas. "Withstanding Extremes: Britain and France, 1918–1940." *Themes in Modern European History, 1890–1945*. Eds Nicholas Atkin and Michael Biddiss. London: Routledge, 2009. 243–72. Print.

Atkinson, Michael. *The Secret Marriage of Sherlock Holmes and Other Eccentric Readings*. Ann Arbor: U of Michigan P, 1996. Print.

Auden, W.H. "The Guilty Vicarage." 1948. *Detective Fiction: A Collection of Critical Essays*. Ed. Robin Winks. Englewood Cliffs: Prentice-Hall, 1980. 15–24. Print.

Auster, Paul. *City of Glass*. 1987. *The New York City Trilogy*. New York: Penguin, 1990. 3–158. Print.

Aydelotte, William O. "The Detective Story as a Historical Source." 1949. *Dimensions of Detective Fiction*. Eds Larry N. Landrum, Pat Browne, and Ray B. Browne. Bowling Green: Popular P, 1976. 68–82. Print.

Bander, Elaine. "Dorothy L. Sayers." *Great Women Mystery Writers: Classic to Contemporary*. Ed. Kathleen Gregory Klein. Westport: Greenwood P, 1994. 309–13. Print.

Bargainnier, Earl F. *The Gentle Art of Murder: The Detective Fiction of Agatha Christie*. Bowling Green: Bowling Green UP, 1980. Print.

Barsham, Diana. *Arthur Conan Doyle and the Meaning of Masculinity*. Burlington: Ashgate, 2000. Print.

Bataille, Georges. *Guilty*. 1944. Trans. Bruce Boone. Venice: Lapis P, 1988. Print.

———. *The History of Eroticism*. 1957. Trans. Robert Hurley. New York: Zone, 1993. Print.

———. "The Notion of Expenditure." 1933. *Visions of Excess: Selected Writings, 1927–1939*. Trans. Allan Stoekl. Minneapolis: U of Minnesota P, 1985. 116–36. Print.

———. *Oeuvres Complètes*. Paris: Gallimard, 1970–1988. 12 vols. Print.

———. *On Nietzsche*. 1945. Trans. Bruce Boone. New York: Paragon, 1992. Print.

———. "The Psychological Structure of Fascism." 1933. *Visions of Excess: Selected Writings, 1927–1939*. Trans. Allan Stoekl. Minneapolis: U of Minnesota P, 1985. 137–60. Print.

———. *Sovereignty*. 1956. Trans. Robert Hurley. New York: Zone, 1993. Print.

———. "The Use Value of D.A.F. de Sade." c. 1930. *Visions of Excess: Selected Writings, 1927–1939*. Trans. Allan Stoekl. Minneapolis: U of Minnesota P, 1985. 91–102. Print.

Bazelon, David T. "Dashiell Hammett's 'Private Eye': No Loyalty beyond the Job." *Commentary* 7.5 (1949): 467–72. Print.

Beck, Ulrich. *The Brave New World of Work*. Trans. Patrick Camiller. Cambridge: Polity P, 2000. Print.

Bell, Ian A. "Eighteenth-Century Crime Writing." *Cambridge Companion to Detective Fiction*. Ed. Martin Priestman. Cambridge: Cambridge UP, 2003. 7–17. Print.

Belsey, Catherine. "Sherlock Holmes: Deconstructing the Text." *Sherlock Holmes: The Major Stories with Contemporary Critical Essays*. Ed. John A. Hodgson. New York: Bedford, 1994. 381–88. Print.

Bentley, Christopher. "Radical Anger: Dashiell Hammett's *Red Harvest*." *American Crime Fiction: Studies in the Genre*. Ed. Brian Docherty. New York: St. Martin's P, 1999. 54–70. Print.

Berger, John. *Ways of Seeing*. London: Penguin, 1972. Print.

Berkeley, Anthony. *The Poisoned Chocolates Case*. 1929. New York: Dell, 1957. Print.

Berkeley, Anthony, Milward Kennedy, Gladys Mitchell, John Rhode, Dorothy L. Sayers, and Helen Simpson. *Ask a Policeman*. 1933. New York: Berkeley, 1983. Print.

Bernasconi, Robert. "What Goes Around Comes Around: Derrida and Levinas on the Economy of the Gift and the Gift of Genealogy." *The Logic of the Gift: Toward an Ethic of Generosity*. Ed. Alan D. Schrift. New York: Routledge, 1997. 256–73. Print.

Biggers, Earl Derr. *Keeper of the Keys*. Indianapolis: Bobbs-Merrill, 1932. Print.

Blake, Nicolas [C. Day Lewis]. *There's Trouble Brewing*. 1937. New York: Harper and Row, 1982. Print.

Block, Walter. "The Gold Standard: A Critique of Friedman, Mundell, Hayek, and Greenspan from the Free Enterprise Perspective." *Managerial Finance* 25.5 (1999): 15–33. Print.

Bordo, Michael D., and Ronald MacDonald. "The Inter-War Gold Exchange Standard: Credibility and Monetary Independence." *Journal of International Money and Finance* 22.1 (2003): 1–32. *OCLC*. Web. 9 Dec. 2009.

Boucher, Anthony. *The Case of the Seven Sneezes*. 1942. New York: Pyramid, 1966. Print.

Brand, Christianna. *Tour de Force*. 1955. New York: Carol and Graf, 1988. Print.

Braverman, Harry. *Labor and Monopoly Capitalism: The Degradation of Work in the Twentieth Century.* New York: Monthly Review P, 1974. Print.

Breit, William, and Kenneth G. Elzinga. "Economics as Detective Fiction." *The Journal of Economic Education* 33.4 (2002): 367–76. *JSTOR*. Web. 3 Aug. 2011.

Broe, Dennis. "Class, Labor, and the Home-Front Detective: Hammett, Chandler, Woolrich, and the Dissident Lawman (and Woman) in 1940s Hollywood and Beyond." *Social Justice* 32.2 (2005): 167–85. *Wilson Web*. Web. 1 June 2012.

Brubaker, Bill. *Stewards of the House: The Detective Fiction of Jonathan Latimer.* Bowling Green: Bowling Green State U Popular P, 1993. Print.

Caillois, Roger. *The Mystery Novel.* Trans. Roberto Yahni and A.W. Sadler. New York: Laughing Buddha P, 1984. Print.

Caputo, John D. "The Time of Giving, the Time of Forgiving." *The Enigma of Gift and Sacrifice.* Eds Edith Wyschogrod, Jean-Joseph Goux, and Eric Boynton. New York: Fordham UP, 2002. 117–47. Print.

Carr, John Dickson. *Castle Skull.* 1931. New York: Berkeley, 1960. Print.

———. *Death Watch.* 1935. New York: Macmillan, 1984. Print.

———. *The Lost Gallows.* 1931. New York: Pocket, 1947. Print.

———. *The Problem of the Green Capsule.* 1939. New York: Bantam, 1956. Print.

———. *The Three Coffins.* 1935. New York: International Polygonics, 1986. Print.

Carrier, James G. *Gifts and Commodities: Exchange and Western Capitalism since 1700.* London: Routledge, 1995. Print.

Cawelti, John G. *Adventure, Mystery, and Romance.* Chicago: U of Chicago P, 1976. Print.

———. "Artistic Failures and Successes: Christie and Sayers." *Detective Fiction: A Collection of Critical Essays.* Ed. Robin Winks. Englewood Cliffs: Prentice-Hall, 1980. 188–99. Print.

Chandler, Raymond. *The Big Sleep.* 1939. *Stories and Early Novels.* New York: The Library of America, 1995. 587–764. Print.

———. *Farewell, My Lovely.* 1940. *Stories and Early Novels.* New York: The Library of America, 1995. 765–984. Print.

———. *The High Window.* 1942. *Stories and Early Novels.* New York: The Library of America, 1995. 985–1177. Print.

———. *The Little Sister.* 1949. *Later Novels and Other Writings.* New York: The Library of America, 1995. 201–416. Print.

———. *The Long Goodbye.* 1953. *Later Novels and Other Writings.* New York: The Library of America, 1995. 417–734. Print.

———. "The Simple Art of Murder." 1944. *Later Novels and Other Writings.* New York: The Library of America, 1995. 977–92. Print.

———. "Spanish Blood." 1935. *Stories and Early Novels.* New York: The Library of America, 1995. 191–234. Print.

Charney, Hannah. *The Detective Novel of Manners: Hedonism, Morality, and the Life of Reason.* London: Associated UP, 1981. Print.

Chesterton, G.K. "The Invisible Man." 1911. *Father Brown Stories.* London: Penguin, 1994. 74–94. Print.

———. "The Strange Crime of John Boulnois." 1914. *Father Brown Stories*. London: Penguin, 1994. 220–38. Print.

Christianson, Scott R. "Tough Talk and Wisecracks: Language and Power in American Detective Fiction." *The Journal of Popular Culture* 23.2 (1989): 151–62. *PAO*. Web. 1 June 2012.

Christie, Agatha. *And Then There Were None*. 1939. New York: St. Martin's P, 2001. Print.

———. "The Jewel Robbery at the Grand Metropolitan." 1924. *Poirot Investigates*. New York: Berkeley, 2000. 112–31. Print.

———. *Murder at the Vicarage*. 1930. New York: Signet, 2000. Print.

———. *The Murder of Roger Ackroyd*. 1926. New York: Berkeley, 2000. Print.

———. *Murder on the Orient Express*. 1934. New York: Berkeley, 2000. Print.

Cohen, Michael. *Murder Most Fair: The Appeal of Mystery Fiction*. Madison: Fairleigh Dickinson UP, 2000. Print.

Collins, Max Allan, and James L. Traylor. *One Lonely Knight: Mickey Spillane's Mike Hammer*. Bowling Green: Bowling Green State U Popular P, 1984. Print.

Cook, Michael. *Narratives of Enclosure in Detective Fiction: The Locked Room Mystery*. Basingstoke: Palgrave MacMillan, 2011. Print.

Cooper, Brian, and Margueritte Murphy. "Taking Chances: Speculation and Games of Detection in Dashiell Hammett's *Red Harvest*." *Mosaic: A Journal for the Interdisciplinary Study of Literature* 33.1 (2000): 145–60. Print.

Copjec, Jean, ed. *Shades of Noir*. New York: Verso, 1993. Print.

Corey, Lewis. *The Crisis of the Middle Class*. New York: Covici Friede, 1935. Print.

———. *The Decline of American Capitalism*. New York: Covici Friede, 1934. Print.

Coxe, George Harmon. *The Camera Clue*. New York: Dell, 1937. Print.

———. *Murder for Two*. New York: Dell, 1943. Print.

———. "Murder Mix-Up." 1936. *The Hard-Boiled Omnibus: Early Stories from Black Mask*. Ed. Joseph T. Shaw. New York: Simon and Schuster, 1946. 181–224. Print.

———. *Murder with Pictures*. New York: Dell, 1935. Print.

———. *Silent Are the Dead*. New York: Dell, 1941. Print.

Crisman, William. "Poe's Dupin as Professional, The Dupin Stories as Serial Text." *Studies in American Fiction* 23.2 (1995): 215–29. *PAO*. Web. 1 June 2012.

Crispin, Edmund. *The Moving Toyshop*. 1946. New York: Felony and Mayhem P, 2011. Print.

Davis, Frederick C. "Crucibles of the Damned." 1936. *Ravenwood: The Complete Series*. Boston: Altus P, 2008. 107–58. Print.

Davis, Norbert. "Red Goose." 1934. *The Hard-Boiled Omnibus: Early Stories from* Black Mask. Ed. Joseph T. Shaw. New York: Simon and Schuster, 1946. 157–80. Print.

Day, Gary. "Investigating the Investigator: Hammett's Continental Op." *American Crime Fiction: Studies in the Genre.* Ed. Brian Docherty. New York: St. Martin's P, 1999. 39–53. Print.

DeFino, Dean. "Lead Birds and Falling Beams." *Journal of Modern Literature* 27.4 (2004): 73–81. *Wilson Web.* Web. 1 June 2012.

Delaney, Bill. "Hammett's *The Maltese Falcon.*" *Explicator* 63.3 (2005): 167–69. *Wilson Web.* Web. 1 June 2012.

Denning, Michael. *The Cultural Front: The Laboring of American Culture in the Twentieth Century.* London: Verso, 1997. Print.

———. *Mechanic Accents: Dime Novels and Working-Class Culture in America.* London: Verso, 1987. Print.

Dent, Lester. "The Death Blast." 1933. *The Weird Adventures of the Blond Adder.* Boston: Altus P, 2010. 1–53. Print.

Derrida, Jacques. *The Gift of Death.* Trans. David Wills. Chicago: U of Chicago P, 1995. Print.

———. *Given Time I: Counterfeit Money.* Trans. Peggy Kamuf. Chicago: U of Chicago P, 1992. Print.

Dickson, Carter [John Dickson Carr]. *The Judas Window.* 1938. Lyons: Rue Morgue P, 2008. Print.

Dollard, John, Neal E. Miller, Leonard W. Doob, O.H. Mowrer, and Robert Sears. *Frustration and Aggression.* New Haven: Yale UP, 1939. Print.

Doray, Bernard. *From Taylorism to Fordism: A Rational Madness.* Trans. David Macey. London: Free Association, 1988. Print.

Dove, George N. *The Police Procedural.* Bowling Green: Bowling Green U Popular P, 1982. Print.

———. *The Reader and the Detective.* Bowling Green: Bowling Green State U Popular P, 1997. Print.

Doyle, Arthur Conan. "The Adventure of the Cardboard Box." 1917. *Complete Sherlock Holmes and Other Detective Stories.* Glasgow: HarperCollins, 1994. 483–96. Print.

———. "The Adventure of the Six Napoleons." 1901. *Complete Sherlock Holmes and Other Detective Stories.* Glasgow: HarperCollins, 1994. 975–88. Print.

———. "The Adventure of the Speckled Band." 1892. *Complete Sherlock Holmes and Other Detective Stories.* Glasgow: HarperCollins, 1994. 368–84. Print.

———. "The Red-Headed League." 1891. *Complete Sherlock Holmes and Other Detective Stories.* Glasgow: HarperCollins, 1994. 297–312. Print.

———. *The Sign of the Four.* 1890. *Complete Sherlock Holmes and Other Detective Stories.* Glasgow: HarperCollins, 1994. 175–243. Print.

———. *A Study in Scarlet.* 1887. *Complete Sherlock Holmes and Other Detective Stories.* Glasgow: HarperCollins, 1994. 83–154. Print.

Durham, Philip. *Down These Mean Streets a Man Must Go: Raymond Chandler's Knight.* Chapel Hill: U of North Carolina P, 1963. Print.

Eagleton, Terry. *Marxism and Literary Criticism.* London: Routledge, 1976. Print.

Erikson, Kai. "On Work and Alienation." *The Nature of Work: Sociological Perspectives*. Eds Kai Erikson and Steven Peter Vallas. New Haven: Yale UP, 1990. 19–35. Print.

Evans, Mary. *The Imagination of Evil: Detective Fiction and the Modern World.* London: Continuum, 2009. Print.

Foucault, Michel. "A Preface to Transgression." 1963. Trans. Donald F. Bouchard and Sherry Simon. *Essential Works of Foucault 1954–1984: Aesthetics, Method, and Epistemology*. London: Penguin, 1994. 69–87. Print.

Freedman, Carl, and Christopher Kendrick. "Forms of Labor in Dashiell Hammett's *Red Harvest.*" *The Critical Response to Dashiell Hammett*. Ed. Christopher Metress. Westport: Greenwood P, 1994. 12–29. Print.

Freeman, R. Austin. "The Case of Oscar Brodski." 1912. *The Best Dr. Thorndyke Detective Stories*. New York: Dover, 1973. 1–41. Print.

———. *The Cat's Eye*. 1923. Kelly Bray: Stratus, 2001. Print.

———. *The D'Arblay Mystery*. 1926. Kelly Bray: Stratus, 2001. Print.

———. *The Eye of Osiris*. 1911. Oxford: Oxford UP, 1989. Print.

———. *The Red Thumb Mark*. 1907. Breinigsville: Resurrected P, 2010. Print.

———. *A Silent Witness*. 1914. Kelly Bray: Stratus, 2001. Print.

———. *The Stoneware Monkey*. 1938. New York: Dover, 1987. Print.

Futrelle, Jacques. "The Haunted Bell." *Mystery and Detection with the Thinking Machine*. Vol 1. Landisville: Coachwhip, 2009. 457–91. Print.

———. "Kidnapped Baby Blake, Millionaire." *Mystery and Detection with the Thinking Machine*. Vol 2. Landisville: Coachwhip, 2009. 7–36. Print.

———. "The Leak." 1907. *Mystery and Detection with the Thinking Machine*. Vol 1. Landisville: Coachwhip, 2009. 504–19. Print.

———. "The Mystery of the Man Who Was Lost." 1907. *Mystery and Detection with the Thinking Machine*. Vol 1. Landisville: Coachwhip, 2009. 96–125. Print.

———. "The Problem of Dressing Room A." *Mystery and Detection with the Thinking Machine*. Vol 1. Landisville: Coachwhip, 2009. 12–27. Print.

———. "The Problem of the Broken Bracelet." *Mystery and Detection with the Thinking Machine*. Vol 2. Landisville: Coachwhip, 2009. 183–99. Print.

———. "The Problem of the Crystal Gazer." 1906. *Mystery and Detection with the Thinking Machine*. Vol 1. Landisville: Coachwhip, 2009. 266–80. Print.

———. "The Problem of the Knotted Cord." *Mystery and Detection with the Thinking Machine*. Vol 2. Landisville: Coachwhip, 2009. 236–46. Print.

Gardiner, Dorothy, and Kathrine Sorley Walker, eds. *Raymond Chandler Speaking*. Berkeley: U of California P, 1997. Print.

Gasché, Rodolphe. "Heliocentric Exchange." Trans. Morris Parlow. *The Logic of the Gift: Toward an Ethic of Generosity*. Ed. Alan D. Schrift. New York: Routledge, 1997. 100–117. Print.

Gatenby, Bruce. "'A Long and Laughable Story': Hammett's *The Dain Curse* and the Postmodern Condition." *The Critical Response to Dashiell Hammett*. Ed. Christopher Metress. Westport: Greenwood P, 1994. 56–67. Print.

Geherin, David. *The American Private Eye: The Image in Fiction.* New York: Frederick Ungar, 1985. Print.

Gide, André. *The Counterfeiters.* 1925. Trans. Dorothy Bussy. New York: Vintage, 1973. Print.

Gilder, George. *Wealth and Poverty.* New York: Basic, 1981. Print.

Goodman, Robin Truth. *Policing Narratives and the State of Terror.* Albany: SUNY P, 2009. Print.

Gouldner, Alvin W. *Against Fragmentation: The Origins of Marxism and the Sociology of Intellectuals.* New York: Oxford UP, 1985. Print.

———. *The Coming Crisis of Western Sociology.* New York: Basic, 1970. Print.

———. *The Dialectic of Ideology and Technology: The Origins, Grammar, and Future of Ideology.* New York: Continuum, 1976. Print.

———. *The Future of Intellectuals and the Rise of the New Class.* New York: Continuum, 1979. Print.

Goux, Jean-Joseph. "Banking on Signs." Trans. Thomas DiPiero. *Diacritics* 18.2 (1988): 15–25. *JSTOR.* Web. 19 Oct. 2007.

———. *The Coiners of Language.* Trans. Jennifer Curtiss Gage. Norman: U of Oklahoma P, 1994. Print.

———. "General Economics and Postmodern Capitalism." Trans. Kathryn Ascheim and Rhonda Garelick. *Yale French Studies* 78 (1990): 206–24. Print.

———. "Seneca against Derrida: Gift and Alterity." Trans. Marila Gackowski. *The Enigma of the Gift and Sacrifice.* Eds Edith Wyschogrod, Jean-Joseph Goux, and Eric Boynton. New York: Fordham UP, 2002. 148–60. Print.

———. *Symbolic Economies: After Marx and Freud.* Trans. Jennifer Curtiss Gage. Ithaca: Cornell UP, 1990. Print.

Greene, Douglas G. *John Dickson Carr: The Man Who Explained Miracles.* New York: Otto Penzler, 1995. Print.

Gregory, Sinda. *Private Investigations: The Novels of Dashiell Hammett.* Carbondale: Southern Illinois UP, 1985. Print.

Grella, George. "The Hard-Boiled Detective Novel." *Detective Fiction: A Collection of Critical Essays.* Ed. Robin Winks. Englewood Cliffs: Prentice-Hall, 1980. 103–20. Print.

Guérin, Daniel. *Fascism and Big Business.* 1936. Trans. Frances Merrill and Mason Merrill. New York: Pathfinder P, 1973. Print.

Hagemann, E.R. "Ramon Decolta, A.K.A. Raoul Whitfield, and His Diminutive Brown Man: Jo Gar, The Island Detective." *West of Guam: The Complete Cases of Jo Gar.* By Raoul Whitfield. Boston: Altus P, 2013. xxiii–xxxv. Print.

Hall, Jasmine Yong. "Jameson, Genre, and Gumshoes: *The Maltese Falcon* as Inverted Romance." *The Critical Response to Dashiell Hammett.* Ed. Christopher Metress. Westport: Greenwood P, 1994. 78–89. Print.

Hammett, Dashiell. "The Big Knockover." 1927. *The Big Knockover.* New York: Vintage, 1989. 349–405. Print.

———. *The Dain Curse.* 1929. *Complete Novels.* New York: The Library of America, 1999. 189–386. Print.

————. "Dead Yellow Women." 1925. *The Big Knockover*. New York: Vintage, 1989. 189–246. Print.

————. "House Dick." 1923. *Nightmare Town*. New York: Vintage, 1999. 42–54. Print.

————. "The House in Turk Street." 1924. *The Continental Op*. New York: Vintage, 1992. 91–119. Print.

————. *The Maltese Falcon*. 1930. *Complete Novels*. New York: The Library of America, 1999. 387–585. Print.

————. *Red Harvest*. 1928. *Complete Novels*. New York: The Library of America, 1999. 1–187. Print.

————. "The Scorched Face." 1925. *The Big Knockover*. New York: Vintage, 1989. 74–114. Print.

————. "Tom, Dick, or Harry?" 1925. *Nightmare Town*. New York: Vintage, 1999. 236–49. Print.

————. "The Whosis Kid." 1925. *The Continental Op*. New York: Vintage, 1992. 179–238. Print.

————. "Zigzags of Treachery." 1924. *Nightmare Town*. New York: Vintage, 1999. 95–128. Print.

Hartman, Geoffrey. "Literature High and Low: The Case of the Mystery Story." *The Poetics of Murder. Detective Fiction and Literary Theory*. Eds Glenn W. Most and William W. Stowe. New York: Harcourt Brace Jovanovich, 1983. 210–29. Print.

Heissenbüttel, Helmut. "Rules of the Game of the Crime Novel." Trans. Glenn W. Most and William W. Stowe. *The Poetics of Murder. Detective Fiction and Literary Theory*. Eds Glenn W. Most and William W. Stowe. New York: Harcourt Brace Jovanovich, 1983. 79–92. Print.

Herzel, Roger. "John Dickson Carr." *Minor American Novelists*. Ed. Charles Alva Hoyt. Carbondale: Southern Illinois UP, 1970. 67–80. Print.

Hilfer, Tony. *The Crime Novel: A Deviant Genre*. Austin: U of Texas P, 1990. Print.

Hilgart, John. "Philip Marlowe's Labor of Words." *Texas Studies in Literature and Language* 44.4 (2002): 368–91. Print.

Hofstadter, Richard, and Michael Wallace, eds. *American Violence: A Documentary History*. New York: Knopf, 1970. Print.

Hollier, Denis. *Against Architecture: The Writings of Georges Bataille*. Trans. Betsy Wing. Cambridge: MIT P, 1989. Print.

————. "The Dualist Materialism of Georges Bataille." Trans. Hilari Allred. *Yale French Studies* 78 (1990): 124–39. Print.

Holmes, H.H. [Anthony Boucher]. *Nine Times Nine*. New York: Penguin, 1940. Print.

Horsley, Lee. *The Noir Thriller*. Basingstoke: Palgrave, 2001. Print.

————. *Twentieth-Century Crime Fiction*. Oxford: Oxford UP, 2005. Print.

Hühn, Peter. "The Detective as Reader: Narrativity and Reading Concepts in Detective Fiction." *Modern Fiction Studies* 33.3 (1987): 451–66. *PAO*. Web. 1 June 2012.

Hulley, Kathleen. "From the Crystal Sphere to Edge City: Ideology in the Novels of Dashiell Hammett." *Myth and Ideology in American Culture*. Ed. Régis Durand. Lille: U of Lille III, 1976. 111–27. Print.

Irwin, John T. "Being Boss: Raymond Chandler's *The Big Sleep*." *The Southern Review* 37.2 (2001): 211–48. *Wilson Web*. Web. 1 June 2012.

Jaffe, Audrey. "Detecting the Beggar: Arthur Conan Doyle, Henry Mayhew, and 'The Man with the Twisted Lip.'" *Sherlock Holmes: The Major Stories with Contemporary Critical Essays*. Ed. John A. Hodgson. New York: Bedford, 1994. 402–27. Print.

Jameson, Frederic. "On Raymond Chandler." *The Poetics of Murder. Detective Fiction and Literary Theory*. Eds. Glenn W. Most and William W. Stowe. New York: Harcourt Brace Jovanovich, 1983. 122–48. Print.

———. "The Synoptic Chandler." *Shades of Noir*. Ed. Jean Copjec. New York: Verso, 1993. 33–56. Print.

Joshi, S.T. *John Dickson Carr: A Critical Study*. Bowling Green: Bowling Green State U Popular P, 1990. Print.

Kayman, Martin A. "The Short Story from Poe to Chesterton." *Cambridge Companion to Detective Fiction*. Ed. Martin Priestman. Cambridge: Cambridge UP, 2003. 41–58. Print.

Keller, Joseph, and Kathleen Gregory Klein. "Detective Fiction and the Function of Tacit Knowledge." *Mosaic* 23.2 (1990): 45–60. *PAO*. Web. 1 June 2012.

Kelly, R. Gordon. *Mystery Fiction and Modern Life*. Jackson: UP of Mississippi, 1998. Print.

Kennedy, J. Gerald. "The Limits of Reason: Poe's Deluded Detectives." *American Literature* 47.2 (1975): 184–97. *MLA International Bibliography*. Web. 6 Dec. 2012.

Kestner, Joseph A. *The Edwardian Detective, 1901–1915*. Aldershot: Ashgate, 2000. Print.

———. *Sherlock's Men: Masculinity, Conan Doyle and Cultural History*. Aldershot: Ashgate, 1997. Print.

Klein, Kathleen Gregory, ed. *Great Women Mystery Writers: Classic to Contemporary*. Westport: Greenwood P, 1994. Print.

Knight, Stephen. "The Case of the Great Detective." *Sherlock Holmes: The Major Stories with Contemporary Critical Essays*. Ed. John A. Hodgson. New York: Bedford, 1994. 368–80. Print.

———. *Crime Fiction, 1800–2000: Detection, Death, Diversity*. New York: Palgrave Macmillan, 2004. Print.

———. *Form and Ideology in Crime Fiction*. Bloomington: Indiana UP, 1980. Print.

———. "The Golden Age." *Cambridge Companion to Detective Fiction*. Ed. Martin Priestman. Cambridge: Cambridge UP, 2003. 77–94. Print.

Latimer, Jonathan. *Murder in the Madhouse*. 1935. New York: International Polygonics, 1989. Print.

Lenin, Vladimir. "The Immediate Tasks of the Soviet Government." Trans. Bernard Isaacs. Vol. 42 of *Collected Works*. Vladimir Lenin. 45 vols. 1946–1970. Moscow: Foreign Languages Publishing House, 1969. 68–84. Print.

———. *Notebooks on Imperialism*. Trans. Clemens Dutt. Vol. 39 of *Collected Works*. Vladimir Lenin. 45 vols. 1946–1970. Moscow: Foreign Languages Publishing House, 1968. Print..

———. *What Is to Be Done?* Trans. Joe Fineberg and George Hanna. Vol. 5 of *Collected Works*. Vladimir Lenin. 45 vols. 1946–1970. Moscow: Foreign Languages Publishing House, 1961. 345–529. Print.

Libertson, Joseph. "Bataille and Communication: From Heterogeneity to Continuity." *Modern Language Notes* 89.4 (1974): 669–98. Print.

Little, William G. "Nothing to Go On: Paul Auster's *City of Glass*." *Contemporary Literature* 38.1 (1997): 133–61. Print.

Mahan, Jeffrey Howard. *A Long Way from Solving That One: Psycho/Social and Ethical Implications of Ross Macdonald's Lew Archer Tales*. Lanham: UP of America, 1990. Print.

Malmgren, Carl D. *Anatomy of a Murder: Mystery, Detection and Crime Fiction*. Bowling Green: Bowling Green UP, 2001. Print.

———. "The Crime of the Sign: Dashiell Hammett's Detective Fiction." *Twentieth Century Literature* 45.3 (1999): 371–84. *JSTOR*. Web. 2 Aug. 2011.

Mandel, Ernest. *Delightful Murder: A Social History of the Crime Story*. Minneapolis: U of Minnesota P, 1984. Print.

Marcus, Laura. "Detection and Literary Fiction." *Cambridge Companion to Detective Fiction*. Ed. Martin Priestman. Cambridge: Cambridge UP, 2003. 245–67. Print.

Marcus, Stephen. "Dashiell Hammett." *The Poetics of Murder. Detective Fiction and Literary Theory*. Eds Glenn W. Most and William W. Stowe. New York: Harcourt Brace Jovanovich, 1983. 197–209. Print.

Margolies, Edward. *Which Way Did He Go?: The Private Eye in Dashiell Hammett, Raymond Chandler, Chester Himes, and Ross Macdonald*. New York: Holmes and Meier, 1982. Print.

Marling, William. *The American Roman Noir: Hammett, Cain, Chandler*. Athens: U of Georgia P, 1995. Print.

Marx, Karl. *Capital: Volume 1*. Trans. Ben Fowkes. London: Penguin, 1976. Print.

———. *Capital: Volume 2*. Trans. David Fernbach. London: Penguin, 1978. Print.

———. *Capital: Volume 3*. Trans. David Fernbach. London: Penguin, 1981. Print.

———. *Economic Manuscripts of 1857–58*. Trans. Ernst Wangermann. Vol. 28 of *Collected Works*. Karl Marx and Friedrich Engels. 50 vols. 1975–2004. Moscow: Progress Publishers, 1986. Print.

Maugham, William Somerset. *The Vagrant Mood: Six Essays*. London: Heinemann, 1952. Print.

Mauss, Marcel. *The Gift*. 1924. Trans. W.D. Halls. New York: Norton, 1990. Print.

McCann, Sean. *Gumshoe America: Hard-Boiled Crime Fiction and the Rise and Fall of New Deal Liberalism*. Durham: Duke UP, 2000. Print.

McGregor, Robert Kuhn, and Ethan Lewis. *Conundrums for the Long Week-End: England, Dorothy L. Sayers, and Lord Peter Wimsey*. Kent: Kent State UP, 2000. Print.

McGurl, Mark. "Making 'Literature' of It: Hammett and High Culture." *American Literary History* 9.4 (1997): 702–14. *JSTOR*. Web. 3 Aug. 2011.

McLuhan, Herbert Marshall. "Footprints in the Sands of Crime." *The Sewanee Review* 54.4 (1946): 617–34. *JSTOR*. Web. 6 Dec. 2012.

Merrill, Robert. "Christie's Narrative Games." *Theory and Practice of Classic Detective Fiction*. Eds Jerome H. Delamater and Ruth Prigozy. Westport: Greenwood P, 1997. 87–101. Print.

———. "Raymond Chandler's Plots and the Concept of Plot." *Narrative* 7.1 (1999): 3–21. *JSTOR*. Web. 13 Sept. 2013.

Metress, Christopher. "Thinking the Unthinkable: Reopening Conan Doyle's 'Cardboard Box.'" *The Midwest Quarterly* 42.2 (2001): 183–98. *Wilson Web*. Web. 1 June 2012.

Mills, C. Wright. *The Power Elite*. London: Oxford UP, 1956. Print.

———. *White Collar: The American Middle Classes*. New York: Oxford UP, 1951. Print.

Mitchell, Gladys. *Death at the Opera*. 1934. London: Vintage, 2010. Print.

———. *The Mystery of a Butcher's Shop*. 1930. London: Vintage, 2010. Print.

———. *The Rising of the Moon*. 1945. London: Virago, 1996. Print.

———. *The Saltmarsh Murders*. 1932. London: Vintage, 2009. Print.

———. *Speedy Death*. 1929. London: Hogarth P, 1988. Print.

———. *When Last I Died*. 1941. London: Vintage, 2009. Print.

Montgomery, David. *Workers' Control in America: Studies in the History of Work, Technology, and Labor Struggles*. New York: Cambridge UP, 1979. Print.

Moretti, Franco. *Signs Taken for Wonders: Essays in the Sociology of Literary Forms*. Rev. ed. Trans. Susan Fischer, David Forgacs, and David Miller. London: Verso, 1988. Print.

Murray, Will. Introduction. *Diamondstone: Magician-Sleuth*. By G.T. Fleming-Roberts. Boston: Altus P, 2012. n. pag. Print.

Nealon, Jeffrey T. "Work of the Detective, Work of the Writer: Paul Auster's *City of Glass*." *Modern Fiction Studies* 42.1 (1996): 91–110. Print.

Nebel, Frederick. "Die-Hard." 1935. *Winter Kill: The Complete Cases of MacBride and Kennedy*. Vol. 4. Boston: Altus P, 2013. 55–92. Print.

———. "He Could Take It." 1932. *Tough as Nails: The Complete Cases of Donahue*. Boston: Altus P, 2012. 301–32. Print.

———. "The Red-Hots." 1931. *Tough as Nails: The Complete Cases of Donahue*. Boston: Altus P, 2012. 43–78. Print.

———. "Red Pavement." 1932. *Tough as Nails: The Complete Cases of Donahue*. Boston: Altus P, 2012. 377–404. Print.

———. "Rough Justice." 1930. *Tough as Nails: The Complete Cases of Donahue*. Boston: Altus P, 2012. 1–38. Print.

———. "Rough Reform." 1933 *Too Young to Die: The Complete Cases of MacBride and Kennedy*. Vol. 3. Boston: Altus P, 2013. 1–34. Print.

————. "Save Your Tears." 1932. *Tough as Nails: The Complete Cases of Donahue*. Boston: Altus P, 2012. 409–40. Print.

————. "Six Diamonds and a Dick." 1932. *The Complete Casebook of Cardigan, Volume 1: 1931–32*. Boston: Altus P, 2012. 71–105. Print.

————. "Spare the Rod." 1931. *Tough as Nails: The Complete Cases of Donahue*. Boston: Altus P, 2012. 163–95. Print.

————. "Ten Men from Chicago." 1930. *Shake Down: The Complete Cases of MacBride and Kennedy*. Vol. 2. Boston: Altus P, 2013. 89–123. Print.

————. "A Truck-Load of Diamonds." 1932. *The Complete Casebook of Cardigan, Volume 1: 1931–32*. Boston: Altus P, 2012. 349–76. Print.

Nolan, William F. *The Black Mask Boys: Masters in the Hard-Boiled School of Detective Fiction*. New York: William Morrow, 1985. Print.

North, Peter. *Money and Liberation: The Micropolitics of Alternative Currency Movements*. Minneapolis: U of Minnesota P, 2007. Print.

Panek, LeRoy L. *Probable Cause: Crime Fiction in America*. Bowling Green: Bowling Green State U Popular P, 1990. Print.

————. *Watteau's Shepherds: The Detective Novel in Britain, 1914–1940*. Bowling Green: Bowling Green U Popular P, 1979. Print.

Panek, LeRoy L., and Mary M. Bendel-Simso, eds. *Early American Detective Stories: An Anthology*. Jefferson: McFarland, 2008. Print.

Parker, Robert B. *The Private Eye in Hammett and Chandler*. Northridge: Lord John P, 1984. Print.

Peach, Linden. *Masquerade, Crime, and Fiction: Criminal Deceptions*. Basingstoke: Palgrave Macmillan, 2006. Print.

Porter, Dennis. "The Private Eye." *Cambridge Companion to Detective Fiction*. Ed. Martin Priestman. Cambridge: Cambridge UP, 2003. 95–113. Print.

————. *The Pursuit of Crime: Art and Ideology in Detective Fiction*. New Haven: Yale UP, 1981. Print.

Pyrhönen, Heta. *Mayhem and Murder: Narrative and Moral Problems in the Detective Story*. Toronto: U of Toronto P, 1999. Print.

Rabinowitz, Peter J. "Rats behind the Wainscoting: Politics, Convention, and Chandler's *The Big Sleep*." *The Critical Response to Raymond Chandler*. Ed. J.K. Van Dover. Westport: Greenwood P, 1995. 117–37. Print.

Reeve, Arthur B. "Craig Kennedy's Theories." *The Silent Bullet*. New York: Harper and Brothers, 1910. 1–3. Print.

————. "The Sand-Hog." *The Poisoned Pen*. New York: Harper and Brothers, 1911. 154–83. Print.

————. "The Silent Bullet." *The Silent Bullet*. New York: Harper and Brothers, 1910. 5–33. Print.

————. "The Truth-Detector." *The Treasure Train*. 1917. Gillette: Wildside P, 2000. 26–53. Print.

————. "The Vital Principle." *The Treasure Train*. 1917. Gillette: Wildside P, 2000. 187–216. Print.

Rhodes, Chip. "Raymond Chandler and the Art of the Hollywood Novel: Individualism and Populism in *The Little Sister*." *Studies in the Novel* 33.1 (2001): 95–109. *EBSCOhost*. Web. 1 June 2012.

Rorty, James. *Our Master's Voice: Advertising*. New York: John Day, 1934. Print.

Roth, Marty. *Foul and Fair Play: Reading Genre in Classic Detective Fiction*. Athens: U of Georgia P, 1995. Print.

Routledge, Christopher. "A Matter of Disguise: Locating the Self in Raymond Chandler's *The Big Sleep* and *The Long Goodbye*." *Studies in the Novel* 29.1 (1997): 94–107. Print.

Rowen, Norma. "The Detective in Search of the Lost Tongue of Adam: Paul Auster's *City of Glass*." *Critique* 32.4 (1991): 224–34. Print.

Rowland, Susan. *From Agatha Christie to Ruth Rendell*. Basingstoke: Palgrave, 2001. Print.

Ruehlmann, William. *Saint with a Gun: The Unlawful American Private Eye*. New York: New York UP, 1974. Print.

Rzepka, Charles J. *Detective Fiction*. Cambridge: Polity P, 2005. Print.

Sayers, Dorothy L. "Aristotle on Detective Fiction." 1946. *Detective Fiction: A Collection of Critical Essays*. Ed. Robin Winks. Englewood Cliffs: Prentice-Hall, 1980. 25–34. Print.

———. *The Five Red Herrings*. 1931. New York: HarperCollins, 1995. Print.

———. *Unnatural Death*. 1927. New York: HarperCollins, 1995. Print.

Scaggs, John. *Crime Fiction*. London: Routledge, 2005. Print.

Shaw, Marion, and Sabine Vanacker. *Reflecting on Miss Marple*. London: Routledge, 1991. Print.

Shell, Marc. *The Economy of Literature*. Baltimore: The Johns Hopkins UP, 1978. Print.

———. *Money, Language, and Thought: Literary and Philosophical Economies from the Medieval to the Modern Era*. Berkeley: U of California P, 1982. Print.

Shershow, Scott Cutler. *The Work and the Gift*. Chicago: U of Chicago P, 2005. Print.

Smith, Erin A. *Hard-Boiled: Working Class Readers and Pulp Magazines*. Philadelphia: Temple UP, 2000. Print.

Smith, Johanna M. "Raymond Chandler and the Business of Literature." *The Critical Response to Raymond Chandler*. Ed. J.K. Van Dover. Westport: Greenwood P, 1995. 183–201. Print.

Spillane, Mickey. *The Big Kill*. 1951. *The Mike Hammer Collection, Volume 2*. New York: New American Library, 2001. 175–346. Print.

———. *I, the Jury*. 1947. *The Mike Hammer Collection, Volume 1*. New York: New American Library, 2001. 1–147. Print.

———. *My Gun Is Quick*. 1950. *The Mike Hammer Collection, Volume 1*. New York: New American Library, 2001. 149–344. Print.

Symons, Julian. *Bloody Murder: From the Detective Story to the Crime Novel*. 3rd rev. ed. London: Penguin, 1992. Print.

Szlajfer, Henryk. "Waste, Marxian Theory, and Monopoly Capital: Toward a New Synthesis." Trans. Maria Chmielewska-Szlajfer. *The Faltering Economy: The Problem of Accumulation under Monopoly Capitalism.* Eds John Bellamy Foster and Henryk Szlajfer. New York: Monthly Review P, 1984. 297–321. Print.

Szondi, Peter. *Theory of the Modern Drama.* 1965. Trans. Michael Hays. Cambridge: Polity P, 1987. Print.

Taylor, Frederick Winslow. *Scientific Management.* Vol. 1 of *The Early Sociology of Management and Organizations.* Ed. Kenneth Thompson. 8 vols. London: Routledge, 2003. Print.

Thomas, Ronald R. *Detective Fiction and the Rise of Forensic Science.* Cambridge: Cambridge UP, 1999. Print.

Trotsky, Leon. "What Is a Revolutionary Situation?" 1931. *Writings of Leon Trotsky [1930–31].* Eds George Breitman and Sarah Lovell. New York: Pathfinder P, 1973. 352–55. Print.

Van Dover, J. Kenneth. *Murder in the Millions: Erle Stanley Gardner, Mickey Spillane, Ian Fleming.* New York: Frederick Ungar, 1984. Print.

Van Gulik, Robert. *The Chinese Maze Murders.* 1957. Chicago: U of Chicago P, 1997. Print.

Wacquant, Loïc. "Crafting the Neoliberal State: Workfare, Prisonfare, and Social Insecurity." *Sociological Forum* 25.2 (2010): 197–220. Print.

Waples, Douglas. *Research Memorandum on Social Aspects of Reading in the Depression.* 1937. New York: Arno P, 1972. Print.

Watson, Colin. *Snobbery with Violence: Crime Stories and Their Audience.* London: Eyre and Spottiswoode, 1971. Print.

Weisenburger, Steven. "Order, Error, and the Novels of Raymond Chandler." *The Detective in American Fiction, Film, and Television.* Eds Jerome H. Delamater and Ruth Prigozy. Westport: Greenwood P, 1998. 13–26. Print.

Werner, James V. "The Detective Gaze: Edgar A. Poe, the Flaneur, and the Physiognomy of Crime." *American Transcendental Quarterly* 15 (2001): 5–21. *MLA International Bibliography.* Web. 27 June 2012.

Whalen, Terence. "Edgar Allan Poe and Horrid Laws of Political Economy." *American Quarterly* 44.3 (1992): 381–417. *JSTOR.* Web. 8 Feb. 2011.

Whitfield, Raoul. "The Caleso Murders." 1930. *West of Guam: The Complete Cases of Jo Gar.* Boston: Altus P, 2013. 143–59. Print.

———. "China Man." 1932. *West of Guam: The Complete Cases of Jo Gar.* Boston: Altus P, 2013. 357–73. Print.

———. "Enough Rope." 1930. *West of Guam: The Complete Cases of Jo Gar.* Boston: Altus P, 2013. 77–95. Print.

———. *Green Ice.* 1930. Harpenden: No Exit P, 1988. Print.

———. "The Siamese Cat." 1932. *Jo Gar's Casebook. West of Guam: The Complete Cases of Jo Gar.* Boston: Altus P, 2013. 377–93. Print.

Willett, Ralph. *Hard-Boiled Detective Fiction.* Halifax: British Association for American Studies, 1992. Print.

Williams, Raymond. "Base and Superstructure in Marxist Cultural Theory." *New Left Review* 82 (1973): 3–16. Print.

———. *Culture and Society 1780-1950*. Harmondsworth: Penguin, 1963. Print.

———. "The Writer: Commitment and Alignment." *Marxism Today* June (1980): 22–25. Print.

Wolfe, Eric R. *Envisioning Power: Ideologies of Dominance and Crisis*. Berkeley: U of California P, 1999. Print.

Wolfe, Peter. *Something More Than Night: The Case of Raymond Chandler*. Bowling Green: Bowling Green State U Popular P, 1985. Print.

Woods, Robin. "'It Was the Mark of Cain': Agatha Christie and the Murder of the Mystery." *Theory and Practice of Classic Detective Fiction*. Eds Jerome H. Delemater and Ruth Prigozy. Westport: Greenwood P, 1997. 103–10. Print.

Worthington, Heather. *The Rise of the Detective in Early Nineteenth-Century Popular Fiction*. Basingstoke: Palgrave Macmillan, 2005. Print.

Žižek, Slavoj. "The Detective and the Analyst." *Literature and Psychology* 36.4 (1990): 27–46. Print.

Index

abstract art 100, 176
"The Adventure of the Six Napoleons"
     (Doyle) 63, 99, 103, 105, 108–11
alienation 2, 21, 50, 127–31, 147, 149, 152,
     181
And Then There Were None (Christie) 31,
     34–6
Ask a Policeman (Berkeley, et al.) 54–6
Auden, W.H. 26n2
Auster, Paul
     City of Glass 64–5, 182

Bataille, Georges
     and economics 18–21, 23, 85
     and expenditure 1, 18–21, 84, 131, 176
     and the *crochet* 2, 59–61, 83, 116, 153
     and the summit 1–2, 27, 60–1, 146
     works
          "Notion of Expenditure, The"
               19–20
          On Nietzsche 60–1
          "Psychological Structure of
               Fascism, The" 19, 20–1
          Sovereignty 60n3
          "Use Value of D.A.F. de Sade,
               The" 19
Berkeley, Anthony
     Ask a Policeman (Berkeley, et al.) 54–6
     Poisoned Chocolates Case, The 22,
          70, 180
Big Sleep, The (Chandler) 58, 64, 69, 80–4,
     119, 130, 144, 159, 161
Biggers, Earl Derr 98
Blake, Nicolas
     Smiler with a Knife, The 51n10
     There's Trouble Brewing 136, 138
     Thou Shell of Death 138
Boucher, Anthony
     Case of the Seven of Calvary, The
          178n3
     Case of the Seven Sneezes, The 139

Brand, Christianna
     Tour de Force 36–7

"The Caleso Murders" (Whitfield) 70–3
Camera Clue, The (Coxe) 65–7
capitalism
     as condition for detective fiction 46–7,
          126, 128
     and crisis 22, 75
     and exploitation 18, 50, 117
     monopoly capitalism 20, 26, 46, 48,
          53, 84, 86, 128–9, 129n6, 175
Carr, John Dickson
     and self-referentiality 7, 38, 42, 98n3
     works
          Castle Skull 139
          Death Watch 55
          Lost Gallows, The 8n7, 139
          Problem of the Green Capsule, The
               40, 42–5, 80, 178–80
          Three Coffins, The 8n7, 38, 40, 95,
               98n3, 122
Chandler, Raymond
     Big Sleep, The 58, 64, 69, 80–4, 119,
          130, 144, 159, 161
     Farewell, My Lovely 130, 162
     High Window, The 64, 105, 115, 118–24
     Little Sister, The 122, 162, 163
     Long Goodbye, The 130, 148, 154,
          161, 162, 163, 164–9
     "Simple Art of Murder, The" 3, 33, 97
     "Spanish Blood" 63, 96, 152
Chesterton, G.K.
     "Hammer of God, The" 39
     "Invisible Man, The" 29
     "Strange Crime of John Boulnois, The"
          98n4
Christie, Agatha
     "Adventure of 'The Western Star,'
          The" 151
     And Then There Were None 31, 34–6

Curtain 12–14, 31, 36
"Four and Twenty Blackbirds" 50
"Jewel Robbery at the Grand
    Metropolitan, The" 8–9
Murder at the Vicarage 98
Murder of Roger Ackroyd, The 29, 31,
    32–3, 34
Murder on the Orient Express 31, 32,
    33–4, 35
"Veiled Lady, The" 76
class
    class interests or bias 2, 5, 9, 20, 24,
        69, 129, 147, 153, 171
    class structure 12, 29, 102, 107
    middle classes 6, 12, 27, 36, 37, 46,
        46n7, 51, 51n10, 54, 55, 66, 128,
        132, 141, 143, 171
    New Class and New Class
        professionals 51, 66, 69, 127–8,
        131, 137, 156
    working class 17, 106, 109
clues
    false clues 31, 32
    and objectivity 18, 38, 63–4
    as signs 4, 64, 65, 93–5, 99, 102
    and value 29, 73, 94, 99, 103, 104, 111,
        140
Collins, Wilkie 30n4
Corey, Lewis 18, 80, 100
counterfeit
    character as 17, 103
    and standard of measure 34, 102,
        103n7, 115
counterfeiting 102–6, 120, 121, 122, 123
Coxe, George Harmon
    Camera Clue, The 65–7
    Murder for Two 96, 155–6
    "Murder Mix-up" 66, 154–5
    Murder with Pictures 66
    Silent Are the Dead 65
Crispin, Edmund
    Moving Toyshop, The 122
    Swan Song 178n3
Curtain (Christie) 12–14, 31, 36

Daly, John Carroll
    "False Burton Combs, The" 96, 144
The Dain Curse (Hammett) 87–91
Davis, Frederick C. 93

Davis, Norbert
    "Red Goose" 58
    Sally's in the Alley 73, 87
"Dead Yellow Women" (Hammett) 78–80
Dent, Lester 63, 93
Derrida, Jacques
    and gifts 146, 147, 148, 152–4
    works
        The Gift of Death 86
        Given Time I: Counterfeit Money
            42n9, 146, 152–3, 154
detectives
    Alleyn, Roderick (Marsh) 98, 136, 137
    Archer, Lew (Macdonald) 57, 63, 64,
        142, 143, 163
    Bradley, Dame Beatrice Lestrange
        (Mitchell) 17, 48–9, 55, 57, 98,
        137, 143, 148, 180
    Father Brown (Chesterton) 29, 98n4,
        137, 143
    Cardigan, Jack (Nebel) 63, 73, 141–2,
        156, 157n2
    Casey, Flash (Coxe) 62, 63, 65, 142,
        154–6, 158, 171
    Chan, Charlie (Biggers) 98
    Inspector Cockrill (Brand) 36
    Continental Op (Hammett) 57, 73–80,
        84–91, 98, 125, 142, 144–5, 171,
        180–1
    Crane, Bill (Latimer) 62, 67–70, 156
    Dee Jen-djieh (Van Gulik) 57n1, 137
    Donahue, Donnie (Nebel) 57, 63, 73,
        142, 156–8, 163–4
    Dupin, C. Auguste (Poe) 4, 38, 69,
        93–4, 128, 131–2
    Fell, Dr. Gideon (Carr) 38, 42, 45, 55,
        95, 137, 143
    Fen, Professor Gervase (Crispin) 98,
        136, 137, 138, 143
    Gar, Jo (Whitfield) 70–2, 157
    Great Merlini, The 90, 137, 143
    H.M. (Dickson) 41, 143
    Hammer, Mike (Spillane) 23, 142, 164,
        169–74
    Holmes, Sherlock (Doyle) 7, 12n10,
        15, 17, 27–8, 29, 37, 39, 45, 48, 60,
        63, 69, 76n10, 94, 97, 101, 102,
        103, 106–11, 116, 117, 120n18,
        122, 125, 127, 128, 131–6, 151

Kennedy, Professor Craig (Reeve) 23, 132, 133n11, 137, 138, 143
MacBride, Captain Steve (Nebel) 63, 98, 142, 152n1, 156
Marlowe, Philip (Chandler) 57, 63, 69, 81–3, 83n12, 119–24, 1301, 142, 143–4, 161–9, 171
Marple, Jane (Christie) 17, 98, 132, 137
Murdock, Roger (Coxe) 62–3, 65–7, 158, 171
Poirot, Hercule (Christie) 9, 34, 76n10, 136, 137, 151
Queen, Ellery (Queen) 74, 98, 137, 138, 178
Sheringham, Roger (Berkeley) 55, 137
Strangeways, Nigel (Blake) 136, 137, 138
Thorndyke, John (Freeman) 23, 28, 30–1, 64, 94, 97–8, 133, 133n10, 136, 137, 143, 171
Van Dusen, Professor S.F.X. (Futrelle) 30, 133, 137
Vance, Philo (Van Dine) 122, 136, 137, 143
Wimsey, Lord Peter (Sayers) 48, 56, 111–16, 132, 136, 137
dialectic 11, 19, 24, 50, 58, 101, 126, 131, 135, 145
Dickson, Carter
Judas Window, The 40–2, 97
Doyle, Arthur Conan
"The Adventure of the Abbey Grange" 48, 151
"The Adventure of the Beryl Coronet" 106n10
"The Adventure of the Cardboard Box" 103
"The Adventure of the Creeping Man" 110n12
"The Adventure of the Devil's Foot" 27
"The Adventure of the Naval Treaty" 106n10
"The Adventure of the Six Napoleons" 63, 99, 103, 105, 108–11
"The Adventure of the Speckled Band" 107, 133
"A Case of Identity" 134
"Charles Augustus Milverton" 76n10
"The Final Problem" 94, 120n18

"The Man with the Twisted Lip" 133–6
"The Red-Headed League" 29, 101, 105, 106–8
A Study in Scarlet 110n12, 132, 134, 135
drama
detective fiction as dramatic performance 11–12, 29, 40, 176–82
enclosure 28–31, 33, 37–8, 40, 43, 44, 177–8, 180
evidence
and the ascription of value 24, 49, 93–9
objectivity of 41–2, 43, 44, 64–5, 67
The Five Red Herrings (Sayers) 50, 105, 111–16
Foucault, Michel 19, 60
Fleming-Roberts, G.T. 120n17
framing of problems
as detective dependent 8, 24, 31, 38, 41, 44, 68, 73, 77, 81, 99, 119, 135, 140, 180
as ideological 12, 29, 42, 58, 85, 124
as institutional 2, 18, 52, 68, 82, 104, 125, 135, 153, 175
in relation to time and space 32, 42, 43, 56, 165
in relation to truth 22, 32, 44, 94, 97, 98, 99
Freeman, R. Austin
"The Case of Oscar Brodski" 30–1
The Cat's Eye 94, 98
The D'Arblay Mystery 133n10
The Eye of Osiris 97, 133
The Mystery of 31 New Inn 50, 178n3
The Red Thumb-Mark 23, 64
A Silent Witness 133n10
The Stoneware Monkey 133n10
Futrelle, Jacques
"The Leak" 30, 133n9
"Kidnapped Baby Blake, Millionaire" 57n1
"The Mystery of the Man Who Was Lost" 133n9
"The Problem of Dressing Room A" 57n1
"The Problem of the Broken Bracelet" 30
"The Problem of the Crystal Gazer" 133
"The Problem of the Knotted Cord" 30

genre
  clue-puzzle 22, 36, 51, 57, 68, 71, 73,
    74, 99, 111, 137, 139, 152
  definitions 2–6, 7n6, 24, 81, 175
  functions 11, 11n9, 28, 85, 130, 131
  historical specificity of detective 2–6,
    46, 143
  locked-room mystery 18, 27, 32, 33,
    34, 37–40, 42, 52, 96, 101, 113
  postmodern detective 24
Gide, André
  The Counterfeiters 103–5
gift
  and economics 2, 127, 146–7, 152–4,
    165, 167, 174
  and genre distinctions 24, 126–7,
    145
  gift-labor 2, 24, 127, 131, 145–6,
    151–4, 158, 164, 170
gold standard 2, 24, 29, 93, 93n1, 94,
    99–102, 105, 123, 176
Gouldner, Alvin W. 47, 132, 182
Goux, Jean-Joseph
  and gifts 127, 147, 153
  on the gold standard 94
  works
    "Banking on Signs" 100, 101
    The Coiners of Language 103–5,
      124, 176n1
    "General Economics and
      Postmodern Capitalism" 18
    "Seneca against Derrida: Gift and
      Alterity" 153–4
    *Symbolic Economies: After Marx
      and Freud* 1, 15–18, 93, 100,
      108
Green Ice (Whitfield) 158–61

Hammett, Dashiell
  "The Big Knockover" 58
  The Dain Curse 87–91
  "Dead Yellow Women" 78–80
  "House Dick" ("Bodies Piled Up")
    74–7
  "The House in Turk Street" 180–1
  The Maltese Falcon 116–18
  Red Harvest 84–7, 98
  "The Scorched Face" 79n11
  "Tom, Dick, or Harry?" 73n7

  "The Whosis Kid" 73n7, 77–9
  "Zigzags of Treachery" 73n7
"He Could Take It" (Nebel) 157–8
High Window, The (Chandler) 64, 105, 115,
  118–24
Holmes, H. H.
  Nine Times Nine 51–4, 96
"House Dick" ("Bodies Piled Up")
  (Hammett) 74–7
"The House in Turk Street" (Hammett)
  180–1

"Jewel Robbery at the Grand Metropolitan,
  The" (Christie) 8–9
Judas Window, The (Dickson) 40–2, 97

Latimer, Jonathan
  Murder in the Madhouse 62, 67–70
  Red Gardenias 67, 69
Lenin, Vladimir 129, 130n7
Long Goodbye, The (Chandler) 130, 148,
  154, 161, 162, 163, 164–9

Macdonald, Ross 64, 142, 163
The Maltese Falcon (Hammett) 116–18
"The Man with the Twisted Lip" (Doyle)
  133–6
Mandel, Ernest
  Delightful Murder 11–13, 176
Marsh, Ngaio 13, 29, 178
Marx, Karl
  Capital 18, 27, 116, 151–2, 176
  Economic Manuscripts of 1857–58
    100
Mauss, Marcel
  The Gift 147–9
metafiction 51, 73n7, 105, 122, 165, 178,
  180
Mills, C. Wright
  The Power Elite 46n7, 47
  White Collar 129, 142–4
Mitchell, Gladys
  Come Away, Death 64
  Death and the Maiden 138
  Death at the Opera 49, 178n3
  The Devil at Saxon's Wall 50
  Laurels Are Poison 137
  The Mystery of a Butcher's Shop 48–9
  The Rising of the Moon 48, 96

The Saltmarsh Murders 49
Speedy Death 148
When Last I Died 49, 138
Murder for Two (Coxe) 96, 155-6
Murder in the Madhouse (Latimer) 62,
    67–70
"Murder Mix-up" (Coxe) 66, 154–5
Murder of Roger Ackroyd, The (Christie)
    29, 31, 32–3, 34
Murder on the Orient Express (Christie)
    31, 32, 33–4, 35

Nebel, Frederick
    "A Couple of Quick Ones" 50n8
    "Death Alley" 141–2
    "Doors in the Dark" 50n8
    "Die-Hard" 98
    "He Could Take It" 157–8
    "Hell's Paycheck" 73
    "The Law Laughs Last" 63
    "Red Pavement" 73, 163–4
    "The Red-Hots" 58, 157
    "Rough Justice" 57, 157n2
    "Rough Reform" 152n1
    "Save Your Tears" 156–7
    "Six Diamonds and a Dick" 157n2
    "Spare the Rod" 156
    "Ten Men from Chicago" 152n1
    "A Truck-Load of Diamonds" 142
Nine Times Nine (Holmes) 51–4, 96

parody
    in Classic/Golden Age fiction 7, 36, 54,
        101, 107, 111, 137, 178
    in hard-boiled fiction 80, 84, 86, 88
photography 63–6
Poe, Edgar Allan
    as innovator 3–4, 38, 101n5, 128
    works
        "The Murders in the Rue Morgue"
            4, 38, 63, 131
        "The Mystery of Marie Rogêt" 4
        "The Purloined Letter" 4, 131
Problem of the Green Capsule, The (Carr)
    40, 42–5, 80, 178–80

Rawson, Clayton 122, 137
Red Harvest (Hammett) 84–7, 98
"Red Pavement" (Nebel) 73, 163–4

"The Red-Headed League" (Doyle) 29,
    101, 105, 106–8
Reeve, Arthur B. 1, 7, 23, 132, 137, 138,
    178
return to order 77, 127, 127n4, 176

Sayers, Dorothy L.
    "The Adventurous Exploit of the Cave
        of Ali Baba" 76n10, 139
    The Five Red Herrings 50, 105, 111–16
    Murder Must Advertise 50, 76n10
    Unnatural Death 48, 97n2
    "The Unsolved Puzzle of the Man with
        No Face" 151
science
    as impacting detective fiction 5, 23,
        37, 96
    representations of 7, 12, 25, 30, 39
    and scientific method 3, 19, 22, 23,
        118, 179
scientific management 128–30, 143, 176
Shell, Marc 1, 14–15, 127
Spillane, Mickey
    The Big Kill 173
    I, the Jury 171, 172, 174
    Kiss Me Deadly 171, 173–4
    My Gun Is Quick 172–3, 174
    One Lonely Knight 173
    Vengeance Is Mine! 173, 174
Szondi, Peter
    Theory of the Modern Drama 176–8

Taylorism, *see* scientific management
totalitarianism 21, 46, 51, 52, 54, 175, 176
Tour de Force (Brand) 36–7
Trotsky, Leon 8, 176

value
    and circulation 2, 6, 103, 106, 110,
        116, 118, 121, 149
    and counterfeit 17, 103
    determination of 2, 17, 22, 24, 41, 58,
        64, 84, 93, 94, 99, 102, 115, 117,
        119, 149, 180, 181
    and equivalence 14, 64
    exchange value 18, 116, 120, 131, 151,
        167
    surplus value 109, 110, 117, 134, 135,
        145, 152

use value 151, 152
Van Gulik, Robert 50, 56n1, 137
verisimilitude 6–9, 120, 169

Whitfield, Raoul
 "The Caleso Murders" 70–3

"China Man" 157
"Enough Rope" 50n8, 157
Green Ice 158–61
"The Siamese Cat" 157
"The Whosis Kid" (Hammett) 73n7, 77–9
Williams, Raymond 6n5, 10n8

For Product Safety Concerns and Information please contact our EU
representative GPSR@taylorandfrancis.com Taylor & Francis Verlag GmbH,
Kaufingerstraße 24, 80331 München, Germany

Printed and bound by CPI Group (UK) Ltd, Croydon, CR0 4YY
01/05/2025
01858454-0001